ROBERT HEWISON

IN ANGER

Culture in the Cold War 1945–60

A Methuen Paperback

A METHUEN PAPERBACK

First published in Great Britain in 1981
by George Weidenfeld & Nicolson Ltd
This new revised paperback edition first published in 1988
by Methuen London
Michelin House, 81 Fulham Road, London SW3 6RB

British Library Cataloguing in Publication Data

Hewison, Robert
  In anger: culture in the Cold
  War, 1945–60. – Rev. ed.
  1. Great Britain – Civilization –
  1945–
  I. Title
  941.085'5   DA588

ISBN 0-413-40900-7

Printed and bound in Great Britain
by Richard Clay Ltd, Bungay, Suffolk

IN ANGER

KINGSLEY AMIS · JOHN ARDEN · FRANCIS BACON ·
JOHN BERGER · JOHN BRATBY · JOHN OSBORNE ·
VICTOR PASMORE · HAROLD PINTER · ARNOLD WESKER ·
ANGUS WILSON · COLIN WILSON

The author, Robert Hewison, published his first book, *John Ruskin: The Argument of the Eye*, in 1976; he is a regular contributor to BBC arts programmes and has written on the theatre for the *Sunday Times* since 1981.

The ten books he has to his credit discuss widely differing aspects of nineteenth- and twentieth-century cultural history. He is a recognised expert on John Ruskin, but he has also examined the effects of censorship on the Monty Python team, and has written a history of the Cambridge Footlights.

The first part of Hewison's series of books on 'The Arts in Britain since 1939', *Under Siege*, was originally published in 1977, and he followed it with two more titles: *In Anger* in 1981 and *Too Much* in 1986. His most recent book *The Heritage Industry*, published in 1987, examines the shift in the cultural climate since 1975.

CONTENTS

LIST OF ILLUSTRATIONS

1. Rodrigo Moynihan *Portrait Group (The Teaching Staff of the Painting School, Royal College of Art)* 1951
2. Rodrigo Moynihan *Grey and Violet* 1955
3. Ceramic mural by Victor Pasmore at the Regatta Restaurant for the Festival of Britain 1951
4. Lucian Freud *Interior Near Paddington* 1951
5. Alan Davie *Entrance to a Paradise* 1949
6. John Bratby *Window, Self Portrait, Jean and Hands* 1957
7. Francis Bacon *Study after Velasquez's Portrait of Pope Innocent X* 1953
8. Jack Smith *Mother Bathing Child* 1953
9. Frank Auerbach *Head of E. O. W. VIII* 1956
10. Robyn Denny *7/1960*
11. The original maquette for *The Monument to the Unknown Political Prisoner* by Reg Butler
12. Richard Hamilton *Just What is it that Makes Today's Homes so Different, so Appealing?* 1956

Front cover photograph
The Suez Crisis: Trafalgar Square 1956

ACKNOWLEDGEMENTS

The sources of all quotations are acknowledged in the notes, but the author wishes to make a special acknowledgement for the use of copyright material to: Kingsley Amis, Macmillan and MacGibbon & Kee; to Robert Conquest, Macmillan and John Calder Ltd; to Donald Davie, Chatto & Windus, Routledge and Kegan Paul Ltd, and Carcanet New Press; to Roy Fuller and Andre Deutsch Ltd for the lines from 'Dedicatory Poem', included in Roy Fuller's *Collected Poems 1962*; to Philip Larkin and Faber & Faber Ltd; to John Lehmann for permission to quote from the *London Magazine*, *The Ample Proposition* (Eyre & Spottiswoode), and *The Craft of Letters in England* (Cresset Press); to the Executors of the Estate of C. Day Lewis for permission to quote from his *Collected Poems* (1954) published by Jonathan Cape Ltd and The Hogarth Press; to John Osborne, Faber & Faber Ltd and MacGibbon & Kee; to Raymond Williams, Chatto & Windus and New Left Books; and to Angus Wilson and the University of California Press.

The author and publishers would like to thank the following for their kind permssion to reproduce the illustrations: The Tate Gallery, London, 1, 5, 6, 8; Rodrigo Moynihan, 2; Victor Pasmore, 3; Walker Art Gallery, Liverpool, 4; Alan Davie, 5; John Bratby, 6; Des Moines Arts Center and Francis Bacon, 7; Arts Council of Great Britain and Frank Auerbach, 9; Robyn Denny, 10; Reg Butler, 11; Kunsthalle Tübingen, 12.

INTRODUCTION

to the Second Edition

In Anger, the second volume in a trilogy which begins with *Under Siege: Literary Life in London 1939–45*, and closes with *Too Much: Art and Society in the Sixties*, is a study of the slow transition from wartime austerity to Sixties affluence. Just as *Under Siege* was the first comprehensive survey of the arts during the war, *In Anger* sets out to give a similar account of a much longer period. That is reflected by the shift of emphasis in the subtitle, from 'literary life' to 'culture'. As a transitional period its pivot, 1956, comes near the centre of the period covered by the whole study. While 1939–45 was externally defined by war, the Fifties move towards the climacteric of 1956, and then on again and, as I argue in *Too Much*, there is no clear point where the Fifties end and the Sixties begin. For practical purposes then, I have for once accepted the arbitrary punctuation of the calendar, and drawn a line at 1960. I have felt free however, to cross that line on occasion and, more important, reserve certain developments in the late 1950s for further discussion in *Too Much*.

The other part of my subtitle, the 'Cold War', requires explanation. 1945 was not the end of the war at all, merely the opening of a new phase. The explosion of the Atom Bomb in 1945 introduced a new element of fear into the world, that of global obliteration. It was intensified in 1949 when Russia proved her nuclear weapon too. By that time Europe, and indirectly the rest of the world, was divided into two armed camps, only occasionally striking at each other, as in Korea, but expending quantities of treasure on armaments, and doing whatever they could by fair means or foul to subvert the morale of the other side. In Britain, military conscription remained in force until 1963.

It was a war fought with propaganda, economics and lies, and it perpetuated the siege conditions under which Britain had lived since 1939. The emphasis on the need for security – mental as much as military – reinforced the conservative responses of a culture that had every reason anyway to want to 'get back to normal'. That Russia, which briefly in the Thirties had held out to intellectuals in the West the image, if not the substance, of a new and just society, proved itself to be a cruel, tyrannical overlord of her own people and all those behind the Iron Curtain (Churchill's phrase), served to reinforce the reaction against social radicalism that had begun during the war. 1945–51 was the period of a reforming Labour government which set in motion many plans for change prepared in wartime, but it did not have the creative support of many artists or writers.

The Cold War, as its imagery suggests, is a climate affecting states of mind, rather than a series of events, although the brutal suppression of the Hungarian rising in 1956 was one such event which had important consequences for intellectual life in this country. Towards the end of the Fifties, again in the imagery of the conflict, there were signs of a thaw, although there were few actual events which justified this alteration in people's states of mind. To a certain extent, it was acceptance of the fact of potential nuclear war – 'the balance of terror' – which created this shift. The Cold War is still not over, and we are still living, if only subconsciously, in siege conditions.

The Cold War affected the cultural climate of the Fifties – which is the subject of this book. The natural feeling of exhaustion at the end of an arduous war coincided with the exhaustion of a cultural movement which had affected all developed societies since the beginning of the century: the optimistic drive of Modernism in the arts, which had moved

forward on a series of formal renewals, supported by a belief
that the arts in themselves were capable of bringing about
social change. It did not end entirely, although artistic change
was less easily understood as progress, but in some fields,
particularly literature, a culturally dominant form in Britain,
there was a feeling that experiment had reached its limits and –
in parallel with a pessimistic political outlook – that this should
be a period of restraint and consolidation. After the romanticism of the Forties, the sceptical realism of the Fifties had a
bracing effect, but scepticism is a narrow base for culture. The
anger of the Fifties was as often a rage of frustration at the lack
of access to a limited number of privileges, as passionate moral
outrage at the caution and spiritlessness of the age.

The problem of cultural pessimism is that it can produce the
very entropy that it fears. (Why bother to experiment, if all
previous experiments have failed?) As *Under Siege* sought to
show, most British writers and artists came out of the war in a
negative frame of mind. *In Anger* begins with a survey of
artistic activity as it stood in the first years of peace, and it is
clear that cultural institutions, such as the newly formed Arts
Council, were better placed than individuals. Reconstruction
came to mean the recovery of old forms, rather than the
evolution of new ones. Some pessimism, at least, was justifi-
able, for by 1947 it was apparent that there was a significant
price to be paid for defending freedom. While externally the
hostility between the former wartime allies in the West and
Russia in the East began to freeze into the Cold War, the arts,
particularly the British cinema, began to suffer the economic
consequences of peace. The collapse in the artificial wartime
book boom had implications for all writers, but especially those
not yet established. To the atmosphere of depression was added
apprehension – or downright fear – with its corresponding
search for security and stability.

  As Chapter 2 shows, the process of bureaucratisation of the
arts which had begun in wartime continued. The foundation of
the BBC's Third Programme followed this pattern, and the

BBC sustained the prevailing cultural conservatism. There was nothing sinister in this; as George Orwell said in 1946 'Any writer or journalist who wants to retain his integrity finds himself thwarted by the general drift of society rather than by active persecution.'

The main area of opportunity – and even then it was not intended as a haven of creative writers – was the university. The 1944 Education Act made higher education a public responsibility, and in theory open to all. But the failure to reform the public school system, or adjust the social dominance of Oxford and Cambridge meant that universities – especially Oxbridge – continued to reproduce most of the cultural values of their privileged prewar existence. Within the universities the prevailing modes of philosophy and criticism tended to promote the ethics of the Cold War by discouraging radical thought.

Oxford and Cambridge, publishing and the BBC, encouraged the perception of British cultural life as a genial club, a co-optive elite. Though their critical standards were more rigorous than those of the Garrick or the Savage, the writings of T. S. Eliot and F. R. Leavis reinforced the prevailing cultural model of an elite. For Leavis this elite was located in the university, and it was in these institutions, as Chapter 4 shows in more detail, that a new generation of writers and poets was forming its ideas.

While the 1945 Labour government lamentably failed to build on the progressive cultural shift of wartime, beyond enacting the Butler Education Act, and transforming CEMA into the Arts Council, it will always be associated with one great cultural event: the Festival of Britain in 1951. This was a popular success, a genuine attempt to restore some colour to a drab and still rationed environment, but although it distributed commissions to architects, designers, painters and sculptors, with the intention of creating something new, its long-term effect was to strengthen the bureaucracies of culture, in particular the Arts Council and the Council for Industrial Design. (It may even be that the institutional approach prepared the way for the heartless town planning of the Fifties and Sixties, although that was not the intention.)

1951 also marked the end of Labour's period in office, and the first of the conflicts at arms-length of the superpowers, the Korean War, which once more postponed economic expansion. Michael Frayn's justifiably famous description of the true celebrants of the Festival of Britain, 'the radical middle-class, the do-gooders' as Herbivores sums up the bloodless achievement of the Labour government in providing conditions in which a nostalgic, class-obsessed culture was able to re-establish itself.

Chapter 3 looks at orthodox literary culture in the early 1950s, the period of the foundation of *Encounter* and the *London Magazine*. It marked the reconciliation of most literary intellectuals to their lot, and is an indication of the political consensus that prevailed as a modest affluence developed. The values of this intellectual aristocracy – though bureaucracy would be a better word – I define as Mandarin.

Mandarin values can be seen most clearly in relation to the values of a secure social order represented by the English country house, a regular setting for plays and novels, of which *Brideshead Revisited* (as I have said before) is the most significant. Yet the celebration of the country house was more an attempt to retrieve the shreds of the institution's former glories, than to use its values as a source of imagination or inspiration.

The theatre was held in check by the power of a close-knit group of commercial managements, and the powers of censorship of the Lord Chamberlain, which ensured that as little as possible would disturb the enjoyment of Terence Rattigan's imaginary Aunt Edna, as she sat at the matinées of a procession of country house plays.

While there was a brief flurry of excitement over the possibilities of verse drama (more a hangover from wartime romanticism than a new development) in the early fifties neither the theatre nor fiction attempted much formal innovation. As I argued earlier, this was at least partially because of the sense that literary modernism was exhausted. Instead, novelists resumed their traditional function of recording the social scene. This was a changed scene, as Evelyn Waugh's *Sword of Honour* trilogy made clear, and Anthony Powell's fine sequence *A Dance to the Music of Time* began to explore at greater length. Angus Wilson drew considerable inspiration from the decay of the Mandarin tradition of which he was a part. And the gradual sense of decay, in spite of the achievements of the best novelists, sapped the confidence of the senior generation. This is most apparent in a remarkable Mandarin symposium, *The Craft of Letters in England*, which, as it happens, was published in the pivotal year of 1956.

While tendrils of romanticism hung on into the 1950s (and never fell away completely) Chapter 4 shows how the process of counter-reaction began first where neo-romanticism had been strongest, in poetry and painting. Critical and creative forces were gathering for the shift that takes place around 1956, and in poetry, before then.

This shift occurred within a changing system of cultural communication: the first most people heard of a new school of poetry was through the medium of radio. This group, which came to be known simply as 'the Movement', included the first beneficiaries of the Welfare State. They were not themselves reared on National Health orange juice, but they were employed in universities and libraries, and some of the sober, clerical associations of their professions touched their verse.

They were not the literary conspiracy that commentators, particularly other literary conspirators, made them out to be, but they did set out as reformers of the decayed condition of English verse. The price was emotional range, but it was unguarded, unconsidered emotion which had led poetry to the demoralized state it was in – a condition worsened by the sheer lack of outlets for new work. It was not until 1956, and the publication of the anthology, *New Lines*, that the shape of the Movement could be seen. It is symptomatic of the prevailing caution that its editor should deny that such a group even existed.

The beneficial effect of the Movement was its call for a return

Introduction

to reality. A similar change was taking place in painting, though here 'realism' has radical overtones not present in the Movement's essential conservatism. Its chief promoter was the Marxist art critic and painter – later novelist – John Berger. But in the early 1950s the most interesting place for a painter to be was not London, but St Ives. The main thrust here was not realism, but abstraction. This native abstraction was pushed aside by the arrival of Abstract Expressionism from America, as was indeed Berger's social realism, neither of which could sustain themselves in the face of the United States' aggressive cultural policies.

John Berger's selection for *Looking Forward* at the White-chapel in 1952 did however suggest that a substantial number of painters were looking at the world as it was, and rendering it with a certain vigour. Similarly, though the Movement was principally interested in restoring order to poetry, their emphasis on the need for clear perception meant that they could not fail to notice that the world was changing. This shows in their non-Mandarin taste for science fiction and American jazz, and it was inevitable that when members of their generation came to depict this world in novels, it was an urban scene of provincial towns and universities, rather than the civilized pastoral of the country house. This was refreshing, and if not quite the revolution it was claimed to be, it did show that in the ten years since the end of the war a new kind of writer was emerging, with different concerns. But it is emblematic of the defensive attitudes of the Cold War period, and the negative atmosphere in which these writers' formation took place, that the 1950s became the age, not of the hero, but the anti-hero.

The most celebrated anti-hero was John Osborne's Jimmy Porter, and in 1956 the series of preparations for his arrival matured in the journalistic slogan, the Angry Young Man. The Angry Young Man was a myth, but marketable, and as the anthology *Declaration* shows, it created a platform for a number of differing protests against the prevailing orthodoxies. As I have argued in *Under Siege*, there is always an underlying

xv

truth to such powerfully persuasive myths, and Chapter 4 explores both its creation and exploitation.

The myth of the Angry Young Man was confirmed by the historical coincidence of Suez and the Hungarian uprising. Both were abhorrent but ultimately timely events. It was not welcome to discover that Britain was no longer a first-class power, and to be taught this lesson by the United States, but it had to be learned (and should have been learned quicker). Hungary was also a reminder of national impotence, but it had an important effect on left-wing thinking. As with Czechoslovakia in 1968, it was a reminder of the lengths the Soviet Union would go to to preserve its European empire, but as I show later, in Chapter 6, by breaking the almost automatic link between Marxism and sympathy for Russian Communism it removed some of the shackles on radical western thought.

The new attitudes apparent in 1956 were the first signs of a break-up in the cultural consensus which was felt in novels, theatre, the cinema and television, and which created space for writers and actors who were not southern, metropolitan and middle class. State institutions took account of the change: the Arts Council increased its subsidy to theatre, the Lord Chamberlain eased his censorship. The theatre also took fresh ideas from the European avant-garde, a degree of expressionism developed alongside the new realism, with implications for the second wave of theatrical development in the 1960s.

After 1956, there was an increasing desire for social and cultural change, not least because growing affluence was bringing change anyway. There were also signs of a thaw in the Cold War, and a relaxation of siege conditions. A party-political consensus remained (and there was no change of government until 1964) and much of the desire for change manifested itself through culture rather than politics, precisely because of the broad consensus between the parties. The exception to this was the Campaign for Nuclear Disarmament, launched in 1958, but as I argue at greater length in *Too Much*, this was to have more profound cultural than political consequences in the coming years.

Introduction

The dispute about change, and the possibility of change, revolved around two key words, sociological and cultural, rather than political in origin: 'the Establishment' and 'Commitment'. The Establishment represented the political, but equally important, cultural and social, dominance of the Mandarin class. (It was not obligatory to be a member of the Conservative Party to be a Mandarin, while, paradoxically some of the Angry Young Men were on their way to voting Conservative.)

The debate received considerable stimulus from former Communist Party intellectuals who had left after 1956, and a younger group disaffected with the Labour Party and encouraged by the formation of CND. Both branches of this new radical movement observed the interpenetration of politics and culture, and called for a new commitment to social change. Two important cultural studies, Richard Hoggart's *The Uses of Literacy* (1957) and Raymond Williams's *Culture and Society* (1958) – both were literary critics – drew attention to the social roots of culture, and gave a theoretical basis for the cultural politics of the movement, which united (though as *Too Much* describes, only briefly) in the foundation of the *New Left Review* at the end of 1959.

Though wider ranging, the debate over the existence or not of an Establishment came down to a matter of defining the ways in which there had *not* been change since 1945. The word came into common currency in 1955, as shorthand for 'elitism' or 'hegemony', and its usefulness and recurrence shows the extent to which the Mandarin tradition had survived, though subtly transformed, by the end of the fifties, into a 'meritocracy'.

In 1960 many prewar institutions, the public schools, Oxford and Cambridge, the BBC, publishing and literary journalism, plus some like the Arts Council and the British Council which had been confirmed in their status by wartime, seemed as secure as ever, indeed strengthened by the effect of developments since 1945. Part of their security – as was demonstrated most clearly by the BBC – was a willingness to absorb change, without ever appearing to promote it.

The pace of change accelerated towards the end of the decade, and particularly under American influence there were signs of a revived romanticism – now termed expressionism – in painting and poetry, which was to have important consequences in the 1960s. New forces were gathering that celebrated the privileged alienation of the artist, as Beat poet or abstract painter, but, in A. Alvarez's phrase, 'the gentility principle' prevailed into the coming decade.

As I have acknowledged, 1960 is an arbitrary date, but it does leave the several opposing forces at a point of balance. The New Left had a positive and dynamic view of what a renewed culture and community might be like, but it did not have the access – except through education – to the means of promoting it. There was also a lingering sentimentalism about the social virtues of the working class, and a failure to appreciate the independence of the individual imagination.

The conflict heralded in 1956 was worked out in the 1960s, in a period of far greater affluence, which had important consequences for mass culture – as anticipated by the 'Pop Art' theorists in the late 1950s, who are discussed in *Too Much*. And as that next volume argues, although there were to be considerable gains in terms of personal and artistic freedom, the Establishment only loosened, rather than relaxed its grip, and tightened it again in the 1970s.

One of the tests of movement in society is the strictness or otherwise of censorship. The passage of the Obscene Publications Act of 1959 showed that a shift had taken place, but it was the successful defence of *Lady Chatterley's Lover* in 1960 that ushered in the new decade.

As with *Under Siege*, I must stress that this is essentially a historical survey, as far as I know the first of its kind and not primarily a work of criticism. As in the previous volume, I have restricted myself to what was done and said, and what was said about what was done, within the period. Unlike *Under Siege*

Introduction

this book has not used any personal interviews with witnesses, for happily the choice would be impracticably large. Instead, I have stayed with published sources, which can be checked. Since nostalgia is one of the weaknesses of our culture, I have not tried to evoke the atmosphere of the period in any nostalgic way, preferring my quotations to speak for themselves.

The story they tell is of a failure to seize a moment of potential after the war, with the effect that when radicalism did re-emerge, it was expressed more in terms of conflict within the structure, than dispute about the nature of the structure itself. That would be the work of another generation, in the 1960s. At all times, of course, individual artists have transcended their circumstances, but individual histories are not the subject of this book.

Once again, I must thank my publisher, Geoffrey Strachan, for making this second edition and its revisions possible. But I would also like to mention the fruitful discussions I had while first preparing the book with Paul Binding, David Britt and Jonathan Barker, who was also a great help in his capacity as Librarian of the Arts Council Poetry Library. Linda Osband was most helpful in the preparations of the first edition, my sister, Anthea Ridett made the original index, and was as ever unfailing in her help.

Annaghmakerrig

CHAPTER ONE

THE GOD THAT FAILED

*'We may allow ourselves a brief
period of rejoicing.'*

Winston Churchill announcing
the German surrender,
8 May 1945

In the spring of 1945 the eminent American literary critic
Edmund Wilson arrived in London to prepare a series of
articles for the *New Yorker*. The war in Europe still had several
weeks to run, and V2 rockets continued to hit London. Wilson
was impressed by the quietness, the orderliness, the shabbiness
and the atmosphere of claustrophobia. He noticed the perva-
sive influence of America and the resentment of Americans.
He was amazed by the quality of London's theatre and, on a
flying visit from Europe later in the summer, he was astonished
by Benjamin Britten's new opera *Peter Grimes*. But when he
came to think seriously about the future of England's cultural
life, he was very worried by what he saw.

It was not simply the prevalent mental exhaustion; that was
only to be expected after six years of war and its necessary
privation. Wilson detected an attitude of regression in the
artists and writers he met. At a literary party given for him by
the publisher Hamish Hamilton he listened to the conversation
of two writers who had done their war service in the Fire
Brigade. They were comparing their experiences to life at

1

public school. What seemed odd to him, as an American, was that the vigorous middle-class writers of the Edwardian age – Bennett, Shaw, Wells – who in the main had not been educated first at a public school and then Oxford or Cambridge, had been succeeded by a generation which shared an attitude strongly influenced by these institutions. This generation, which for convenience – and thinking of Virginia Woolf and Lytton Strachey – Wilson called 'the Bloomsbury circle', left its mark on the generation that had in turn followed it, and which was now represented at Hamilton's party. Though the more vigorous of them had tried to break away from the upper-class élitist atmosphere of Bloomsbury during the 1930s, the war that followed on the failures and disappointments at the end of that decade drove them back on their social origins. The public school was an institution for which they felt both nostalgia and contempt – blaming it for their own inadequacies and the general debility of English life. This regression made Wilson ask whether anything had survived that was positive in English culture:

Must we conclude that the articulate middle class that thought it was working for democracy and freedom is now almost completely dead, having failed, in the time of its prosperity, to create a lasting civilization, so that there is nothing today left but a labouring and shop-keeping people, more and more equalized by the pressure of war services and wartime restrictions, over whom hangs a fading phantom of the England of the public school?

Not surprisingly, the British literary intelligentsia were irritated by Edmund Wilson's articles for the *New Yorker*. As Wilson himself had noted, the strain of war had made the British irritable. It was equally galling when W. H. Auden arrived a few weeks later in the uniform of an American major to work on a survey of the effect of strategic bombing in Germany. Auden had broken with Bloomsbury to the extent of emigrating to America in 1939, and his British colleagues had had to take much criticism on his behalf for his abandonment of the political commitment he had encouraged in the

2

1930s. Now the war was over he was back, but it was felt that if his job was to study the psychological effects of bombing, it was a pity that he had not had the opportunity to experience it at first hand, as his former friends had done.

These irritations were recorded by John Lehmann in the second volume of his autobiography *I Am My Brother* (1960). Lehmann had been at the party for Edmund Wilson, and was very much the literary figure for whom Wilson felt such insulting concern. This was not just because he had been educated at Eton and Cambridge. He was linked to the older Bloomsbury generation by his partnership with Leonard Woolf in The Hogarth Press (which he failed to take over in 1945); he was a prominent spokesman of the younger generation as editor of *New Writing* since 1936; and whatever uncertainty he felt in 1945 about his former political convictions, Lehmann, like other participants in London's literary life, had every reason to feel proud of the achievements of the war years. Literature – indeed, all the arts – had flourished in seemingly impossible conditions of scarcity and distraction. It was very unfair of well-fed Americans to come and cast doubts on their future.

It was also a little odd – or so many people must have felt – that Wilson should be so anxious about the prospects of democracy and freedom in Britain. In 1945, to everyone's surprise, not least that of the defeated Winston Churchill and the victorious Clement Attlee, Britain elected a Labour government with an overwhelming majority, giving it a free hand to carry out the social and economic transformation that had been the object of left-wing hopes in the 1930s. The young Bloomsbury intellectuals had done much before the war to keep those hopes alive; now Fascism was defeated and Socialism stood ready to open a new era of British history.

And yet Edmund Wilson turned out to be right, not so much about political developments as the nostalgic and regressive culture that came with them. Britain continued to be free and a democracy, but the next five years saw more social and economic disappointment than transformation. By the end of 1950 the Labour government was struggling without a proper working majority, rationing and shortages were still a normal part of everyday life and, as a junior partner of America, Britain was fighting a war at arm's length with Russia and China in Korea. There had been social and economic alterations, but these had been mainly a consolidation of the political consensus created by wartime necessity. That no more than that had been done was all to the good as far as the reorganized and reinvigorated Conservative Party, poised to regain power in 1951, was concerned.

This is a study of the cultural rather than the political history of post-war Britain, but it is impossible to separate the two themes entirely. The failure of the Labour government to achieve its programme or to hold on to power (though more people actually voted Labour in 1951 than ever before) is a matter of political history, but this lack of achievement is matched by a lack of achievement over the same period in the world of literature and the arts. In both cases a gradual reaction set in as the decade came to its end. J. B. Priestley, the one still active representative of that Edwardian style of writer so missed by Edmund Wilson, the supporter of Socialism whose wartime broadcasts, according to the demonology of the Conservative Party, had done so much to bring Labour to power in 1945, expressed the general sense of disillusion in the *New Statesman* in July 1949:

We are revolutionaries who have not swept away anything. We are Tories loudly denouncing taxes and regulations chiefly invented by Tory Ministers. We are Socialists busy creating peers and cheering pretty princesses. We are a dreary self-righteous people with a passion for gin, tobacco, gambling and ballet. We are a nation of Sabbath-keepers who do not go to church. We toil to keep ourselves alive, with three tea-breaks, a five-day week and Wednesday afternoon off for the match. We spend so much time arguing about food we have no time to cook it properly. We spend fourpence on our culture, and several million pounds a year advertising it. We get free spectacles and false teeth and, for lack of hospital beds, may die in a ditch. We have probably the best children and the dullest adults in Europe. We are a Socialist-Monarchy that is really the last monument of Liberalism.

4

Priestley, a novelist and playwright, chose to express his disappointment in political terms (and, it should be noted, in the most important of the government-supporting magazines); the sociologist Donald MacRae expressed his in cultural terms, in the (also Socialist) *Political Quarterly* in January of the same year:

> there has been . . . an enormous failure of nerve and a massive indifference to the true context of life, the creation of personality. The newest houses are abominably ugly and, in urban England, intensely inurbane. The creative arts gain less than the executant from the Arts Council, while the BBC Light Programme combines the cinema and the elementary arithmetic of the Pools to produce a contempt for the higher pleasures that is infinitely more strongly founded than the call to these pleasures uttered rather stuffily by the Workers' Educational Association, the Third Programme, and so on . . . the English, indeed, have largely lost that passion for words and verbal creation that has characterized them in Europe for nearly 400 years.

A sense of failure and disappointment might be expected from the supporters of a government that was losing ground, but those on the Right were equally certain that things were wrong. T. S. Eliot, the most respected cultural figure of the Right, wrote in *Notes Towards the Definition of Culture* (1948): 'We can assert with some confidence that our own period is one of decline; that the standards of culture are lower than they were fifty years ago; and the evidences of this decline are visible in every department of human activity.'

It is not a new judgment to say that the second half of the 1940s produced little in the way of great literature or art. What must be stressed is that people were embarrassedly aware of the fact at the time. It was both symptomatic and symbolic that Cyril Connolly should announce the 'temporary' (in fact permanent) suspension of his magazine *Horizon* at the end of 1949. The launching of *Horizon* in January 1940 had been equally symbolic, and its survival through bombing and shortage had been an emblem of the cultural survival of Britain. Connolly's last editorial is well known for its judgment of the period:

'Nothing dreadful is ever done with, no bad thing gets any better; you can't be too serious.' This is the message of the Forties from which, alas, there seems no escape, for it is closing time in the gardens of the West and from now on an artist will be judged only by the resonance of his solitude or the quality of his despair.

The trouble was that everyone agreed with him. And though T. C. Worsley, in his *New Statesman* obituary for *Horizon*, pointed out that the magazine itself had been getting progressively duller and heavier, he also sympathized with Connolly's problems: 'Five years after the war there is still no sign of any kind of literary revival; no movements are discernible: no trends.' That was the general view, and the closure of John Lehmann's *New Writing* in 1950 helped to confirm it.

The whole post-war period received a swift obituary in Alan Ross's *The Forties*, published in 1950:

Literature took a temporary turn to the Right. The days of social realism, of proletarian art and documentary reporting were gone forever. The political coat-hangers on which well-cut literary jackets had been laboriously and nonchalantly draped were put away in the attic. The moth was gingerly removed from dinner-jackets and bright, linen trousers, from espadrilles and travelling-rugs. The Marxists shut up shop. There appeared to be no minority causes left for the writer; only a retreat to private conflicts, to an imaginative romanticism that turned its back on the outworn political clichés of an earlier generation. The best writing was upper-middle-class and upper-middle-aged; and that too was a sign of the times. Those teeth that had ground so successfully a decade ago had already made their impression. The war had extracted the best of the newer ones.

Ross was making a snap judgment, and it is not enough to record it and press on. There were good reasons for the failure of cultural life to revive after the war, or even to fulfil the promise shown in wartime. Ross's comment on the shift of literature to the Right suggests that politics continued to be as important an issue as it had been during the 1930s, but with different results. Another reason for the difficulties in which the arts found themselves was Britain's disastrous economic position, and that too had a significant effect on political developments. But beyond these external influences there was an inherent weakness afflicting the arts themselves, so that they found it difficult to adapt to the economic and political climate that developed after the war.

None of these problems was fully perceived in the latter half of 1945 or in 1946. One of the unexpected effects of the war had been heightened awareness of the importance of the arts; people had realized spontaneously that 'culture' was one of the things for which they were fighting. True, such art as was available had to be spread thin, but scarcity itself acted as a stimulus. The government recognized the importance of culture when it started to subsidize the Council for the Encouragement of Music and the Arts, launched in 1940. CEMA's success was confirmed when, in 1945, it became the Arts Council, and, under a new constitution in May 1946, was enabled to make capital grants and interest-free loans, instead of simply providing guarantees against loss. The BBC emerged from the war with its reputation enhanced and proceeded to crown its cultural achievements with the formation of the unashamedly highbrow Third Programme, which started broadcasting in September 1946. There is no doubt that war created – or discovered – new audiences for serious music and drama. One recognized weakness was the emphasis on the performing arts, but painting and literature also benefited from the new appetites sharpened by the stress of war.

The re-opening of Covent Garden Opera House in February 1946 (during the war it had been a Mecca dance hall) with the Sadler's Wells Ballet in Tchaikovsky's *Sleeping Beauty*, starring Margot Fonteyn and Robert Helpmann, was a mark of the particular achievement of ballet in not only staying alive, but creating new work. James Redfern wrote in the *Spectator*:

In the Sadler's Wells Ballet this country truly has something to be proud of, for it has shown a creative activity in the art of ballet to which neither our contemporary drama nor music can offer a parallel.

7

Our opera is of inferior quality, and lives – with the exception of one solitary new English work, *Peter Grimes* – on the past. Our theatre, although superior in technical standard to our opera, lives wholly on the past. It is only in ballet that we have managed to assemble a veritable host of new and truly creative talent.

Redfern's comparisons with the other performing arts were ominous. While the Sadler's Wells Ballet passed under the control of Covent Garden and its administrator David Webster (leaving a 'Theatre Ballet' at the Wells), Sadler's Wells Opera did not, and there were rumblings in the operatic world when the Sadler's Wells producer, Eric Crozier, and two of their best singers, Joan Cross and Peter Pears, seceded (although they had to be re-engaged to keep *Peter Grimes* in the repertory). Benjamin Britten went with them, supplying a chamber opera, *The Rape of Lucretia*. This secession led to the founding of the English Opera Group. Meanwhile, Covent Garden had begun its own programme of opera productions, and with the Carl Rosa Company and the unsubsidized Cambridge Opera, Britain's meagre operatic resources quickly became stretched, as the critics soon pointed out. 'Anybody might suppose that the country was chock-a-block with suitable theatres, well-trained opera singers, and highly experienced conductors and producers. Whereas the truth is exactly the reverse: there is an absolute famine of the whole lot!' complained Desmond Shawe-Taylor. 'The fact is that, on top of our endemic complaints, we are suffering from six years of operatic isolation: we have no standards, no models, not even a school of opera; our singers drift on to the stage with the minimum of general culture and musical taste.' There was a popular theory that British soldiers who had fought in Italy had acquired a liking for Italian opera, and the producers were ready to exploit it. ' "When it's not *La Bohème* it's probably *Tosca*" seems to be a fairly safe bet on operatic productions,' commented Martin Cooper, editor of the *Musical Times*, in the *Spectator* in December 1946.

Over-production and over-reliance of old favourites became a general problem in the concert-halls as well as the opera houses. Desmond Shawe-Taylor returned to his theme in October 1947:

Half-empty houses proclaim the sad truth: the boom has been unintelligently over-exploited, too much music is going on to compete with the sustained interest of the Third Programme. In the field of opera, though radio is here a less dangerous competitor, the mutually destructive *guerre des bouffons* reaches new heights of fantasy. This very day eight operatic performances are announced in and around London: three *Rigolettos*, two *Carmens*, a *Faust*, a *Barber*, and a *Herring*. Could anything be madder?

Judging from the music critic Ernest Newman's comments in the *Sunday Times* in May 1949, over-production also worried the performers. Newman and the conductor Sir Thomas Beecham had begun a campaign about the poor state of orchestral music. 'Everywhere among really musical people one hears the same complaints – too much music-making, hackneyed programmes (even the orchestral players tell us in private that they are sick to death of performing certain works), a low standard of performance in general, and the too great dependence of it all for its existence on a feckless use of the taxpayer's money.'

As with music, the theatre enjoyed an immediate post-war boom, but again the emphasis was on revivals. The Old Vic Repertory Company mounted a splendid season with Laurence Olivier and Ralph Richardson at the New Theatre, and John Gielgud was having equal success at the Haymarket, but Shakespeare, Sheridan, Maugham and Wilde were keeping the new playwrights out. One of them, Peter Ustinov, who had begun to make his reputation during the war, complained:

There is very little reason for the dramatist to be confident in these hard days. Like Ibsen's Mrs Alving he is haunted before he begins to work by ghosts – ghosts of the past. For instance, Oscar Wilde may be dead, but his plays carry a guarantee of popular success with them, and that is enough to provoke incessant revivals. . . . It is slyly suggested that it is the paucity of new plays which necessitates these elegant creations, creations which cause the dead to turn in their graves and the living to twist in their seats.

Excluded from the West End – James Agate calculated in September 1945 that out of thirty London theatres only six might conceivably be ready to risk experimental productions – the writer with a new play had to try his luck with the uncommercial tiny club theatres, The Torch, The Gateway, Unity Theatre, The Lindsay, The Boltons, The Embassy, The Lyric Hammersmith, the Arts Theatre Club or The Mercury. And it was at the Mercury Theatre that verse drama saw a false dawn in the following years.

The problem was institutional. In the West End, money was made by owning theatres, not putting on plays. In wartime, theatre ownership had become concentrated; soaring rents and production costs meant restricted sets and casting, and risk-taking was increasingly discouraged. The limitations were even stricter because of the dominance of 'The Group' – theatre-owners and managers who through a complex network of directorships and shareholdings had a lien on twenty-one of the West End theatres. At the centre of the Group was the leading play-producing management of H. M. Tennent, whose managing director was Hugh 'Binkie' Beaumont. Through its non-profit-making subsidiary, Tennent Productions Ltd, the firm co-operated with the Arts Council in putting on plays of merit. But H. M. Tennent's chairman, Prince Littler, was interested in making money, and he and his brother, Emile Littler, had a monopolistic control of theatrical enterprise that extended through the West End to the provincial theatres as well.

In February 1948, J. B. Priestley acted as chairman at a serious attempt to call into question the state of contemporary British theatre, a grand three-day Theatre conference of all sides of the theatre business. The Chancellor of the Exchequer, Sir Stafford Cripps, gave his support by addressing the conference, but the Group managers boycotted the meeting and there was an attempt to smear the conference on the grounds that the organizing secretaries – Ossia Trilling, and Ted Willis of the Unity Theatre – were Communists. The theatres remained in the hands of the managers, and by the end of 1948 hopes that wartime enthusiasms could be built on had evaporated.

The God that Failed

The *New Statesman*'s drama critic, T. C. Worsley, explained the lack of new plays and playwrights in terms of the post-war upheavals:

At times of flux the novelist and the poet can continue speaking to the isolated individual; but the playwright may have lost his old audience and not yet found a new. . . . So it comes about that the post-war theatre inevitably looks a little old-fashioned; it is still addressing itself to the left-overs of the old audiences, perhaps trying to reassemble them; and being naturally conservative, it relies on the conventions that succeeded in the immediate past.

Though at first the book boom had shown no signs of weakening, by the end of 1948 the poet and the novelist were also wondering where their audiences had gone. The boom was the biggest paradox of wartime. Publishing had suffered every kind of restriction and difficulty, paper was severely rationed, printing and binding staff were conscripted, bombing destroyed stocks and held up production and distribution, yet the demand for books, especially new books, soared. A sign of the times was that 200 new publishing firms had been set up during the war, surviving on whatever stocks of unrationed paper they could find.

The economic conditions which created this paradoxical boom were not immediately altered by the coming of peace, although in November 1945 the publishers' ration of paper was increased from 50 per cent to 65 per cent of their pre-war consumption. The problem was that there was an even stronger case than in the theatre for revivals. It was calculated that 44,000 standard works were out of print at the end of 1945. In Dent's Everyman's Library series 550 volumes were unavailable; of the 440 in Oxford's World's Classics series only twenty-nine were in print, and only fifteen of the one hundred Oxford Standard Authors. At the same time, wartime reading habits had stimulated interest in the English classics, and publishers were happy to play safe. Oxford University Press launched *The Oxford Trollope*, Hamish Hamilton *The Novel Library*, John Lehmann Ltd (a new firm) *The Chiltern Library*, Spottiswoode

The Century Library of twentieth-century classics. Penguin, besides starting their series on architecture, archaeology and history, launched their Penguin Classics with *The Odyssey*. Not surprisingly, living authors became worried about the way publishers were using their increased ration. Anna Kavan wrote in *Horizon* in January 1946:

One might expect preference to go to new names and experimental forms appropriate to the inchoate fluidity of a time when culture as previously known is almost certainly ending. In fact, most, if not all the fresh allocation is devoted to reprints – often excessively long. Works, familiar to us since childhood, crowd new writers and non-traditional writing out of a list reminiscent of the catalogue of a school library. The truth is, of course, that inner and outer reality do not so much correspond as balance each other. Chaos and uncertainty outside must be compensated by a solid stability within.

Conversely, post-war uncertainty encouraged demand for the security of familiar forms.

The exception as far as new authorship was concerned was the steady stream of war memoirs and documentaries. Out of office, Winston Churchill settled down to produce his account of the Second World War, while his publishers hoarded paper to meet the expected demand. It was speculated that the memoirs, serialized in the *Daily Telegraph, New York Times* and *Life* magazine, would make him the highest paid author in the world. Of the inevitable war novels Alexander Baron's *From the City, from the Plough* (1948) was judged the most convincing, and Jocelyn Brooke's *The Military Orchid* (1948) the most exotic, but none could match the brutal force of Norman Mailer's *The Naked and the Dead*, published in Britain in 1949.

Whatever the complaints of writers less fortunate than Churchill, the book boom was still going strong at Christmas 1946, and the *Spectator* was already warning readers in November that 'the wise buyer is taking early advantage of the comparatively catholic choice which is seen at the moment on [booksellers'] shelves, and it is certain that those who leave their shopping till much later will only find very scant leavings.' The artificial element in this prosperity was the sheer scarcity of supply. This was the time when booksellers had to order a hundred copies of a book in the hope of getting twelve. Scarcity was also affecting the art market. In the same number of the *Spectator* a letter appeared complaining that 'it is now more difficult for an English artist to obtain canvas and other painting materials than at any period during the last hundred years . . . Artists' materials, textbooks and classics become unobtainable, while the shops are flooded with hideous ceramic ornaments and low-grade literature.' Meanwhile the art dealer could not supplement his stock with Continental or American work: the government had banned the import of all paintings.

At the same time, the British found it difficult to get abroad, except as members of the armed forces. After six years under siege people were avid for travel, but they were not allowed, and could not afford, to go. Sartre's new play *Huis Clos*, published by *Horizon* in 1945 and directed by Peter Brook with Alec Guinness in 1946, had an unexpected relevance for Britain. Its three characters discover that they are dead and condemned to an eternity together in the same room. *Horizon*'s more privileged contributors managed to take British culture abroad to the occupied countries through the British Council (Stephen Spender for instance was sent to de-nazify German libraries), and they sent back reports from France, Italy and Germany which are full of the delights of being allowed out after so long. But Sartre's metaphorical hell was being exchanged for a real one; the reports from Belsen, Berlin and Vienna recorded the devastation and exhaustion of Europe.

Britain, too, was exhausted. At the moment when all the efforts of wartime should have been rewarded, economic and political developments outside her control nullified them – or almost. A Labour government was in power and was laying the foundations of a more just society than that of between the wars. The cultural efforts of 1939–45 had helped to create the atmosphere in which the Labour government was elected; the disgruntled Conservative opposition were quick to blame the success of the arts in wartime for at least part of their defeat. Malcolm Muggeridge's sneering attack in the right-wing *New English Review* in May 1946 is an acknowledgment of the part 'culture' had played:

This new post-war Parliament can fairly claim to be representative. It is the legitimate fruit of much earnest endeavour. Classes, discussion groups, summer schools, brains trusts, BBC talks, instruction in world and other citizenship, chairs of international relations, book clubs, and bureaux of current affairs, have brought it into being. A vast wash of words, both written and spoken, has prepared the way for its coming, and now it has come. Leftism has arrived and is installed in Westminster. It may be seen there – earnest faces, slight tendency to premature baldness; company suggestive of concert or art gallery or British Museum reading-room, of lost causes which produce seven hundred a year, of little out-of-the-way places at home or abroad, of sherry parties thronging small rooms, voices penetrating rather than loud, clothes loose, hands wayward, and eyes restless; intourists now indubitably in. They are bores.

On the Left, in his pamphlet *The Arts Under Socialism* (1947), Priestley warned that such progress as had been made was not enough:

We are by no means devoid of art here – and our recent progress in the communal arts of music, ballet, drama, has been considerable and astonishing – but I declare without hesitation, as one still bleeding from the battle, that every bit of art we achieve is almost a miracle. Artists of every kind are faced with a nightmare obstacle race, and this is not simply because of the transition from a wartime to a peacetime economy and production in a half-ruined world, for this we can all understand; but it is also because there are too many people in authority here who fail to appreciate the importance of art to a society like ours.

1947 was the year when optimism disappeared. The British economy succumbed to a crisis that finally brought home the country's true position. One important factor in the crisis was beyond anyone's power, the vicious winter weather – but this only exposed inherent problems. Britain had ended the war a debtor nation; the vast overseas investments whose earnings had served to mask the long-term decline in the country's industrial strength had been sold off; at home worn-out people were working with worn-out machinery that somehow had to be reconverted to peaceful production at a time when the traditional European markets were in ruins, some of them no longer accessible. Britain also had heavy overseas military commitments, besides sharing the responsibility for feeding a starving Europe.

Britain's chief creditor was America, but the two Allies had a contradictory relationship. They had fought the war as equals (and some politicians thought they were about to go to war again, against Russia), but America was both jealous of Britain's imperial past and suspicious of her socialist present. Lend-lease, which had kept both Britain and Russia going during the war, was ended abruptly in May 1945. Britain's needs were met by a large American loan, but only after hard bargaining and the imposition of conditions which were to increase her difficulties. In 1946 prospects appeared to improve, and the pre-war level of exports was passed in May. (The export drive had its advantages for the Victoria and Albert Museum, which was able to get priority in war damage repairs in order to house the *Britain Can Make It* exhibition, an important forerunner of the Festival of Britain in 1951. The unpleasant fact was that so many of the tantalizing consumer goods on display were labelled 'Export Only'.) But America was also rapidly moving from a war economy, and inflation eroded the value of the dollar loan, which began to run out faster than expected.

At the beginning of 1947, after a summer drought that badly hurt European agriculture, Britain was paralysed by the worst winter conditions for a hundred years. Production and distribution, particularly in the vital coal industry, virtually came to a halt. The balance of payments swung downwards. By the spring the leader writers were comparing the economic disaster which had struck the United Kingdom to the military disasters that had struck her in 1940 at the end of the phoney war. This, though, was the end of the phoney peace. In July one of

Britain's obligations under the terms of the American loan came into force. Previously Britain's financial reserves had been maintained by the large accounts of trading and colonial partners held in sterling in London. The Americans had demanded that sterling should be freely convertible to dollars. Not surprisingly, many countries took the opportunity to exchange a weak currency for a strong one, and the last of Britain's precious dollars seemed about to disappear. In August the British government had to go back on its agreement and suspend the convertibility of the dollar. Later, in 1949 when the American economy went into recession, Britain was forced to devalue drastically.

Britain's economic troubles were only part of the failure of the European economy to recover, and as the fear of Russia's readiness to exploit this weakness increased, the American government realized that a more thorough European recovery programme was necessary. From a combination of economic and political circumstances the Marshall Plan was born in 1948. By that time the relationship between Britain and America had altered. In April 1947 the now characteristically melancholic Cyril Connolly contrasted the 'confident, affable and aggressive' Americans with the demoralized British:

Here, the ego is at half-pressure, most of us are not men or women but members of a vast, seedy, overworked, over-legislated, neuter class, with our drab clothes, our ration books and murder stories, our envious, strict, old-world apathies and resentment – a care-worn people. And the symbol of this mood is London, now the largest, saddest and dirtiest of great cities, with its miles of unpainted half-inhabited houses, its chopless chop-houses, its beerless pubs, its once vivid quarters losing all personality, its squares bereft of elegance, its dandies in exile, its antiquities in America, its shops full of junk, bunk, and tomorrow, its crowds mooning round the stained green wicker of the cafeterias in their shabby raincoats, under a sky permanently dull and lowering like a metal dish-cover.

The crisis was not simply one of morale; the arts, and especially the arts that depended on new work, were prominent victims

16

of the austerity measures the British government was forced to take.

Worst hit was what was left of the British film industry. This had already been virtually destroyed by the Americans after the First World War, and its dependence on American money symbolized Britain's debtor relationship. Thanks to the realization of the propaganda value of the cinema, and the tradition of British documentary film-making, the British film industry had come out of the war with some critical credit, 4,500 cinemas, and a regular audience of thirty million people. But most of the films the thirty million saw were American. Further, an even tighter version of the 'Group' system in theatre managements controlled distribution. The 1,000 key cinemas, taking three-fifths of all receipts, were in the hands of two powerful chains which were closely tied to American interests. ABC was controlled by Warner Brothers, and showed Metro-Goldwyn-Mayer films for thirty-four weeks of the year; the Methodist millionaire J. Arthur Rank had a similar arrangement to show the films of Twentieth-Century Fox in his nominally separate Odeon and Gaumont British cinemas. Through associated companies at all stages of the chain of production Rank and ABC had a virtual monopoly of the British cinema. The only viable independents were Michael Balcon's Ealing Studios (which had a distribution link with Rank) and Alexander Korda's London Film Productions. The indigenous film-making industry was partly protected by a quota which specified the showing of a minimum proportion of British-made films, but many of these were cheap American-financed 'quota-quickies'. Meanwhile, at a time of desperate dollar shortage, American companies were taking $70 million a year from Britain.

In August 1947, at the height of the dollar crisis, Britain placed a 75 per cent import duty on foreign films. The Americans retaliated by boycotting the British market, while the stock of American films already in the country continued to circulate. J. Arthur Rank announced that he would step into the breach with a £9¼ million production programme for forty-seven 'first feature' films. But his efforts to break into the American market following the success of *Henry V* (1945) came to nothing, while *Caesar and Cleopatra* turned out to be an expensive and embarrassing flop. (The costs included exporting sand and a sphinx to Egypt.) In October 1948 Rank was forced to announce that he was £13 million in the red.

The American boycott was successful, and in March 1948 the duty was withdrawn and an agreement made by which the Americans would limit the return of their dollar earnings to £4¼ million a year, with a further sum matching any British film earnings in America (about £1 million). The money left in Britain could be used for film production, which meant continuing American influence. At the same time, Harold Wilson, in his first important post as President of the Board of Trade, was tackling the problems of finding new British finance and fixing a new quota. The National Film Production Council was set up with £5 million to invest, and in October 1948 a new quota was set requiring that 45 per cent of films shown be British.

The British film industry, which had produced roughly fifty feature films in 1947, was now expected to supply over 150, and it could not meet the demand. (In February 1949 it was reported that 1,600 cinemas had obtained exemption from the quota.) The film technicians' leader George Elvin commented in April 1948, after eight months of American boycott, 'the British film industry has earned itself the doubtful honour of being the first industry to fail to respond to protection. And it failed deliberately.' In March 1949 the *New Statesman* reported that the industry was 'On the Rocks'. Seventeen out of the twenty-six major studios were idle, and the rest not at capacity; 3,000 out of a total of 10,000 technicians were laid off. In recognition of the impossibility of meeting the quota it was reduced to 40 per cent, and then 30 per cent in October 1950. By then most of the National Film Production Council's first £5 million had been lost, and the British were producing about forty feature films a year. The 1948 Film Act had failed to answer the challenge of the Americans, and it had also failed to alter the near monopoly structure of the domestic industry.

Under the Act the Board of Trade had acquired powers to force the big cinema chains to show an independently produced film if it merited it. These powers were not used until 1950, when Bernard Miles's *Chance of a Lifetime* was given a showing in Rank's cinemas. The plot concerned a factory where the managing director invites his workers to run the business themselves. After some difficulties they succeed. The distributors objected to the film on the grounds that it was propaganda.

The live theatre also ran into difficulties as the financial crisis deepened. The Old Vic Repertory Company had two very successful seasons in 1944–5 and 1945–6, and further encouraged by the link-up with the long-standing National Theatre Committee in January 1946, which meant that the Old Vic would eventually become the National Theatre (a promise finally achieved in 1963), the governors of the Old Vic decided on an ambitious programme of expansion. There were to be two number one companies, one in London while the other toured abroad. There was to be a repertory centre for provincial tours, an Old Vic Centre covering an experimental studio, a drama school, and a Young Vic children's theatre. But the 1946–7 season made a loss, and when Laurence Olivier took the cream of the actors on a tour to Australia, the company left behind at the New Theatre was not up to standard. One play had to be withdrawn and a tour to America hurriedly cancelled. While the Young Vic and the school were launched under the enthusiastic direction of Michel Saint-Denis, Glen Byam Shaw and George Devine, they were hampered by lack of funds. The Old Vic Theatre itself, which had been bombed, did not reopen until autumn 1950, and the following spring the expansion plans, the Young Vic and the school collapsed in recriminations between the board of governors and the creative personnel. The Old Vic was not the only theatre to have a bad season in 1947–8. It was no longer true that 'anything will run', as an attempt to exploit the Hollywood reputation of Robert Donat in a 'special season' proved when it was abandoned after one play.

Publishers were already beginning to feel the effects of

increased costs through higher wages and the introduction of a five-day working week, when the freeze-up of 1947 forced the government to reduce the fuel allocation to the paper mills. The raw material for paper was an expensive import item, and the ration had been cut again by 10 per cent, but the slow-down at the paper mills made it doubtful that they would get even their meagre entitlement. Rising costs for block-making, and bottlenecks at the binderies added to their troubles. Faced with the prospect of cutting back orders by a third or a half, the publishers pointed to the export value of the book trade. Books were earning £6¾ million a year from overseas, but British publishers were facing increasing competition from the Americans. (At home American firms were buying up the copyrights of British authors freed when their London publishers could not find the paper to keep their work in print.) The general American hostility to imperial preference forced Britain to limit the import of Australian and Canadian books on the grounds that if they did not, American books should be allowed in on equal terms. From January 1947, in an effort to reduce book imports from America, running at £3 million a year, American publishers were required to obtain a special licence for each title they wished to sell in Britain, though fiction and children's books were unrestricted provided that 50 per cent were re-exported.

The book boom burst resoundingly. In July 1947 a publisher who could get no paper at all for his new firm from the Paper Control wrote a letter of protest to the *New Statesman*:

The plain fact of the matter is that the halycon days are over, and the five-year boom in books, which already looked a little shaky last Christmas, was dealt a major blow by the events of the winter, and does not show any signs of recovering this summer. Most booksellers complain that their stocks are dangerously high, and some even go so far as to say that they have never been offered so many new books as during the last few months. They are cutting down orders right and left, in some cases in a spirit that almost borders on panic. What are the reasons for this paradoxical situation? Some attribute it to a general lack of economic confidence since the fuel crisis, some to a gradual increase of other long-awaited goods in the shops, others to more motoring and more holidays abroad, others again to the number of books that are already being printed abroad for the British market. Whatever the true reason or the mixture of reasons, the ideal sellers' market no longer exists in the book trade.

For fear of offending the paper controller, the publisher signed himself 'Ishmael'. Squeezed by rising costs and falling sales, a number of publishers went bankrupt.

Naturally these difficulties had their repercussions on writers. Publisher Michael Joseph wrote in April 1948: 'These are hard times for authors . . . new authors, unless they are promising enough to elbow their established competitors aside, are denied publication; cheap editions are a thing of the past. Production delays, due to the scarcity of skilled labour and materials, make quick reprinting impossible, and the success of a novelist depends on a rapid succession of new impressions while the demand for his book is at its height.' Joseph was sympathetic to new writers, but established authors like the novelist Elizabeth Bowen felt equally aggrieved. Her books, she wrote, were non-existent. 'That is to say, they do not exist commercially . . . the income, however modest, that we should have expected to be deriving from their continuous sales is lost to us. Twenty or twenty-five years of work is of prestige value only; not worth a farthing.'

The most serious consequence of the crisis in publishing was the widespread destruction of little magazines. This was to have long-term effects, for the little magazines are the seed-bed of literature. Their existence is always precarious and never financially profitable, but they provide the freedom to experiment with new ideas and develop fresh lines of criticism. In 1940 it actually became illegal to start a new magazine, and officially there was no paper to start one anyway, but if paper could be obtained from somewhere it was possible for one to appear masquerading as a miscellany. Wartime conditions proved particularly favourable to miscellanies, anthologies and magazines, of which *Penguin New Writing*, the wartime format

21

of *New Writing*, was the leading example. In 1946 there was a
fresh burst of activity as people released from the forces and
war work set out on literary careers. Paper was still a problem,
and the regulations against new magazines technically still in
force. An Austrian refugee who had worked during the war for
the BBC, George Weidenfeld, wanted to start a magazine,
Contact, but found he could only produce it as a series of
miscellanies. The younger son of Harold Nicolson, Nigel,
joined the staff from the army in January 1947; the firm of
Weidenfeld and Nicolson was launched on 10 November 1949.

Adam and *Outposts* are the only literary magazines launched
in wartime still in business. In the depths of the winter fuel
crisis of 1947 the Ministry of Fuel and Power decided that the
entire periodical press was not an essential industry, and for a
fortnight no magazines of any kind, from *Punch* to pornography, were published. For good measure the BBC's Third
Programme was taken off the air. Denys Val Baker's *Little
Reviews Anthology 1947–8* (itself delayed by production difficulties) reported that in the previous eighteen months the
number of little magazines had almost doubled, and listed
seventy-one, though some had already collapsed. In the *Little
Reviews Anthology* for 1949 Baker wrote:

> Despite the fact that it is technically easier now to bring out new
> reviews than during the war, there are probably fewer literary maga-
> zines today than in, say, 1944. A number of reviews of high quality,
> such as the *Bell, Selected Writing, Now, Polemic, Writing Today, Irish
> Harvest*, and *Transformation* have ceased publication.

To these may be added *Khaki and Blue, Oasis, Voices, The
New Savoy, The Mint, Dint, New Theatre, Orion, Counterpoint,
Gangrel, The Critic, Politics and Letters, Pilot Papers, Focus,
Future, Million, The Arts, Orpheus, The Windmill* and *London
Forum*, and this is not a complete list. Baker commented, 'The
most hard-hit appear to have been the various short story
collections', and true to his own prognosis, the *Little Reviews
Anthology* never appeared again. Other magazines succumbed
by the end of the decade: *Horizon, New Writing, Our Time*,

The God that Failed

The Wind and the Rain, The Strand, The New English Review and *Life and Letters Today*. V. S. Pritchett summed up in November 1950: 'It is pointless to say "there are no young writers"; there are no young periodicals to publish them.'

In order to maintain full employment and the standard of living of the working population, the Labour government was forced to continue austerity measures long after the end of the war that once had made them acceptable. They got small thanks for their ends, and none for their means. Exasperation with shortages and controls led to articles such as barrister C. K. Allen's 'The Pinpricked Life' in the 5 November 1948 number of the *Spectator*. Reviewing the alarming rise in crime, particularly among juveniles, Allen suggested that everyone was having to become more or less criminal to survive:

> There is the whole demoralizing under-the-counter rigmarole, and, worst of all, the pervading atmosphere of petty corruption, direct and indirect, in cash and in kind. Not only kissing but all life goes by favour, and it becomes a maxim, grinned or groaned at, that 'you can't get anything done unless you know somebody'. One must either belong to the commissar class, or sedulously cultivate acquaintanceship among it.

Corruption was very much in the headlines at the time of Allen's article. A dubious entrepreneur, Sidney Stanley, was currently before a judicial enquiry on the grounds that he had tried to gain favours from officials in the Board of Trade. Justice Lynskey's report, with its revelations of the world of spivs, greyhound tracks, football pools, black-market restaurants and coupon-free clothes, became a bestseller.

In October 1948 the *New Statesman* was comparing life in London unfavourably with Munich. 'At any medium restaurant in Munich you can eat better and more than in the best West End restaurants in London. There is no limit to the number of courses one is permitted to consume. If you like you can have soup, *hors d'oeuvres*, beef tartare, joint, poultry, fish, sweet, savoury and coffee.' In March, workmen had at last begun to demolish the air-raid shelters in Lincoln's Inn Fields. The very

23

next day the Home Secretary Sir John Anderson recommended that the government should start building new shelters – against the atom bomb.

The harsh facts of Britain's economic difficulties between 1945 and 1950 would have had the depressing effect that they did have on cultural life regardless of what happened politically, but the lowering atmosphere of deprivation and frustration was further embittered by the development of the Cold War. Indeed, Britain's economic difficulties played their part in causing it. The Cold War which, as the term implies, is a climate rather than a series of events, has two aspects: the external and easily discernible opposition of the military and diplomatic forces of East and West, and the much more subtle internal conditions that opposition creates, the mood of fear and suspicion that affects both opponents. The Cold War climate was felt in areas a long way from the political events that created it.

That climate set in over a number of years. Britain, America and Russia remained technically allies after the partition of Germany became a constitutional fact. America and Britain had their own differences over the British Empire and Social-ism. The summer and autumn of 1945 was a period of chaos, followed by a series of intensifying arguments between the Allies over the terms of the peace. By the autumn of 1946 the Russians and Americans were plainly in opposing camps, with Britain being drawn by her economic dependence into the American; not without some protests, however, from the 'Keep Left' group who wanted to see Britain lead a revived Europe as a 'Third Force'. But Britain's Foreign Minister was Ernest Bevin, staunchly nationalist and staunchly anti-Communist as a result of his long experience of battles with Communists within the trades union movement. It was said that Bevin's foreign policy was Winston Churchill's, and Churchill's 'Iron Curtain' speech at Fulton Missouri in March 1946 did much to set the tone of the developing conflict. Churchill, of course, was out of office, and his speech was officially disowned, but it helped to create a favourable attitude in the United States Congress towards continuing to lend money to Britain. Again, it was Britain's decision to withdraw from Greece early in 1947 (where British troops were supporting a right-wing government against Communist guerillas) which led America to fill the power vacuum. This in turn led to the 'Truman Doctrine' of opposition to all potential Communist threats, and the military aspects of the Marshall Plan.

By the end of 1947 the four-power approach to Germany was clearly at an end, and Britain, France, and America decided to take action to revive the economy of their sectors by reforming the currency. This had a miraculous effect on the German economy, but the Russians objected to the inclusion of Berlin in the reform, and the blockade and airlift (which ran from July 1948 to May 1949) began. American bombers returned to bases in Britain. Meanwhile the last non-Communist coalition government behind the Iron Curtain, Czechoslovakia, fell in a *coup d'état* in the spring of 1948. In April 1949 the North Atlantic military treaty was signed. In July Russia successfully exploded an atomic bomb.

The existence of the atom bomb, even when only America possessed the weapon, was enough to create an atmosphere of fear. But the source of the insidious anxiety that so weakened the imaginative wills of artists and writers lay deeper. Writing – a little wearily one feels – yet another article on 'The Future of Fiction' in 1947, V. S. Pritchett commented: 'The real political subject of the last fifteen years has not been the clash of beliefs, but the vacillations and disillusions accompanying the wish to believe.'

In the 1930s the predominant political attitude of the British (and American) intelligentsia had been liberal or left-wing. Communism was more than fashionable; it represented the logical point of opposition to Fascism in Germany and Italy, and the Spanish Civil War provided a stage on which to rehearse the approaching conflict. Russia supported the Republican government, Germany and Italy backed the Franco rebels, and the liberal democracies stood aside. But gradually disillusion with Communism set in. There was the slow seep of rumours about the trials and purges in Russia, there were George Orwell's and Franz Borkenau's revelations about the Communist commissar's activities in Spain. The Russian–German Non-Aggression Pact of August 1939 was the first turning-point, and although Communism was legitimized again by the German invasion of Russia in 1941, the drift away from Communism continued, encouraged by the writings of ex-Communists such as Arthur Koestler's *Darkness at Noon* (1940). The wartime mood was summed up in the title of John Spink's article 'The Strategic Retreat of the Left' in *Horizon*, January 1943 (see *Under Siege*, page 79).

The sense of disillusion was in no way altered by the Labour victory in 1945, though Alan Pryce-Jones, for one, questioned if disillusion was the right word for the attitude that had prevailed since 1939. He wrote in 1956:

a kind of numbness seized us. The war of experience was already over before our war began. Abyssinia and Spain and Austria and Czechoslovakia were the battlefields of the mind, and the real battlefields which followed later never touched the imagination half so closely. Indeed, for many of the more articulate British participants, the process of war, once experienced, was no more than an enormous and sometimes dangerous game of cops-and-robbers. The leaders pronounced noble words, but in the light of events whatever they said was greeted with the utmost cynicism by those who were actually doing the fighting. There was no question of disillusionment, because there had never been an illusion.

Whatever illusions the arrival of Socialism might have encouraged were soon dispersed. Connolly had supported Labour in 1945, in 1947 he declared:

the honeymoon between literature and action, once so promising, is over. We can see, looking through these old *Horizons*, a left-wing and sometimes revolutionary political attitude among writers, heritage of Guernica and Munich, boiling up to a certain aggressive optimism in the war years, gradually declining after D-Day and soon after the victorious general election despondently fizzling out. It would be too easy to attribute this to the policy of the editors, their war-weariness and advancing years. The fact remains that a Socialist Government, besides doing practically nothing to help artists and writers . . . has also quite failed to stir up either intellect or imagination; the English renaissance, whose false dawn we have so enthusiastically greeted, is further away than ever. . . . Somehow, during the last two years, the left-wing literary movement has petered out.

One effect of this disappointment was for writers to turn away from political commitment of any kind, to retreat into the 'ivory tower' from which the conflicts of the 1930s had drawn them. But to renounce politics is a political act, and the drift from the Left became a move to the Right. Those who had committed themselves to Communism in the 1930s had done so out of despair at western values, and the experience was often like a religious conversion. Now despair ruled again. When, in 1950, six ex-Communists published a collective account of their loss of faith, they chose the title *The God That Failed*. This testament of loss of faith by members of the senior generation had its effect on their juniors. Arnold Wesker has said that it was 'one book that really shattered me, as it must have shattered other people'.

Loss of faith in Communism was inevitably accompanied by a change in perception of the USSR (and *vice versa*). Anti-Soviet talk had begun as soon as the war ended, when stories started to filter back about Russian behaviour in their occupied zone of Germany. Concern for what might happen if the Germans in all the four zones continued to be allowed to starve, led Victor Gollancz in 1946 to publish one of the earliest of a flood of Cold War books. Gollancz's change of attitude had followed the wartime pattern exactly. In the 1930s he was the publisher of the highly successful Left Book Club, which (in Cold War terms) had been a Communist 'front organization', by virtue of the number of Communists who wrote for it, and the prominent position of a pro-Communist, John Strachey, on the selection panel. Strachey had also broken with the Communists and was now a Labour minister. Strachey contributed to Gollancz's *The Betrayal of the Left* (1941), which marked completion of the first stage in the process of disenchantment. In 1946 Gollancz published *Our Threatened Values*:

> While I by no means underestimate the dangers of a resurgent fascism in many parts of the world, and particularly, owing to our own follies, in Germany, I am certain that it is in the spread of what is today called communism, and in the growing power throughout Europe of Soviet Russia, that the strongest positive forces opposed to the stability and development of our western civilization can now be found.

This may be said to represent the external aspect of the Cold War. There was also the internal: 'Just as communists inside Russia must safeguard the foundations of the new society by any means, so must communists outside Russia, also by any means, serve the interests of Soviet power.'

The interest of *Our Threatened Values* is that it comes from a committed left-wing publisher. Most British publishers contributed at least one Cold War volume in the following years. Books and broadcasts, leading articles in the serious newspapers and magazines and scare stories in the popular ones, created an atmosphere in which there was safety in conformity, and no encouragement at all to think freely. The young literary critic Raymond Williams, a Communist Party member for eighteen months before the war, commented in 1948:

> it is an open season for communists, and unctuous anti-marxism will pass for genuine liberalism in its shooting clothes. One is reminded how difficult any contemporary path of political goodwill must become. Perhaps at least one can say this: that the public fantasies and indulgences of popular commercial writers, the prejudices and abstractions which these produce, and the absence of a criticism which actively guards the quality of political and other writing, are factors which impressively contribute to this moral chaos of which one manifestation is war.

The criticism that Williams was calling for was not forthcoming.

Fortunately, the Cold War mentality which developed in Britain did not reach the state of paranoia which sometimes afflicted the United States. No House of Commons committee solemnly examined the works of art chosen for exhibition abroad by the British Council, in search of Communist tendencies, as did a House of Representatives committee with a group of paintings chosen by a cultural arm of the State Department. (Out of forty-five painters 'no fewer than twenty were definitely New Deal in various shades of Communism'.) Charlie Chaplin's 1947 comedy *Monsieur Verdoux*, in which a bank clerk applies the capitalist ethic to murder, was warmly greeted in London. In New York it was considered subversive. Britain had no Senator McCarthy.

The difference between British and American attitudes is conveyed in Pamela Hansford Johnson's *A Summer to Decide* (1948), a novel very consciously evocative of the period. In New York the hero asks if Americans are really afraid that Russia will start a war, and is told that they are, to the point of being ready to strike first. He then explains why the possibility is less discussed in Britain:

One, the ordinary person is too busy. I mean he's too busy coping with the daily problems of his rationed life, and trying to see a clear road for his own future. Two, he sees the ruins of war all round him – along the railway lines as he goes to work, along the bus routes. He sees the place where the pub was, and the children's playground on the cleared site. He's still wondering how long it'll take to tidy them all up. He hasn't got round to contemplating new ruins. And despite sporadic hullaballoo in the newspapers, he simply doesn't see Russia as a threat to himself.

Nonetheless, the British government ordered a purge of Communists from the Civil Service at the beginning of 1948, of which the most prominent victim was the eminent scientist J. B. S. Haldane; a similar prejudice was felt in academic circles. When the British Communist Party proposed affiliation with the Labour Party in 1946, the Labour Party's chairman Harold Laski replied with a pamphlet, *The Secret Batallion*.

Organized as a conspiracy, their major desire is not to select the best possible leadership in ability and character for the end Socialism

29

desires; it is to get those on whom they can count for uncritical and devoted obedience to their orders into the key positions of a movement or party they enter to use for their own purposes.

One may wonder if fears of communist conspiracies in the furniture department caused the John Lewis Partnership in April 1949 to order the dismissal of any employee in its department stores who refused to sign an anti-Communist declaration.

Richard Crossman, assistant editor of the *New Statesman*, and who as a leading MP in the 'Keep Left' movement could not be accused of Conservative prejudice, summed up the Socialists' dilemma as 'The "Russia" Complex'. Many early Labour Party members could recall the inspiration of the Russian Revolution and, in now perceiving Russia as an aggressive totalitarian state out to sabotage the Marshall Plan, 'they find themselves at war with themselves. They are involved, personally and inescapably by their own political past, in the Soviet Union.' Younger members, whose political formation had taken place during the era of the Popular Front and the Spanish Civil War

may now convince themselves by reason that a break with the Communists is essential and that the comrades of the Spanish War and the Resistance Movement must now be crushed; but such a policy leaves a psychological wound, compensated, as in the case of a successful careerist, by vulgar anti-Communism, or unconcealed, as with the unfortunate intellectual who cannot make up his mind.

The discomforting ambivalence of the Labour Party's position had created 'among many Labour leaders an anti-Communism not unlike anti-Semitism in its emotional violence.'

The British Communist Party, with two MPs and a number of close sympathizers in the 1945 Parliament, and a membership of fewer than 50,000, was hardly an overt threat to the constitution. Its most powerful influence was in the trades union movement, but Labour Party members were so much on the alert for 'penetration' and 'infiltration' that there was not much subversive that the Communists could do, even if they wanted to. (Soviet espionage was another matter, as the Fuchs case of 1950 demonstrated.) In 1947 the Communist Party reversed its position on the production drive, in line with the recently established Cominform organization, which the Russians had set up in response to the Marshall Plan. Previously Communists had led the drive, but this was now presented as part of the capitalist anti-Communist policy of the Marshall Plan. However, there was no switch to sabotage, and the key National Union of Mineworkers, which had a Communist General Secretary, voted in favour of the Marshall Plan. In 1949 the Trades Union Congress withdrew from the Communist-dominated World Federation of Trades Unions.

The problem was not what did happen, but the fear of what might happen. J. B. Priestley wrote in October 1948:

We don't live in a world of neat plots, but in a foggy atmosphere of prejudices and cross purposes, silly rumours, tragic blunders. . . . The point here, I believe, is a very important one. We are deafened and bedevilled now by people who believe in enormous elaborate plots. Like most public men, I have had from time to time letters from unhappy victims of persecution mania, giving me in bewildering detail their accounts of fantastic conspiracies, sometimes involving hundreds of people, to kidnap or murder them. I find the same hysterical tone, the same nightmare atmosphere, in much writing and talking, these days.

It was in this atmosphere that George Orwell published *Nineteen Eighty-Four*. Completed in 1948, and published the following year, the reversal of digits points to a strong contemporary reference in his projection of a future totalitarian Britain, renamed Airstrip One and solidly part of an Atlantic block, Oceania, perpetually at war with Eastasia or Eurasia. But Orwell's consistently anti-Communist position was taking on a new meaning as political circumstances altered. He had found it very difficult to find a publisher for his anti-Stalinist allegory *Animal Farm* (1945), but by 1948 his reputation had changed. 'Ask any Stalinist today what English writer is the greatest danger to the Communist cause, and he is likely to answer "Orwell". Ask the ordinary reader what is the most familiar of Orwell's books and he is likely to answer *Animal Farm,*' wrote George Woodcock in *The Writer and Politics* (1948).

Clearly the world of *Nineteen Eighty-Four* contains many elements derived from the Russian Communist model: the one-party state, the cult of the single omniscient leader, the secret police, the false confessions and the trials, the constant re-writing of history and suppression of inconvenient evidence, the total subordination of the intelligentsia to the requirements of the state; there were those who took Orwell seriously when he wrote that the thought-killing language Newspeak had been developed 'to meet the ideological needs of Ingsoc, or English Socialism'. The material aspects of the novel, the sprawling seedy city, the power cuts and shortages, the limited world of the proles and the existence of a privileged inner group who could obtain rare luxuries, reflect those of London in wartime and after. But equally, the idea of Britain as a vast stationary aircraft-carrier for the forward defence of America, a common reference at the time of the Berlin airlift, may have contributed to the re-naming of Britain as Airstrip One. And Airstrip One is in the Oceanic, not the Eurasian block. It is a Marxist idea that perpetual war is a necessary consequence of capitalism.

A Cold War has many of the advantages, and misses some of the disadvantages, of a hot one. Apart from the economic advantage to those whose energies are devoted to preparing for the war they say they are trying to prevent, it reinforces the virtues of patriotism and conformity, and justifies an emphasis on security which undermines the position of anyone who wishes to question the *status quo*. Orwell had observed the totalitarianism of Nazi Germany and Russia, and in wartime he had seen the liberal democracies forced to use similar methods of state direction and propaganda. *Animal Farm* and *Nineteen Eighty-Four* seem to fall into the category of Cold War books, but that was not Orwell's intention. When in 1946 the Communist writer Randall Swingler accused him of doing well out of attacking Russia, he replied:

32

The God that Failed

For some years past, orthodoxy – at least the dominant brand of it – has consisted in not criticising Stalin, and the resulting corruption has been such that the bulk of the English literary intelligentsia has looked on at torture, massacre and aggression without expressing disapproval and perhaps in the long run without feeling it. This may change, and in my opinion probably will change. In five years it may be as dangerous to praise Stalin as it was to attack him. But I would not regard that as an advance. Nothing is gained by teaching a parrot a new word. What is needed is the right to print what one believes to be true, without having to fear bullying or blackmail from *any* side.

Orwell's prophecy of 1946 proved correct. He commented in *The English People* (1947) that in general 'the English are not sufficiently interested in intellectual matters to be intolerant about them', and only among the intelligentsia did orthodoxies flourish. By 1950 the dominant orthodoxy had become conservative, or, if you prefer, 'non-political', which often meant reflecting conservative moral and aesthetic views at one remove from political statements. Doris Lessing's semi-autobiographical left-wing heroine in *The Four-Gated City* (1969) took the temperature of the time:

Two, three years, had changed the climate completely. 'Out' was humanitarianism, warmth, protest, anger. What was 'in' was the point of view put by the able Miss [Dorothy] Sayers. Why? Very simple indeed. The 'cold war' was spreading, had already spread, from politics, to the arts. Any attitude remotely associated with 'communism' was suspect, indeed, dangerous. Few intellectuals had not been associated with the left, in some form of it, during the 'thirties and the 'forties. Precisely these intellectuals were now running, in one way and another, the arts. Tom, Dick and Harry, they were now peddling, for all they were worth, a point of view summed up by the slogan: The Ivory Tower. This was admirable, subtle, adult, good, and above all, artistic. Its opposite was crude, childish, bad, inartistic.

The collapse of morale of the literary Left had a largely negative effect on English cultural life; the intellectual climate, any more than the economic climate, did not encourage an expansive attitude. But at the same time there was a positive revival of the Right. Politically, the period 1945–50 saw Lord

Woolton's reorganization of the Conservative Party machine, so that it had both funds and, through the creation of a research department, means to put a much more closely argued Conservative case. It was also assisted by the strong Conservative bias in the political spectrum of the national press, for out of the seventeen daily and Sunday newspapers, only the *Daily Mirror*, the *Daily Herald, Reynold's News* and the *News Chronicle* were committed to the Labour government. *The Times* was officially neutral, while the two leading 'quality' newspapers, Lord Camrose's *Daily Telegraph* and Lord Kemsley's *Sunday Times* were strongly Conservative, as were Lord Beaverbrook's papers centred on the *Daily Express* and the *Evening Standard*, and Lord Rothermere's group centred on the *Daily Mail*. While the Labour Party had to cope with the extreme difficulties of office, the Conservatives could prepare themselves for the day when the unpopular measures forced on the government would swing opinion in their favour. Assisted by the redistribution of Parliamentary constituencies, they almost succeeded in gaining power in 1950, and then finally took office in 1951, after the Labour government collapsed in disarray. They were to continue in office throughout the rest of the period covered by this book.

It may be that the emphasis on the external pressures affecting cultural life has made this account excessively gloomy. The arts, after all, survived. This was the period of the founding of the Edinburgh Festival, the Aldeburgh Festival and the Institute of Contemporary Arts; the state's commitment to patronage of the arts was steadily growing. New writers, poets and painters did begin to establish themselves, and established ones continued to work and be published. But the Labour government failed to capture the imagination. As Priestley put it:

The artists wonders rather dubiously about the Socialist atmosphere of co-operation, committees, and common sense . . . he is doubtful about a society that no longer has either magnificent palaces or picturesque hovels but only nice bungalows and tidy communal flats;

and he is ready, secretly perhaps, to regret the dramatic values that will disappear from a society abolishing all terrific social inequalities.

Evelyn Waugh, for one, made no secret of his regret for the passing of privilege. But he had the advantage of consistency. Others, the majority, were driven back from the progressive positions that they had held before the war. Stephen Spender, one-time member of the Communist Party, now wrote, 'Socialism is afraid of ideas and ideals, of a conception of humanity which includes the rich as well as the poor, of the unfettered imagination.' The artist turned in on himself and, like Elizabeth Bowen, asserted that his responsibilities were only towards his craft: 'writers should keep out of pulpits and off platforms, and just write.' And being an artist was not much fun any more, as Alan Ross, a poet reared by wartime Fitzrovia, recorded in 1950: 'There was a perceptible change in the relation of the artist to society. Bohemianism, like Bloomsbury and Chelsea, was dead as a term applicable to Art. Painters, like writers, could no longer afford *la vie bohème*. Artists, with the slight rise in the respectability of their professions, became bourgeois. The best painters and writers preferred to be taken for stockbrokers or professional men of leisure, rather than reveal their trade by their appearance.' This is virtually a programme for Rodrigo Moynihan's 1951 Festival of Britain picture, *Portrait Group (The Teaching Staff of the Painting School, Royal College of Art, 1949–50)* (Plate 1).

In November 1948 the publisher Geoffrey Faber contributed an article titled 'The Critical Moment' to the *Spectator*. He complained of government pressures to produce technical, informative work instead of imaginative fiction, and of the difficulty of producing anything at all in the current economic circumstances. He then turned to the decline of contemporary literature:

During a routine conference for the purpose of going over my own firm's forthcoming publications, I found myself wondering aloud where 'literature' had got to. Almost every book seemed to deal with some more or less specialized subject. That evening I attended a meeting of a society whose members include editors, critics, librarians, authors and literary agents, as well as booksellers and publishers. We were addressed by the editor of a famous periodical; and the burden of his utterances was precisely the doubt I had expressed in the afternoon. There were one or two dissentients in the discussion that followed; but the general opinion was overwhelmingly with the speaker. . . . Signs of exhaustion are only to be expected. As a nation, or an island group of nations, we have suddenly exchanged riches for poverty, and power for insecurity. This change in our status and prospects has come as a reward for our 'finest hour'. Until we have realistically and courageously adjusted ourselves to it, we are not likely to produce very much worthwhile literature. The process of adjustment is going to be slow and painful.

CHAPTER TWO

CRISIS IN THE UNIVERSITY

'The voice of the lively don rings throughout the land.'

The *Listener*, July 1948

When Geoffrey Faber wrote of Britain's cultural life undergoing a slow and painful adjustment to post-war conditions he had the country's economic and political weakness most in mind. But what was also needed was an adjustment in the attitude of writers and artists themselves, an institutional adjustment – if the loosely related official and unofficial formations governing Britain's cultural life can be called an institution. While external economic and political factors discouraged change, expansion or experiment, there were few attempts to revitalize cultural life from within.

In some ways writers and artists had done well out of the war, certainly those who had stayed behind in London. Tom Harrisson, one of the originators in 1936 of the sociological group Mass Observation, who had left London to be parachuted into Borneo in 1944, noted on his return two years later in a 'Demob Diary' for the *New Statesman*:

How well off the intellectuals are. The fine standard of living of friends, who were, pre-war, penniless. For years, people insisted in *New Writing* (and in their cups), that the artist *must* have financial security before he could do his best work – that the economic position

37

of the artist was the root of all his frustration. Now, free from the shadow of overdraft, some of them are making thousands where before they made tens. When, then, does the big creation begin?

It was a fair question, although from the inside things did not look quite so prosperous. Cyril Connolly, at the centre of the literary world as editor of *Horizon*, decided in 1947 that the magazine would not publish its customary annual review of poetry – because the poetry of 1946 was so bad. He detected signs of institutional atrophy in the world he inhabited. 'Viewing the scene of 1947, moreover, one is conscious of the predominance of a certain set of names, the literary "Best People", who somewhat resemble a galaxy of impotent prima donnas, while around them rotate tired businessmen, publishers, broadcasters and Civil Servants who once were poets, novelists, and revolutionary thinkers.' Prosperity was all very well, but Connolly could still dream of the Filmore Van Rensselaer Crutch Society for the Redemption of Middle-Aged Hacks. This generous foundation would relieve the hack of all reviewing and broadcasting duties for a year (even of reviewing gardening books for the *Financial Times*), and send him to the Bahamas to do nothing. The following year the hack would actually be able to write a good book.

The unofficially institutional nature of cultural life was reinforced on 29 September 1946 with the launching of a new institution, the Third Programme of the BBC. Tom Harrisson's criticisms as an outsider became more specific, this time in a letter to the *Listener* in January 1947. He complained that the Third Programme had become

'cliquey', a bit of a mutual admiration society. . . . A relatively small number of persons, nearly all between the ages of thirty and fifty, and many of them personal friends, exercise a major influence on the cultural side of a large proportion of our newspapers, weekly journals, arts bodies and the plethora of new monthlies and quarterlies. The Third Programme has further helped those who have 'arrived' to widen their prestige and to ensure their getting a larger slice of the income cake. There is a real danger that today, when there are more new media for writing, etc., than ever before, it may become more difficult than ever before for the younger generation to make good, especially since their generation lost more than any other in time, opportunity, output during 1939–46.

Harrisson feared that the Third Programme was setting up a closed shop of cosy criticism. Not along afterwards he returned to Borneo and remained there until 1970.

The unofficial connections underlying British cultural life can be traced in the links between those who staffed, and broadcast on, the Third Programme. For instance, its first Controller, George Barnes, was related to 'Bloomsbury' through his mother, a member of the Strachey family; E. M. Forster, a regular BBC contributor, was a close friend. The Third Programme *was* experimental, in that it had no fixed points, beyond beginning at six in the evening; it had no news bulletins and aimed at the highest level of achievement in music, drama and the spoken word, without 'educational' compromise. 'There will be few "hearing-aids" for listeners to the Third Programme,' promised Barnes.

Strictly speaking, the Third Programme employed no producers itself, being supplied with material from production departments which also serviced the Light Programme and the Home Service (the names indicate their functions). The most important department was Features, re-organized in 1945 under Laurence Gilliam. It was important because unlike the departments concerned with drama, music or, for that matter, talks, Features was a specific product of radio techniques, and used the means of original writing, adaption, interviews, drama, poetry and music for exclusively radio ends. Features had established its reputation during the war, and already employed a number of poets and writers, prominent among them Louis MacNeice, who were known for more than their BBC work. The department employed some forty people, fifteen or so of them producers, and from 1945 on many of them besides MacNeice were literary men: the poets Terence Tiller and W. R. Rodgers, the satirist Stephen Potter, writers Christopher

Sykes, Paul Dehn and Rayner Heppenstall. These were on the BBC staff, but the list of those who worked as outside contributors extends to virtually all those who were active in the world of letters during the late 1930s and wartime. (A glance at the 1956 selection *From the Third Programme*, edited by the then Controller, John Morris, will show which contributors were considered suitable for the Third Programme.)

Though working for the bureaucratic BBC, the personnel of the Features Department (and its complementary, Talks) behaved as uninstitutionally as possible, following the practice of Fleet Street or the independent man of letters, in that they stayed out of the office as much as possible. The literary origins of most of the group probably account for the creation of a miniature Bohemia in the pubs conveniently near the BBC. This lesser Bohemia supplanted the decaying Fitzrovia of Charlotte Street in the post-war years; its pubs were The Windsor Castle in Weymouth Mews, The Stag's Head on the corner of Hallam Street and New Cavendish Street, the 'Whores' Lament' (The Horse and Groom) in Great Portland Street, the 'Gluepot' (The George) in the same street, so called because once inside it was very difficult to get out, Shirreff's Wine Bar off Upper Regent Street, and an afternoon drinking-club known as the ML. In his autobiography *Portrait of the Artist as a Professional Man* (1969) Rayner Heppenstall, who joined the department in 1945, states candidly that he preferred to drink in The Stag's Head at lunch-time (when most office days seem to have begun) rather than The George, because drinking in The George tended to lead to an afternoon in the ML, followed by a return to The George at 6 p.m. 'It would be there that one encountered any such of one's colleagues as a whole day's *désœuvrement* had rendered very drunk indeed.' The pub was of course the place for conducting business between BBC staff and contributors, and Heppenstall has supplied a fascinating list of those who circulated at one time or another in this BBC Bohemia: C. P. Snow, Pamela Hansford Johnson, Rose Macaulay, Andrew Young, Norman Cameron, Sean O'Faolin, Michael Innes (J. I. M. Stewart), George

Orwell, Angus Wilson, Laurie Lee, Henry Reed, Muriel Spark, W. H. Auden, Theodore Roethke, Robert Graves, Lawrence Durrell, Bernard Spencer, George Barker, Hugh MacDiarmid, William Empson, Roy Campbell, and, of course, Dylan Thomas. Significantly the short-story writer Julian Maclaren-Ross, a prince of Fitzrovia, tended to be frozen out; later he was banned from The Stag's Head altogether.

Although there is no doubt about the quality of these writers, for whom the BBC could be a useful source of income, it is questionable how much work they were able to do as *writers*. The Drama Department, for instance, did very litle to encourage original radio plays – producing only three specially written for radio in 1946, one in 1947 and two in 1948 – preferring to concentrate on adaptations of the classics. A radio feature, too, is in a sense an adaptation, in that it is about something else – though Louis MacNeice's *The Dark Tower*, Laurie Lee's *The Voyage of Magellan* and Henry Reed's translations were distinguished works. (The Italia prizes for drama were regularly won by the Features, not the Drama Department.) And, though Louis NacNeice announced 'Writers Wanted' in the BBC *Yearbook* for 1947, it is questionable how far the producers looked outside the established circle of their regular contributors for new blood. The old writers, too, were not satisfied with the terms under which they worked; in June 1947 the Society of Authors held a press conference to protest at the meanness and avarice of the BBC in paying low fees to contributors and exploiting the monopoly position of the *Listener*. The campaign was sponsored by Sir Osbert Sitwell, J. B. Priestley, Rosamond Lehmann, Storm Jamieson, John Masefield and Herbert Read, but such protests have hardly died away in the years since then.

Beyond the inevitable dissatisfaction over who did and who did not get work from the BBC, and how much was paid for it, there was a more serious problem. V. S. Pritchett, another sponsor of the 1947 protest, commented:

The novelist, the poet, the biographer of today are broadcasters, film script writers, publishers, journalists of all degrees; they begin by

41

saying they are doing this work in order to buy for themselves the leisure to write the next book; they end by having no time for the book at all. They cannot afford to write it. Nor are these contemporaries the failures in their art; on the contrary, many are the outstanding talents. All that can be said when they complain is that they are luckier than the very young who cannot get their books published at all and who have been absorbed from the start by full-time jobs at the BBC, the COI [Central Office of Information] and other intellectual bureaucracies.

In spite of the bohemianism of the Features Department, the BBC remained an intellectual bureaucracy, and writers new or old were not encouraged to make their contributions controversial. A. J. P. Taylor, for instance, was banned for a while in 1948. Geoffrey Bridson, Laurence Gilliam's assistant head of the Features Department, writes in his autobiography *Prospero and Ariel* (1971):

The excessive timidity of the BBC Higher Command in the early post-war years is truly ludicrous to remember, especially in the light of what was seen and heard on the air in the permissive sixties. But the fact remains that until the advent of Hugh Carlton Greene as Director-General in 1960, the BBC Home Service had never regarded itself as a pacemaker for public opinion. Its role, as the BBC saw it, was to reflect the most respectably orthodox opinion as it already existed – and that meant conservatism of the pre-Macmillan kind.

Harman Grisewood, who succeeded Geoffrey Barnes as head of the Third Programme (Barnes was promoted to be the awesome-sounding Director of the Spoken Word), has admitted that he failed to get the Third to put on any talks which 'dealt directly with the principles of contemporary culture'.

This timidity, or, if you prefer, institutional prudence, was quickly noticed. Reviewing the first year's work of the Third Programme, W. E. Williams (himself an important institutional figure in adult education, the Army Bureau of Current Affairs, a Director of Penguin and later Secretary-General of the Arts Council) noted that the Third 'jibs at full-blooded controversy on current affairs, religion, or sociology'. This is one reason why the Third Programme found itself speaking to such a tiny audience. To be fair, the Third had never pretended to have mass appeal – that was its virtue; its object was to act as a centre of excellence, and as such it gained the BBC much prestige, though the people who accorded this prestige were in foreign countries where the Third was inaudible. In an analysis for the quickly defunct magazine *Pilot Papers* in 1947 Peggy McIver concluded that 'the BBC is now geared in both policy and organization to serve audience groups as they already exist rather than affect public taste'. At most, the Third Programme was attracting 5 per cent of the adult population, and had 1¼ million listeners on a typical evening. This, she argued, was about a third of the potential – the potential of the new audiences created in wartime but which were now being allowed to lapse. Much the same thing was said by Bruce Belfrage on the Third's fifth anniversary in 1951. One per cent of the BBC's total audience listened to the Third Programme; sometimes the audience was so small that it could not be measured by the BBC's own listener research techniques. Again, Bruce Belfrage recognized that it was not the Third's intention to have mass appeal, but his argument was that it was missing even its possible audience, which he put at between three and four million. He also had a familiar criticism to make: 'There is no doubt at times a faint and carefully diluted touch of Bloomsbury in evidence which puts a great many people off.' George Orwell had put things more bluntly in 1947: 'the language of the BBC is barely intelligible to the masses.'

The arguments over the Third Programme were the opening phrases of the continuing debate over the role of mass communications in cultural life. For the moment we are concerned with the problems of the writer, and Orwell, as during the war, was wary of encroaching institutionalization. In *Polemic* No. 2 (1946) he wrote:

In our age, the idea of intellectual liberty is under attack from two directions. On the one side are its theoretical enemies, the apologists of totalitarianism, and on the other its immediate, practical enemies,

43

monopoly and bureaucracy. Any writer or journalist who wants to retain his integrity finds himself thwarted by the general drift of society rather than by active persecution. The sort of things that are working against him are the concentration of the Press in the hands of a few rich men, the grip of monopoly on radio and the films, the unwillingness of the public to spend money on books, making it necessary for nearly every writer to earn part of his living by hack work, the encroachment of official bodies like the Ministry of Information and the British Council, which help the writer to keep alive but also waste his time and dictate his opinions, and the continuous war atmosphere of the past ten years, whose distorting effects no one has been able to escape. Everything in our age conspires to turn the writer, and every other kind of artist as well, into a minor official.

The institutionalization of culture had its most serious consequences for those who had not yet found a niche in an institution, official or unofficial. Those who had found a position were at least able to survive economically, if not creatively. It was not for nothing that Peter Ratazzi's short-lived organization, Front Line Generation (described by a former member, Derek Stanford, as 'a sort of Old Comrades Club for the long-haired boys out of battle-dress'), declared opposition to all 'restrictive monopolies from financial monopolies to literary cliques'. There is no need to repeat the evidence given in the last chapter of the shrinking opportunities for new work, but the physical limitations placed on starting a new publishing house are a good example. Whereas the established publisher could, at a pinch and with loss of quality, just about produce as many books as he had published in 1939, an ex-serviceman who wanted to go into publishing was allowed a meagre forty-four hundredweight of paper a quarter, or enough to publish 21,000 copies of one novel a year. Magazines, as has been shown, were equally difficult to launch and sustain. The Indian writer and critic Balachandra Rajan complained:

What these restrictions have done, in effect, is to petrify our literary structure in the obsolescent formations of 1939. Those formations had a value then, though perhaps a value which was even then diminishing; they have no value today except as an impediment to the more honest

44

writer's powers of survival. Always the task of living letters has been to break down the barriers of literary vested interests, barriers fortified by the equipment of civilization, the newspapers, the radio, and the commercial highbrow press. . . . But publishing restrictions make this challenge impossible. Established magazines stand firm behind the shield of their quota and the opposition, unable to take shape or devise a strategy, remains an ineffective welter of pamphlets, polemics and ephemeral little reviews.

From the relatively independent viewpoint of a literary agent, A. D. Peters assessed the chances of a new writer as 'very, very slender indeed. The publisher is harassed on the one side by his regular established authors, none of whom is satisfied with his allocation of paper. He is harassed on the other by the necessity to reprint his backlist, on which his security depends, and to bring out educational books. He wants new writers, of course. But if the new writer turns out to be successful, the publisher is in a worse mess than if he had never taken him on at all.' Painters, whose opportunity for showing their work was restricted to a half-dozen galleries within a quarter of a mile of Piccadilly, found it difficult to make a living, even when they had broken into this magic circle. The newly appointed Director of the National Gallery, Philip Hendy, commented in 1946 that only a handful of middle-aged artists could price their pictures at more than £100, and so live off their work: 'still more ironical: the fact that there has never been a time in English history when young and original artists were so much pampered by the state, so artificially boosted.' Their work was being shipped around for exhibitions all the time, but apart from a small hiring fee from the Arts Council, they got nothing from it. Throughout the late 1940s, the opportunities of a new artist in any field were slim indeed.

There was, however, one area where there was opportunity and expansion: the universities. As the *Listener* reported in July 1948, 'in modern England many promising authors are perforce Civil Servants, newspaper-men or employees of semi-public concerns. Only in the universities is much opportunity provided for artistic expression, and the voice of the lively don rings throughout the land.'

Up to 1939 official policy towards the universities had been one of almost complete *laissez-faire*, with the then sixteen self-governing universities developing along their own lines. With the exception of Scotland, the system was dominated by the seniority and prestige of Oxford and Cambridge, which enjoyed influence and respect well beyond all the other institutions (including London) that were colloquially known as Redbrick. The war led to greatly increased state interest in the universities, particularly in the field of science. While student numbers declined drastically between 1939 and 1945, especially in art subjects, this period was the prelude to a shift in policy which meant that within ten years university education changed from being an almost entirely private to a public responsibility. The Butler Education Act of 1944 meant that education was no longer the privilege of wealth, for by 1949 68 per cent of the student population were receiving financial help from government or local authority grants. At the same time the pre-war university population of 50,000 had increased to 83,000. London was still the largest single university, but Oxford had increased its numbers by 50 per cent and Cambridge by 17 per cent, and these remained, after London, the biggest universities by far, retaining their cultural dominance.

The universities were especially crowded immediately after the war because of the large numbers of ex-service personnel who wanted to catch up on or start their interrupted studies. It was during this period, when universities were most over-crowded and underequipped, that Evelyn Waugh's nostalgic evocation of a lost, sybaritic, 1920s Oxford in *Brideshead Revisited* (1945) had its most poignant, and pernicious, effect. Not only this, but succeeding generations of undergraduates have been misled into trying to recover a lost and probably never-existent Eden, oblivious of the social values it represented. While the expansion of the universities was in theory capable of causing a social revolution, the government was scrupulous in not interfering with the universities' policies, appointments, standards of research – or methods of selection. Although when the number of state scholarships was increased in 1947 it was decreed that not all should be available at London, Oxford or Cambridge, nothing was done that would change the preponderance of 'Oxbridge' over Redbrick. Traditionally, the public schools, outside the state system, had been the most effective producers of candidates for Oxford and Cambridge, and this did not change. Nor has it changed.

The effects of the 1945 Labour government's commitment to a new state system of education was to reinforce the power of institutions which stood outside it, and whose social influence was enhanced rather than decreased. While 'Bruce Truscot' (Edgar Peers) might protest in *Redbrick University* (1943, revised 1951) that Oxbridge 'half-strangled' the other universities, these two remained the target of every student's ambition, like Richard Hoggart's 'scholarship boy' in *The Uses of Literacy* (1957). If he did get there, he tended, as Hoggart observed, to be translated into membership of another, higher class, as he learned the unchanged values of Oxford and Cambridge. 'Becoming middle-class is in itself a process of education,' wrote Angus Maude and Roy Lewis in *The English Middle Classes* (1949). One might add, becoming educated is in itself a process of becoming middle-class.

At a time when people's minds were chiefly on getting back to normal, there seems to have been little criticism of Oxford and Cambridge's reinforcement of their privileged position. The Professor of Sociology at London University, David Glass, noted in a talk on the Third Programme in 1951 that the problems of social mobility had received very little study in the United Kingdom. Indeed, it seemed that there was something indecent in asking questions about such matters:

To look at the underside of recent contemporary social processes has sometimes been regarded as something not quite respectable. A statement implying a disparity between ability and opportunity, or suggesting that working-class children have disproportionately poor prospects of getting a university education had a pretty fair chance of starting an extended argument – at least that was true in the nineteen-thirties.

As with the BBC, there was little attempt to challenge the accepted educational arrangements; in fact, criticism of university expansion took a completely different direction – that expansion had been taken far too far.

The one work discussing post-war higher education to have any significant impact on public opinion was Sir Walter Moberly's *Crisis in the University* (1948). As Honorary Fellow of three Oxford colleges, with a career that led from a lectureship at Aberdeen to a professorship at Birmingham, the Principal-ship of University College, Exeter, the Vice-Chancellorship of Manchester University, and finally chairmanship of the University Grants Committee which channelled government money to the universities, Sir Walter Moberly was in a good position to judge the condition of the system. But the crisis he detected was moral and religious, not social or financial. The demands for specialization and departmentalization (the results of the state's policies, however much at arm's length) had created divisions within the universities, particularly between the arts and science. But while the state was demanding, and paying for, more and more students, these students were receiving no Christian guidance. The universities represented in microcosm the problems of Great Britain, where there was a fundamental refusal to confront the changes forced by war. ' "Safety first", to let well alone, *quieta non movere*, to wait for the saecular movement of thought to come to its natural climax, is no missionary policy for Great Britain in the world today, or for the universities in Great Britain. It may sound plausible in our own pleasant, and seldom war-scarred Common Rooms; it would be much less so in the universities of Central Europe.' This is an effective polemic against the complacency and inherent conservatism of privileged academic life, but Moberly wished to replace the 'morbidly exaggerated cult of neutrality' with a vigorous intellectual commitment to Christian – and traditional – values. 'For western civilization at least, and notably for Great Britain, reconstruction is to be achieved, not by abandoning our tradition, but by rediscovering and reinvigorating it.' This is a challenge to the universities not from the Left, but from the Right.

Crisis in the University certainly struck a chord, for it was generally agreed that there was a problem; but the crisis was perceived as being the result of change, certainly not of the need for change. Some felt that Moberly had not gone far enough. One of these was a Cambridge don, Michael Oakshott, an avowed conservative who was to succeed the former Labour Party chairman Harold Laski as Professor of Economics at the London School of Economics in 1951. Reviewing *Crisis in the University* in the *Cambridge Journal* (which he edited), Oakshott commented, 'oddly enough, Sir Walter pays very little attention to the "crisis in the university" which springs from the altogether excessive number of undergraduates.' Oakshott detected a threat to the traditional values of Cambridge from these new arrivals:

The leaders of the rising class are consumed with a contempt for everything which does not spring from their own desires, they are convinced in advance that they have nothing to learn and everything to teach, and consequently their aim is to loot – to appropriate to themselves the organization, the shell of the institution, and convert it to their own purpose.

If that really was the purpose of the undergraduate classes of 1946, 1947 and 1948, or of Socialists who wanted to challenge the old system, they were remarkably unsuccessful in producing any institutional change. Oxbridge continued to ensure that, in the words of the Bidding Prayer of Cambridge University, 'there may never be wanting a supply of persons duly qualified to serve God in Church and State'. In 1949, of the 4,000 people working in the Administrative Class of the Civil Service, 60 per cent had been to public school, and 80 per cent to Oxford or Cambridge, the same proportions as before the war. Between 1949 and 1951 all recruits to that class came from Oxbridge.

There was, in the words of the title of American journalist Virginia Cowles's 1949 study, *No Cause for Alarm*. Her account of post-war British society was specifically written to reassure American readers that the 1945 Labour government was not dangerous. Rightly, she points to the influence of Oxford and Cambridge educations on the leaders of both the Left and the Right:

The fact that so many men of all parties share a common intellectual background has had a profound effect in narrowing contentions between the various leaders of political thought. And for this reason Oxford must take large credit for the civilized way in which Britain's social revolution is being carried out.

In post-war Oxford and Cambridge the atmosphere was (where it was not positively Conservatve) apolitical. At Oxford the most fashionable topic for intellectual discussion was A. J. Ayer's *Language, Truth and Logic*, first published in 1936, but reissued in 1946. In an article for the *New Statesman* another academic, Graham Hough, subtly teased out the significance of this vogue for Logical Positivism, a vogue which did not imply that the intellectual rigour of Ayer's original argument was fully understood. By its concentration on language, and the question of whether or not statements can be logically tested, *Language, Truth and Logic* led to the conclusion that since they could not be objectively tested, all metaphysical, theological and ethical propositions were neither true not false, merely meaningless. Hough commented, 'there are many ways of suppressing free discussion, and to shoulder a certain class of arguments out of the accepted range of discussable subjects is one of them.' In the context of the Cold War, Hough was concerned that a philosophy that suggested that ethics were meaningless might be too expedient. Again, this was an exaggeration of Ayer's argument, but Hough goes on to link Logical Positivism with another popular post-war book, James Burnham's *The Managerial Revolution* (1941).

Burnham's book much concerned George Orwell when he was writing *Nineteen Eighty-Four*, for Burnham forecast a change towards not a classless society but one dominated by a new class of managers, whose one object is to manage in its own interest, without ethical considerations. '*Language, Truth and Logic* may yet become the *Summa Theologia* of the managerial society,' was Hough's parting shot.

The effect of Logical Positivism was to narrow down the areas about which it was safe to speculate; questions outside those areas had to be resolved on rigidly practical grounds, and politics were considered in terms of empirical, not moral, choices. The key work of political philosophy was Karl Popper's *The Open Society and its Enemies* (1945), which attacked the authoritarian prescriptions of Plato, and the historically determinist theories of Marx. The one Oxford philosopher to take an interest in the contemporary work in France of Jean-Paul Sartre, Iris Murdoch, has deplored the effects of Logical Positivism in removing ethical questions from politics:

A curious result of this development is that liberal and progressive thinkers who are touched by modern philosophy come on what they take to be logical grounds to the same conclusions about political theorizing to which conservative thinkers come on frankly moral grounds. [Isaiah] Berlin and [Thomas] Weldon and Popper agree with T. S. Eliot and Michael Oakshott that systematic political theorizing is a bad thing. The former think it so because it is 'metaphysical' and opinionated and obscures the scientific business of altering our society for the better. The latter think it so because it interferes with the deep operation of traditions which should not be tampered with by critical reflection.

While Existentialism had fruitful literary results, both on the Continent and for Iris Murdoch herself, Logical Positivism promoted the ethics of the Cold War. In 1948 there was a lively debate in the correspondence columns of the *New Statesman* when an anonymous 'Oxonian' suggested in an article that Ayer's book encouraged 'an anti-aesthetic Philistinism'. The same article described the prevalent right-wing atmosphere at Oxford, and reported undergraduate flirtations in the Corporate Club with Sir Oswald Mosley's Neo-Fascist ideas.

* * *

51

The failure of Oxford and Cambridge either to change or to relax their grip on the education of the country's leadership had profound cultural significance. It is absurd, of course, to argue that there were no other channels through which cultural life could flow; individual writers and artists could make their way perfectly well without an Oxbridge degree. But Oxbridge – or the Oxbridge-fed institutions like the BBC – largely determined the conditions under which they were to work. Oxbridge was central, a point made by Stephen Spender in 1949: 'to a great extent, Oxford and Cambridge provide a literary tradition which widens later into Bloomsbury, the Twenties, the Thirties, the New Romantics, into which the life of writers who have not been educated at those universities merges, albeit sometimes rebelliously.' 'Bloomsbury', or whatever that wider formation which still dominated literary life should be called, was indeed co-optive, but co-option implied some acceptance of common values, derived ultimately from university training. Spender continues a little later: 'The older writers are nearly all acquainted with each other personally. Apart from the tendency of older and more successful English writers to petrify into public monuments in their lifetime, a general consciousness of shared values which can be maintained or betrayed, informs English literary life.'

T. S. Eliot, not quite a national monument in 1948, stressed the importance of a co-optive cultural élite in his *Notes Towards the Definition of Culture* (1948). He too was suspicious of the expansion of the universities, and feared that education was in danger of being used in order to pursue social ideals rather than wisdom. He also regretted 'the exaggerated estimate of the social importance of the right school and the right college at the right university, as giving a status which formerly pertained to mere birth'. (His comment reveals the extent to which Public School and Oxbridge *were* perceived as essential to a child's future.) For Eliot, the pursuit of status through education was a sign of the disintegration of the former neat relations of the social classes; in his view, 'education should help to preserve the class and select the élite.' The cultural élite was not the same as the ruling class, since there are the culturally interested and the ignorant in every class. Eliot's description of the past constitution and function of the cultural élite is in fact a description of how it operated in his own day, including the co-option of talent. 'I think that in the past the repository of this culture has been *the* élite, the major part of which was drawn from the dominant class of the time, constituting the primary consumers of the work of thought and art produced by the minority members, who will have originated from various classes, including that class itself.' It was the duty of the élite to communicate culture to all classes, but it would remain, nonetheless, a minority interest. (Dare one say, the Third Programme?)

Further questions were how this cultural élite should be sustained, and located. T. S. Eliot, London-based critic and publisher, suspicious of the abuses of education, seemed to believe that the cultural élite would find its sustenance in the Metropolis. F. R. Leavis, Fellow of Downing College, Cambridge, believed it should be in the University. An account of Leavis's influence is complicated by his relations with the hierarchy of his own university, to which he was implacably opposed, and which he considered implacably opposed to him. 'No pupil of mine was ever appointed to a post in the Cambridge English Faculty,' he said in 1967. But his influence, particularly during the 1940s and 1950s, was broad, both directly through his teaching at Cambridge and through his critical magazine *Scrutiny* (1932–53), which was particularly influential with schoolteachers. Leavis was also opposed to the later Eliot, although he had championed him in the 1930s. In *Notes Towards the Definition of Culture*, Eliot wrote of the 'danger that education – which indeed comes under the influence of politics – will take upon itself the reformation and direction of culture instead of keeping its place as one of the activities through which a culture realizes itself.' In *Education and the University* (1943) this is what Leavis suggested the University, and particularly the English Faculty, should do.

Leavis wanted to turn the study of English into a real discipline, not a course which

> tends to foster a glib superficiality, a 'literary culture' too like those *milieux* in which literary fashions are the social currency – *milieux* of which the frequenters cultivate quickness in the uptake, knowingness about the latest market-quotations, and an impressive range of reference, all at the expense of real intelligence and disinterested understanding, or interest in anything but *kudos*.

Leavis is describing his image of Bloomsbury, and it is not an unfair one. Instead, his School of English would rigorously confront the student with problems of literary and moral discrimination that would reveal to him the nature of the central tradition of English life and thought. The Faculty would be a 'real humane focus in a university', and the University would be the moral pivot of the nation.

> The real university is a centre of consciousness and human responsibility for the civilized world; it is a creative centre of civilization – for the living heritage on which meaning and humane intelligence depend can't, in our time, be maintained without a concentrated creativity somewhere.

Fine as these feelings are, there is something about this conception of a university which reminds one of the monasteries of the Middle Ages, areas of calm in a violent and unsettled world, but also places of inwardness and retreat. Leavis argued that the value of English as a discipline was that it led constantly outside itself to other disciplines, but that there remained an attitude of hostility to the outside world. John Gross, a bitter critic of Leavis, has commented that Leavis regarded the ruling order as corrupt, but did not suggest any alternative. 'This is one reason, it seems to me, why his influence was particularly strong during the early Cold War years, when the intellectual appeal of active radical movements was at its lowest.'

Leavis was a radical, but he was radically conservative. It is true that there was a need for new discipline in writing about literature; that was something that even a despised metropolitan critic like Cyril Connolly would admit. The economics of newspapers and magazines meant that criticism had declined into reviewing. Connolly wrote in 1946, 'Mr Desmond MacCarthy is generally considered our best [Leavis would not have agreed] but it must be a long time since he has written (except occasionally on the theatre) an article of more than 800 words – the length required by the opulent Sunday newspapers. Critics, in fact, may be divided into the 800 Sunday and 1,600-word weekly classes.' The poet Kathleen Raine complained in 1949 that contemporary poets had no forum in which to discuss their work at its own level. 'Most of the critical writing of the 1940s has been journalism – that is, addressed to a public assumed to know less than the author himself.' But criticism cannot substitute for creativity, and creatively frozen by the economic and political conditions of the Cold War, more and more writers found themselves teaching rather than writing English literature. (In America this was the period of the rise of the 'New Criticism', whose textual concentration preferred to exclude biographical, social and political context.) It is significant that the poets whose reputations were made during this period were older men – Robert Graves, Edwin Muir and (though he was no longer writing poems) William Empson – whose work was most susceptible to critical explanation. Both Muir and Empson were themselves academic critics. A much younger academic and poet, John Wain, remarked in 1950: 'In an age when nine out of ten people who bother about literature do so because they are drawing a salary for it, it may well be that criticism will be remembered when poetry is forgotten, for criticism breeds fresh criticism more easily than poetry breeds fresh poetry.'

John Wain had made his living as an academic since 1946, and others of a rising generation were finding that only in the universities, where teaching staffs had doubled, was there the economic security in which to work. The post-war expansion of higher education was a great achievement in itself, but by itself, was it enough? J. B. Priestley asked precisely that question:

55

what is the use of spending hundreds of thousands of pounds every year teaching children that Shakespeare is a great dramatist, if every playhouse accessible to those children and their parents is controlled by men who are determined to present nothing but leg shows and stupid farces? Why have art teachers if real painters are nearly starving? Why teach music and then offer conductors and symphonic players not a glimpse of security? . . . why feed a British Council to spread British culture abroad, and yet go on starving that culture at home?

In 1951 there came a chance to make up for these mistakes.

THIS FESTIVAL OF BRITAIN
What a chance for budding writers!

There will be a big demand for stories and articles on Britain and her way of life. The LSJ shows by personal postal tuition how to find subjects, work out plots, develop a theme and round off work for the Editor's OK.

The London School of Journalism's advertisement was one of the more unusual (though not more obscure) contributions to the Festival of Britain. The idea of marking the centenary of the Great Exhibition of 1851 had been proposed as early as 1943; in 1945 Gerald Barry, editor of the pro-Labour *News Chronicle* suggested that an international post-war exhibition should be held in 1951, and the idea was officially taken up by a Board of Trade committee, who saw it as a chance to demonstrate Britain's 'moral, cultural, spiritual and material' recovery. As we have seen, that recovery was slow in coming, and the proposal nearly foundered in 1947, but thanks largely to Herbert Morrison, a Labour politician with a strong London base, it was agreed that a *national* exhibition could be held, which would cost about one-sixth of the original proposal. A Festival Council was established in 1948 and Gerald Barry became Festival Director.

The main thrust of the Festival was towards advertising British achievements in science, technology and design, subjects outside the scope of this book, but the Festival was a significant cultural phenomenon, both in its conception and its

56

reception. It is interesting to see how literary its treatment was, for the theme, in the words of the official guide, was 'The Autobiography of a Nation'. Those responsible for arranging the various sections of the shows were officially known as script writers, with the exhibition on the South Bank (the centre piece, but by no means the only piece) divided into chapters of the 'island story'. The literary approach was essentially didactic and propagandist. This was to be 'a challenge to the sloughs of the present and a shaft of confidence cast forth against the future', said the official guide, falling back on the language of the King James's Bible.

Both in its approach and its selection of personnel, the Festival of Britain betrayed its origins in the efforts and experience of the Ministry of Information and CEMA in wartime, when the idea of theme exhibitions with a confident message was first put into practice. The Festival was to be, in Gerald Barry's phrase, 'a tonic to the nation' – the title chosen for an exhibition in 1976 reviewing the Festival's work. Mary Banham, one of the creators of the 1976 show, has written, 'The overall intention of the Festival of Britain was that, through its diversity, the people who visited its various manifestations should not only be entertained but also educated; people were in fact encouraged to come *expecting* to be educated.' And just as the *Daily Express* had attacked the launching of CEMA in 1940 with the slogan that there was no such thing as culture in wartime, it and the other Beaverbrook newspapers attacked the Festival as a waste of time and resources.

As in 1940, the *Daily Express* was proved wrong. The Festival was a popular success in lifting some of the post-war gloom, in spite of the unhelpful weather. Two thousand cities, towns and villages in the United Kingdom organized a Festival event of some kind, with no more than encouragement (for there were no resources) from the Festival Office. Eighteen million people visited officially-sponsored Festival events, and the BBC found material for 2,700 broadcasts.

Essentially, the Festival offered a first chance to a generation of architects and designers who had spent the war building military installations like aircraft hangars (an appropriate experience, it turned out, for the designers of exhibition spaces). Some fifty architects and one hundred designers were commissioned to work on the Festival, most of them aged under forty-five, and it was in tune with the theme of post-war reconstruction that this should be so. John Summerson noted in the *New Statesman* in October 1951, as the South Bank exhibition closed, that the Festival architects were

the troublesome students of around 1935 – troublesome, 'left', self-opinionated, with a marked tendency to instruct their teachers how and what to teach. They are the students who, at that date, discovered Lloyd Wright, Gropius and Le Corbusier for themselves – and behaved as if nobody had discovered them before. It was a second rush of discovery and, as it seems now, the one which was to carry English architecture out of one age into another. This is not to generalize outrageously on the evidence of the South Bank; for wherever you look architects of this generation are doing the same kind of thing, talking the same language and looking for the same opportunities to talk it. A situation singularly unlike that prevailing in painting and sculpture.

Summerson was right about the international sources of the exhibition buildings, which with their furniture and fittings became in turn the sources of a degenerated 'contemporary' architecture and design during the 1950s. His reference to painting and sculpture needs discussion.

It was certainly the intention of the Festival's organizers that the exhibition should be a cultural event as well as a shop window. Misha Black, a member of the Exhibition Presentation Panel and the co-ordinating architect of the 'upstream' half of the South Bank show, has said, 'from the earliest planning exercises, the Festival Design Group were determined to celebrate the talents of British artists simultaneously with those of its architects and designers. We sought the collaboration both of the famous and those who were not yet renowned.' He has also said that the attempt to unify art and architecture on the South Bank was a failure, for although every section had its mural or sculpture, and usually both, the individual works were overwhelmed by the devices and designs around them, and the sheer mass of exhibits clamouring for attention. The murals were obscured, the sculptures crowded. The artists cannot be blamed for the positions in which the designers placed them, but most of them were content to scale up work in the style in which they were already working. If architects and designers were learning to use a new language, most of the artists were not. Of the major artists who could expect commissions, only Victor Pasmore had undergone a major development since the war, and he did seize the chance to extend the scale of the abstract themes he had turned to in 1947 as a response to the post-war mood of reconstruction and renovation (Plate 3); but in general the South Bank murals and sculptures represented no new ideas. It may be because of the crowded nature of the site, but there is an atmosphere of what Reyner Banham has called 'the English Picturesque' about the South Bank art, a picturesqueness most successful in the Festival Gardens at Battersea, where John Piper and Osbert Lancaster were allowed their head and encouraged to be whimsical.

Nonetheless, the South Bank did provide commissions for some fifty painters and two dozen sculptors; it is as an act of patronage on a wide scale that the Festival of Britain must be appreciated. In 1940 the state had committed itself to propping up existing institutions; now for the first time it had committed itself to a creative act. While the specially appointed Festival Office arranged the South Bank and other exhibitions, and the Council of Industrial Design selected the exhibits, responsibility for the associated cultural activities fell to the Arts Council. Since its formation from CEMA in 1945, the Arts Council had been gradually extending its influence, a process reflected by the steady increase in its annual grant from the government from £235,000 in 1945 to £570,000 in 1949 (plus an additional £25,000 for Covent Garden, as the Royal Opera House had already established itself as a major client for funds). In 1950 the Council found itself with an extra allocation of £400,000 to spend on the Festival.

The need for a nationwide celebration was met by backing twelve new arts festivals, besides bringing eleven established ones into the scheme, of which the Edinburgh International Festival, Aldeburgh and the Cheltenham Contemporary Music Festival (launched in 1945) were the most significant. London was treated to a loosely co-ordinated Festival of the Arts in May and June which included 300 concerts, a Wagner season at Covent Garden, thirty public exhibitions (eleven arranged by the Arts Council), and seven plays in repertory at the Old Vic. London's major gain was the opening of the Royal Festival Hall on the South Bank, a London County Council project which coincided with the Festival. (At the same time the LCC caused a scandal by withdrawing its grant to the London Philharmonic Orchestra on the grounds that it was under Communist influence.) There had been a desperate need for a new concert hall in London ever since the Queen's Hall was destroyed in the Blitz. The government made two gestures towards a permanent improvement in the capital's facilities by laying the foundation stone of a National Theatre building and announcing plans to rebuild the Queen's Hall. The foundation stone later had to be moved and the Queen's Hall plans were scrapped. The South Bank buildings of today, almost hygieni-cally separated from the main flow of the capital's life, are the heirs of the Festival.

The way the Arts Council spent its £400,000 reflects the history of its growth. (In fact £50,000 was not spent and remained a useful surplus.) The Council was most adventurous in opera and music, where it took its policy of support a step further by commissioning work for the first time. Direct com-missions went to Benjamin Britten and George Lloyd for their operas *Billy Budd* and *John Socman*, and after a competition which drew no fewer than sixty entries, Arthur Benjamin, Alan Bush, Berthold Goldschmidt and Karl Rankl received commis-sions to complete their opera scores. Constant Lambert had a new ballet commissioned for the Sadler's Wells at Covent

Garden, and Richard Arnell a new ballet for the Sadler's Wells Theatre Ballet at the Wells. Choral and orchestral works were commissioned from Sir Arnold Bax, William Alywn, Sir Arthur Bliss, Sir George Dyson, Gordon Jacob, Alan Rawsthorne, Edward Rubbra and Thomas Bush, and the Welsh Committee of the Arts Council commissioned a further five Welsh composers.

In the theatre the Arts Council's co-ordinating role was less established than in music, and there were some failures. The best that it could do with commercial managements was to try to persuade them to put on the most appropriate work for the Festival. The Old Vic's season, and the Sir Laurence Olivier/Vivien Leigh double *Antony and Cleopatra* and *Caesar and Cleopatra* at the St James's Theatre were a success, but the season was dominated by classics and revivals. Of new work, Christopher Fry's religious drama *A Sleep of Prisoners* toured churches across the country. Priestley's *The Golden Door* and N. C. Hunter's *Waters of the Moon* were modest successes, William Douglas-Home's *The Thistle and the Rose* a flop. In its report on the Festival, the Arts Council had to admit that 'it was disappointing that so few contemporary plays of merit emerged for the occasion'. The one flicker of controversy was over John Whiting's *Saint's Day*, which won the Arts Council competition 'for a new play of contemporary significance'. Universally damned by the critics, more progressive members of the theatre like Tyrone Guthrie, Peter Brook, John Gielgud, Peggy Ashcroft and George Devine protested in letters to the press that, on the contrary, *Saint's Day* was an important development. Retrospectively, they have been proved right.

For the visual arts, the Council played a central role, since there was no other organization that exhibited, commissioned and bought work on such a scale. £12,540 went on purchases and commissions in 1952. Twelve sculptors had work commissioned by the Arts Council, of which the major works were by Frank Dobson, Jacob Epstein, Barbara Hepworth and Henry Moore, while Moore received confirmatory recognition of his position as national sculptor with a retrospective at the Tate

Gallery. A grand anthology show, *British Painting 1925–1950*, was organized but proved to be an administrative nightmare since the Council's New Burlington Galleries were too small to hold all the exhibits, and it had to be shared with the Whitechapel Art Gallery. This allowed for a division between the more progressive painters in Anthology One and the more traditional in Anthology Two, but both the enclosing dates and the material available were somewhat arbitrary, and the show was too broadly based for any clear pattern to emerge. The South African painter Le Roux Smith Le Roux commented in the *Listener* that there was one group of painters 'whose work has a certain broad affinity . . . John Craxton, Prunella Clough, Robert Colquhoun, Robert MacBryde and John Minton', adding sourly, 'some critics are already regarding them as the spoiled darlings of present-day British painting.' This group was benefiting from the start it had had during and immediately after the war, and was working in a direction that British painting was not going to take in the later 1950s. More significantly, Le Roux noted the growing institutional influence of members of the pre-war Euston Road School, which might be compared to Summerson's 'troublesome' student architects. William Coldstream had become head of the Slade School, Laurence Gowing was Professor of Art at Durham, and Rodrigo Moynihan was Professor of Painting at the Royal College of Art.

The Arts Council's boldest move was to invite sixty selected painters to create an especially large picture for the Festival. It is a reminder of the continuing post-war austerity that the only bait was that the Arts Council would supply the actual canvas free. The motivation was a double one: to release the artists' energies cramped by the shortage of materials, and to encourage a more monumental, 'public' style of painting – which clearly relates to the possibilities offered by the murals for the Festival exhibits. (Ten artists produced both murals and paintings.) As with the anthology shows, the numbers involved were too large for any single tendency to emerge, and the minimum size, 45 inches by 60 inches, was still uncomfortably large for

some contributors. As a further inducement, five of the resulting pictures were to be bought for £500 each on the recommen-
dation of three independent judges. The final selection showed
a prudent spread across the spectrum from non-figurative to
figurative, from William Gear's abstract *Autumn Landscape*,
through Ivon Hitchens's huge *Aquarian Nativity*, to Robert
Medley's decorative *Bicyclists Against a Blue Background*,
Lucian Freud's disturbing *Interior Near Paddington* (Plate 4)
and Claude Rogers's quasi-academic figure study, *Miss Lynn*.
Neither anthology shows nor prize panels can satisfy everybody, but the Arts Council had made a positive step towards
encouraging contemporary art and, by taking the exhibition to
twelve cities throughout the country, showed it to as wide a
public as possible. It failed in the further intention of attracting
sponsors for large public paintings, or in selling more than a
few paintings in the exhibition to public organizations. In
general 'big' painting had to wait for more expansive economic
circumstances.

Considering the literary nature of the Festival, literature
received the least attention of all the arts. Apart from the
employment of Laurie Lee as chief caption writer for the South
Bank, plus one or two others on a freelance basis, the Festival
hardly created any work for writers (unless you count Priestley's novel *Festival at Farbridge*, 1951). The National Book
League organized eight touring exhibitions, a show of rare
books at the Victoria and Albert Museum and an exhibition of
books by one hundred contemporary writers. Evelyn Waugh
commented on the accompanying portrait photographs, 'if you
wish to preserve the Festival spirit, shun the hundred best
authors.' PEN and the Apollo Society organized two series of
poetry readings, and eminent writers lectured at the Victoria
and Albert Museum, but this was hardly patronage on a big
scale. The Arts Council had come late to supporting literature,
and had only given small sums to the Apollo Society and the
Festival of Spoken Poetry, launched in 1947. In 1950 it was
forced to form a small poetry committee (Joseph Crompton,
Richard Church, John Lehmann, G. Rostrevor-Hamilton,

Cecil Day Lewis, Christopher Hassell and L. A. G. Strong), in order to administer a Festival poetry competition. £1,100 in prize money was offered, but unfortunately the Council seems to have been taken with the idea that there should be something epic in poetry to complement the monumental in painting, and prizes were offered for poems of over 300 lines in length, in addition to the category for a collection of six to twelve short ones. (The BBC Third Programme also wanted to do something grand and commissioned Cecil Day Lewis to translate all twelve books of Virgil's *Aeneid*.) 2,093 were entered and eight prizes awarded, but as John Hayward admitted in his introduction to the prizewinners published as *Poems 1951*, the vast majority of entries were extremely bad, 'revealing from every point of view but that of literary criticism . . . it was disturbing to find such widespread ignorance of the nature of poetry and such technical incompetence'. Still, it was, as Hayward pointed out, just about the first public support for poetry since the creation of the Poet Laureateship, and it came at a time when the publishing of poetry had become completely uneconomic.

The Festival of Britain invited the participation of so many people throughout the country that it could not avoid being both a success and a failure. It did bring back colour and a little gaiety, in spite of economic troubles, re-armament and the Korean War. For most people it made itself felt in just one or two striking images in a kaleidoscope of exhibits and events: J. B. Priestley, haunted throughout the pomp and circumstance of the inaugural concert at the Royal Festival Hall by 'the homely and rather melancholy smell of moth balls'; the author at the age of eight disappointed to discover that the soaring narrow pod of the Skylon was held up by wires. The music critic of the *New Statesman*, Desmond Shawe-Taylor, has contributed a telling double-image. Delighted by the feast of music, he wrote:

I feel as though our Philistine old Albion, so solid and beefy, has turned overnight into Prospero's insubstantial isle; an impression fostered by the strange glamour and glitter of the South Bank. But not for long is Anglo-Saxon reality to be held at bay. Lured on by the novelty and freshness and colour, I drop into one of the Festival resturants, dreaming perhaps of *cannelloni* or *quenelles de brochet*; and then, ah then, I am soon back in familiar old England. Not indeed in the fine old England of beef sirloins and saddles of mutton, but in our latter-day, take-it-or-leave-it England of lukewarm tomato soup and custard with a skin on the top.

The Festival year of 1951 marks a kind of watershed and, with the Conservative victory in the general election, an end as well as a beginning. For the Arts Council and the Council of Industrial Design, the Festival marks a coming of age, and the effect of the Festival was more important for these two institutions than for any individual. The Council of Industrial Design proceeded to try to impose a design orthodoxy on public taste, while the Arts Council was confirmed in its role of leading public taste in the arts to the light, and acting as a judge of artistic quality. After the Festival, a more confident and polemical note is sounded in the Arts Council's annual reports, beginning in 1951 with 'Some Reflections on Policy', which rebut the now familiar charges that the Arts Council was metropolitan in bias and indifferent to the provinces, that it supported frivolity and tried to provide too much itself directly.

Michael Frayn's brilliant essay on the Festival in *The Age of Austerity* (1963) establishes 1951 as an end, much more than a beginning. Further, he points out that the actual balance of power between the consumers and administrators of public taste had not changed at all:

With the exception of Herbert Morrison, who was responsible to the Cabinet for the Festival and who had very little to do with the actual form it took, there was almost no one of working-class background concerned in planning the Festival, and nothing about the result to suggest that the working classes were anything more than the lovable human but essentially inert objects of benevolent administration. In fact Festival Britain was the Britain of the radical middle classes – the do-gooders; the readers of the *New Statesman*, the *Guardian*, and the *Observer*; the signers of petitions; the backbone of the BBC. In short, the Herbivores, or gentle ruminants.

The Herbivores, who in Frayn's terms were shortly to be replaced by a more aggressive ruling class of Carnivores, had been in power *de facto* since 1940, when the institutions in which they ruminated had first become important. They had favoured the efforts of the Labour government to produce social justice, and missed an opportunity for social change. In short, they became a well-meaning élite. This was done almost by default, when the narrowed circumstances of war had left the responsibility for the preservation of cultural life in a few hands. Six years after the war they were still in charge, and there had been few opportunities for younger men to bypass the system by finding new outlets. The Festival did provide an opportunity for architects and designers, but the same opportunities were not offered by the Arts Council commissions.

It is not surprising, then, that the younger generation should begin to feel a little frustrated, even a little carnivorous. Though its social values did not change, the University did offer more chances than the Metropolis, and it is at Cambridge that one of the first signs of frustration can be detected, in the founding of the literary magazine *Politics and Letters* in 1947, edited by Clifford Collins, Raymond Williams and Wolf Mankowitz. The editors were very much under the aegis of F. R. Leavis, who contributed to the magazine, but they took a more committed line as far as the political responsibility of literature was concerned. In the first number Raymond Williams wrote:

We have seen critics selling out to commercial literary standards. And, most important because least easily recognized, we have seen a dereliction of duty by those who have assumed cultural responsibility, the participation of most of the surviving literary reviews either in the new commercialism, or in an assertion of minority social standards which have been assumed to be identical with the standards of our literary tradition, but which, on the evidence of their practice, are as destructive of the tradition as their grosser neighbours.

This shows the moralistic, anti-metropolitan attitude of Leavis, but it was a sincere criticism of what was perceived as the London literary establishment. In the following number of *Politics and Letters* Henry Gibson named names:

It is important that the respectable literary organs and institutions which we can connect with this word [Bloomsbury] are various and influential. They include some of our University Schools of English, the book page in the *Observer* and in the *Sunday Times, Horizon, New Writing*, not a few publishing houses, and the Third Programme. And for the purveyors of its standardized and standardless opinions, many of the old names, and many more who have come after them – Mr Kingsley Martin, Editor of the *New Statesman*, Mr Cyril Connolly, one of its directors, Mr Desmond MacCarthy, a past literary editor, Mr Raymond Mortimer, and Mr V. S. Pritchett. And in addition – Mr Edward and Miss Vita Sackville-West, Mr George Rylands, Mr Cecil Day Lewis, Mr Nicholas Blake [a C. Day Lewis pseudonym], Mr Henry Reed, Mr John Lehmann, Mr G. W. Stonier, Mr T. C. Worsley, and Mr Philip Toynbee. And more recently – Mr Stephen Potter, Mr Patric Dickinson, and Mr P. H. Newby.

Gibson had a point. A comparison of the April and October literary pages of the *Sunday Times* and the *Observer* for 1945 and 1951 shows month for month and year for year the same cast of contributors, and more significantly, no fresh names at all. Again, this was not a plot on the part of those who had gathered to meet Edmund Wilson at Hamish Hamilton's party in 1945, but the persistence of the old names was bound to have a dulling effect on cultural activity already suffering from economic restriction and the pressures of Cold War politics. This institutional debility was as responsible as external threats for the failure of artistic life to revive in the latter half of the 1940s.

For it to revive in the 1950s, it needed new opportunities, new men and women and, ultimately, renewed means of expression.

CHAPTER THREE

THE CRAFT OF LETTERS IN ENGLAND

About us lie our elder writers
Small, guilty, like detritus:
Resistance to the epoch's rage
Has not survived their middle age.

Roy Fuller
Epitaphs and Occasions
(1949)

In October 1951 Winston Churchill and the Conservative Party
returned to power; the temporary buildings of the Festival were
demolished. By the end of Festival year the cultural patterns of
the 1950s became set, both in terms of the attitudes that
dominated the early part of the decade and the new ideas that
emerged in reaction to them. In their negative aspects, the
challenges to the established pattern only reflect the climate
that created them.

In spite of the Korean War, the Conservative government
gradually lifted the wartime controls that Labour had retained.
Peacetime consumer industries revived, and Britain began to
enjoy a modest affluence. The ownership of television sets and
motor cars was on the increase; in London a sign of new times
was the spread of the coffee bar, which became a new kind of
social centre, particularly for the young. The imported Italian
espresso coffee machines were only the most obvious elements
of the décor that suggested a Continental style of living: Italian,

French, Spanish – anything, in fact, rather than English. Like the décor, the bohemianism associated with the coffee bars was bogus, but it showed that there was a relaxation after post-war austerity and a strong desire, at least on the part of the younger generation, for something new.

The truth was that Britain was at last moving out of the post-war period, but there was great uncertainty as to what sort of period it was moving into. By April 1956 Rayner Heppenstall was ready to risk a definition:

> More than half of the Fifties is now behind us. We ought to be able to guess at the myth they will leave. It depends, of course, whether (or in the length of time by which) atomic warfare anticipates the Sixties. With a bit of luck, we may be remembered as the generation which lived in fear of a weapon that never killed a European, what time our favourite plaything, the motor car, was killing 50,000 Europeans a year. There will certainly be seen to have been a right-wing orthodoxy, and, unless there is now a marked change, its literature is bound to be regarded as a butlers' and antique-dealers' cult of gracious living and more spacious ages. . . . It will be seen how extraordinarily few full-time, professional literary intellectuals there were in the Fifties, and it may be understood how, for monetary reasons, the plums have been picked by people who, before Hitler's war, had lived or could have lived on private income. The names of Mr Wain and Mr Amis are unlikely to figure in the stereotype. If, individually, their work comes to anything, and, even more, if they become *chefs d'école*, they will be claimed by the Sixties themselves.

This is a fair summary of the 1950s as they looked at that moment; Heppenstall's one miscalculation was to assume that it would not be until the 1960s that a new generation would be able to challenge those in charge of literary taste. Even by the close of 1956, the myth of the 1950s was beginning to look different.

In April 1956, however, Heppenstall's miscalculation was perfectly understandable. The two new literary magazines launched in the 1950s, the *London Magazine* and *Encounter*, exactly fit Heppenstall's description of a right-wing orthodoxy dominated by survivors of the 1930s. As early as 1945 Humphrey Slater's magazine *Polemic* had tried to introduce a brisk new note of intellectual discipline into the over-ripe romanticism of the period; *Polemic* was anti-Marxist, anti-Existentialist and in favour of Logical Positivism, but like other new ventures it was crushed by the economic crisis of 1947, after eight issues. In September 1953 *Encounter* was launched as the house magazine of Conservative intellectual orthodoxy. Edited by Stephen Spender and Irving Kristol, it was backed by the Paris-based Congress of Cultural Freedom, an organization set up to combat the cultural efforts of the Russian 'Peace Offensive' masterminded by the Cominform. It was not until 1966 that it finally came out that the Congress for Cultural Freedom was funded by the American Central Intelligence Agency, but *Encounter* was recognized from its very first number as another weapon of the Cold War and was described as such by those who reviewed it. *Encounter* was a political as well as a literary journal, and its pro-American editorial line was consistent in both fields. Commenting on the anti-Communism of its book reviews and articles on music and science, A. J. P. Taylor wrote in the *Listener*: 'The culture, whose freedom we are defending, is genuine, but it seems to have been going for a very long time, and it is getting a little thin on the top.' Indeed, *Encounter* was born middle-aged; the source of its funds was not nearly as significant as the convinced anti-Communism of the people who ran it. *Encounter*'s negative conservatism matched the times.

John Lehmann's *London Magazine* reflected former glories rather than contemporary political tensions. Although he was the most respected literary editor of the wartime period, John Lehmann's career had not prospered. *Penguin New Writing* was killed off in 1950, and there was also disappointment over the fate of his publishing house, John Lehmann Ltd. Having failed to take over The Hogarth Press from Leonard Woolf, Lehmann launched his own firm in the autumn of 1946, in association with the printing firm of Purnell. The 1947 economic crisis forced him into complete ownership by Purnell's, but Lehmann continued to build up a reputation and a backlist, publishing 100 books by the end of 1949, including the London edition of

Saul Bellow's first novel, *A Dangling Man*, and the first of Elizabeth David's cookery books. John Lehmann Ltd, however, failed to produce profits for Purnell's, who became increasingly dissatisfied. In December 1952 they sacked John Lehmann and wound up the firm.

There was, then, something backward-looking about Lehmann's decision to return to editing a literary magazine, even though one was badly needed. Backed by the chief executive of the *Daily Mirror* newspaper group, Cecil King, the first number of the *London Magazine* appeared in February 1954. It was more elegantly styled than *Penguin New Writing*, but was essentially its successor, and the advisory board of John Hayward, Rex Warner, William Plomer, Elizabeth Bowen and Veronica Wedgwood represented the established literary world that *New Writing* had helped to create. The *London Magazine* was already a little dated in its conception as a purely *literary* magazine to the exclusion of the other arts; other journals, such as the revived *Twentieth Century Magazine*, were finding that more general sociological topics were an essential ingredient to attract a readership.

The *London Magazine* was worthy and a little dull, for it could not help reflecting the lack of urgency in the literary scene as a whole. Too often it relied on translations and memoirs, congratulating itself in January 1955 for acting as 'a crystallizing agent for many personal recollections of famous literary people and literary circles of the recent past'. But backward-looking reminiscence, often to the more glorious days of *New Writing*, does not make for a lively magazine if there is nothing to balance it, and this may be one reason why the circulation did not reach the magic figure of 10,000, the figure to which *Horizon* had always aspired and never reached. In 1956 there was a crisis when the Mirror Group withdrew its support, but the magazine continued under John Lehmann's editorship until 1961, when he sold the magazine to Alan Ross.

Where the *London Magazine* favoured literary reminiscence, *Encounter* had a leaning towards the self-portrait. An article in

1955 on the British intellectual produced this complacent picture of the typical *Encounter* reader:

Who criticizes Britain now in any fundamental sense, except for a few Communists and a few Bevanite irreconcilables? There are complaints here and there and on many specific issues, but – in the main – scarcely anyone in Great Britain seems any longer to feel that there is anything fundamentally wrong. On the contrary, Great Britain on the whole, and especially in comparison with other countries, seems to the British intellectual of the mid-1950s to be all right and even much more than that. Never has an intellectual class found its society and its culture so much to its satisfaction.

The author is an American, Edward Shils, a sociologist who had taught at the London School of Economics and Manchester University, and he argues that the reconciliation that had taken place between British intellectuals and their society was the result of their assimilation into the wartime bureaucracy, followed by the ending of class conflict with the Labour and Conservative support for the Welfare State. The institutional power of the London–Oxbridge axis helped to ensure the dominance of aristocratic, or at least 'gentry', cultural values over provincial bourgeois culture, demonstrated by the way in which the cultural establishment behaved as though universities other than Oxford or Cambridge did not exist. But what, according to Shils, were the values to which the new, reconciled British intellectual subscribed?

Continental holidays, the connoisseurship of wine and food, the knowledge of wild flowers and birds, acquaintance with the writing of Jane Austen, a knowing indulgence for the worthies of the English past, an appreciation of 'more leisurely epochs', doing one's job dutifully and reliably, the cultivation of personal relations – these are the elements in the ethos of the emerging British intellectual class.

It is difficult to believe that Shils did not have his tongue at least partially in his cheek when he came to these precise details, but the idea of a conforming intellectual class as opposed to a dissenting one was very much in the air at that time. It was the subject of an essay, also published in 1955, by the social historian Noel Annan. Its title, 'The Intellectual Aristocracy', became a catch-phrase used to describe the alliance between the political and intellectual leadership of the country. As a historian, Noel Annan's main concern in his essay is with the rise to power of a group of upper middle-class families who began to form 'an aristocracy of intellect' in the academic and administrative fields in the first half of the nineteenth century. But his point is that through this group's strong propensity to intermarry it retained considerable influence on academic and cultural policy, right down to the mid-twentieth century:

The influence of these families may partly explain a paradox which has puzzled European and American observers of English life: the paradox of an intelligentsia which appears to conform rather than rebel against the rest of society. The proclivity to criticize, of course, exists. . . . But the pro-consular tradition and the English habit of working through established institutions and modifying them to meet social needs only when such needs are proven are traits strongly exhibited by the intelligentsia of this country. Here is an aristocracy, secure, established and, like the rest of English society, accustomed to responsible and judicious utterance and sceptical of iconoclastic speculation. As a corollary of this it is often contended that they exert a stultifying effect upon English cultural life by monopolizing important posts and thus excluding a new class who, unbeneficed and indignant, eat out their hearts in the wilderness. Certainly the charge of monopoly is far-fetched: during the last hundred years the number of academic and editorial posts have multiplied far faster than these families, and when to these posts are added the new institution of the BBC, the British Council, the Arts Council and the National Trust, their members are spread very thin over the crust of English intellectual life.

Nonetheless, the co-optive attitude of the cultural élite, plus the influence of these families in forming the institutions (chiefly Oxbridge) from which the new recruits were drawn, ensured that its values were generally held and reinforced.

Annan's essay confidently concludes: 'Here at any rate seems to be an aristocracy that shows no signs of expiring.'

Before considering their expression in drama and the novel, it is necessary to define more precisely the cultural values to which this intellectual aristocracy subscribed – at least, define them more precisely than as a fondness for Continental holidays and the connoisseurship of wine. In 1938, in *Enemies of Promise*, Cyril Connolly appropriated the adjective applied to the intellectual and literary bureaucrats of the old Chinese empires in order to describe a certain style of writing – and thus an attitude to life – as Mandarin. Thanks to the war and its consequences, Mandarin values dominated the early 1950s. Having abandoned the mild socialism that had given Bloomsbury a radical edge even up to 1945, the intellectual aristocracy fell back on a system of values that was more appropriate to the function they performed, and the caste from which they came. These values were truly aristocratic in origin, in that they were conservative of tradition, pastoral as opposed to industrial, and most detectable when it came to nuances of class. The mood can properly be described as reactionary, since its effect was to reassert the importance of hierarchy and tradition, and protect the influence of institutions that encouraged respect for such values. The conservative mood was in tune with the majority of the population, as can be seen from the succession of Conservative Party election victories and the warm response to the presentation of Queen Elizabeth II's coronation in 1953. Within a glittering framework of pomp and circumstance, government and aristocracy performed their rituals while the whole population took part in this ceremony of assimilation and unity, gathered round their television sets. The Coronation was an elaborate piece of romantic theatre that managed to be both a celebration of hierarchy and Empire, and a family affair. It also confirmed the importance of television as a cultural force.

Literature and art remained central to the Mandarin way of life, for although relatively few were occupied in creating art, many were employed in disseminating it and the values that it expressed. The existence of an avant-garde was tolerated, even promoted, though this was most evident in painting, where the function of an avant-garde was most institutionalized. The wartime avant-garde had produced a picturesque, English-rooted neo-romanticism that was most strongly expressed in painting and poetry, though it was also felt in music and ballet. Since this neo-romanticism was in itself backward-looking, it suited the prevalent nostalgic hankering after an idealized earlier period, before modernism and before world wars, when cultural and social values seemed retrospectively more secure. Delicacy, gentility and sentiment were preferred to candour, vigour or passion; irony was felt a more suitable mode than satire. Faith in Communism having long been abandoned, it was replaced in many cases by Christianity, which was seen as the only countervailing force to the beliefs that had been repudiated – often with much personal anguish. The Roman Catholic Church offered a fresh faith with both aesthetic and hierarchic appeal, but the majority were satisfied by the softer outlines of the Church of England, the established Church which offered in its dogma the most personal way to reconcili-ation with God, and reflected in its social attitudes just those conservative, pastoral and genteel values with which the Man-darin felt at home.

For novelists and playwrights the typical metaphor for the values to which they subscribed was the country house, which not surprisingly was also a regular location for their novels and plays. The image was set by Evelyn Waugh in 1945 with *Brideshead Revisited*, where, in the prologue and epilogue, the great house of Brideshead, on which the novel centres, is shown beleaguered by soldiers' huts. The country house stands for a pre-war society of established values and social relations; its very fabric is the product of a uniquely English artistic tradition, and its occupants, in their family relationships, employment of servants, and ownership and rule over the surrounding countryside, reflect a secure social order. That the great days of the country house were over added a sealing touch of romantic nostalgia, so that it was admired with passive regret rather than as a positive image of life for the present. This retrospective valuation of the country house as a symbol for all that Britain had lost was turned inside out by Nigel Dennis's novel *Cards of Identity* in 1955, when members of the mysterious Identity Club take over a country house and re-create the identities of its former servants and occupants:

This sort of house was once a heart and centre of the national identity. A whole world lived in relation to it. Millions knew who they were by reference to it. Hundreds of thousands look back to it, and not only grieve for its passing but still depend on it, non-existent though it is, to tell them who they are. Thousands who never knew it are taught every day to cherish its memory and to believe that without it no man will be able to tell his whereabouts again. It hangs on men's necks like a millstone of memory; carrying it, and looking back on its associations, they stumble indignantly backwards into the future, confident that man's self-knowledge is gone for ever. How appropriate it is that these forlorn barracks, these harbours of human nostalgia, should now be in use once more solely as meeting-places for bodies such as ours! How right that we should assemble this summer in one of the last relics of an age of established identities!

By locating his fantasy in a country house, and by making it the scene of the activities of a club, Nigel Dennis united two aspects of British upper-class culture that seemed to be threatened. Although in many novels country houses are shown to have undergone a change of use, both country house and London club managed to adjust themselves to the post-war world, for nostalgia for former glories proved a powerful motive for their continuation into the present. In his introduction to a modified *Brideshead Revisited* in 1960, Evelyn Waugh was forced to acknowledge that things had not turned out so badly after all.

In one part of England the country house continued to flourish as though there had never been a war: on the London stage. The drawing-room, with its telephone and french windows, was the almost permanent setting for a series of light romantic comedies, family melodramas and detective thrillers, of which

Agatha Christie's *The Mousetrap*, first played in 1952 and still playing in 1988, remains a venerable example. These plays, almost exclusively concerned with the problems and pleasures of the upper-middle classes were presented in a style of polite naturalism by actors whose performance was gentlemanly and unhistrionic, as repressed as the characters they portrayed. The 'Oxford' accent (a little over-projected to reach the back of the stalls) defined the standard actor's voice; the working classes hardly appeared at all except as servants or comic relief, and all other social types were reduced to 'character' or 'dialect' parts. Outside Shakespeare, there was little opportunity to show any emotional range, though Chekhov permitted more sentiment than was usual. Edwardian and Victorian settings sanctioned a greater gorgeousness of costume, but the plots remained fundamentally the same. Contemporary references flattered middle-class prejudices: in William Douglas-Home's comedy *The Chiltern Hundreds* (1948) a member of the landed gentry stands for Parliament as a Socialist, and is defeated by the Conservative candidate – his butler.

This state of affairs, which genuinely reflected the wishes of the audience that paid to see such plays, was reinforced by the firm grip of semi-monopolist managements of the West End that we saw in Chapter 1, who needed to ensure financial success in an increasingly expensive business. Terence Rattigan, who was always looked to to provide commercial success *and* something more, tried to explain the circumstances in his introduction to the second volume of his *Collected Plays* (1953) by inventing the character of Aunt Edna, who was

a nice, respectable, middle-class, middle-aged, maiden lady, with time on her hands and the money to help her pass it. She enjoys pictures, books, music, and the theatre and though to none of these arts (or rather, for consistency's sake, to none of these three arts and one craft) does she bring much knowledge or discernment, at least, as she is apt to say to her cronies, she 'does know what she likes'.

She knows that she dislikes the novels of Kafka, the paintings of Picasso and the music of William Walton. 'She is, in short, a hopeless lowbrow, and the great novelist, the master painter, and the composer of genius are, and can afford to be, as disregarding of her tastes as she is unappreciative of their works. Not so, unhappily, the playwright, for should he displease Aunt Edna, he is utterly lost.' In the changed climate of 1964, when a third volume of his plays appeared, Rattigan regretted the invention of Aunt Edna, but he was always mindful of her in his plays.

Aunt Edna had a double protection from anything adventurous or shocking in the form of the commercial managements and the Queen's Lord Chamberlain. It was the latter's duty to censor any new play to be given a public performance anywhere in the British Isles, a duty exercised since 1737. In the 1950s the Lord Chamberlain was the Right Honourable Lawrence Roger Lumley, Viscount Lumley, Baron Lumley of Lumley Castle, Earl of Scarborough, KG, GCIE, GCVO, TD, DL, JP, a former Governor of Bombay and author of a history of the 11th Hussars; and in his capable hands no play appeared unless it was trimmed of offensive sexual and religious reference. Political censorship could be imposed under the rules against offensiveness, but self-censorship made that unnecessary. It was possible to avoid censorship by presenting a play as a club performance (although this was strictly outside the terms of the 1843 Theatres Act) and the device only served to widen the gap between the commercial theatre and the small club theatres where the experimental and the avant-garde were tolerated. Like little magazines, the little theatres were an essential adjunct to the profitable commercial sector, for it was only here that talent had a chance to develop. There were about a dozen theatre clubs operating in London at the beginning of the 1950s, but they were even more exposed to economic problems than the commercial theatre, and their number gradually declined. By 1955 only the Arts Theatre Club, conveniently near Charing Cross Road and Shaftesbury Avenue, remained a going concern. The penalty was to be treated more and more as a 'try-out' theatre for the West End.

Outside London about 100 permanent repertory companies

and 150 seasonal companies struggled to make ends meet by replaying West End successes. A dozen of these were more secure and so more adventurous, thanks to local government and Arts Council support – though at this time the government was taking about £4 million a year from the theatre as Entertainment Tax, and only returning 0.03 per cent in the form of subsidy. In 1952 a young repertory actor wrote to the *New Statesman* protesting at the conditions under which he was forced to work:

> The general policy is reactionary to say the least of it. Even the plays they present (under admittedly difficult conditions, which, however, they resolutely do nothing to overcome by decent endeavour) have changed little in twenty years. Indeed, so often they are the very same plays, only too familiar to any actor who has had the experience of working for these play factories, which turn out their perennial and vulgar farce-drama-thriller cycle twice nightly to audiences who would be as well served by a nude review.

The writer is John Osborne. In 1955 a play he had written with Anthony Creighton, *Personal Enemy*, was presented by the Opera House, Harrogate, but only after it had been cut to ribbons by the Lord Chamberlain's office. 'It is not surprising,' commented its producer, 'that it has not been heard of since.'

It is not surprising, either, that few new playwrights emerged between 1945 and 1956, nor that those who did were in the main unadventurous. The one exception to the country-house monotony was the flurry of interest in verse plays; but in spite of their divergence from the prevailing naturalism verse plays reflected particularly Mandarin prejudices. To begin with, their chief exponent was T. S. Eliot, and the revival of verse drama had begun in a specifically religious context, in the drama commissioned for the Canterbury Cathedral Festivals begun in the 1930s. Eliot's first two verse plays, *The Rock* (1934) – for which he supplied a group of choruses – and *Murder in the Cathedral* (1935), were not written for the theatre at all. In 1945–6 E. Martin Browne, a specialist in religious drama and founder of the Pilgrim Players, which had toured the country during the war with CEMA support, presented a season of verse plays at the Mercury Theatre in Notting Hill Gate, with Ronald Duncan's *This Way to the Tomb*, Anne Ridler's *The Shadow Factory* and Christopher Fry's *A Phoenix Too Frequent* – the last proved the hit of the season. Other Mercury Theatre productions in the following years were Norman Nicholson's *The Old Man of the Mountains* (1947) and Patric Dickinson's *Stone in the Midst* (1949).

The justification for verse drama was that a theatre of ritual using the heightened speech of verse enabled the dramatist to deal with the universals of God and Man by transcending the petty naturalism that made the discussion of such subjects look absurd. The Mercury performances attracted a fashionable côterie, but there seemed little prospect of seducing West End playgoers from their normal diet, precisely because of the absence of naturalistic presentation. E. Martin Browne wrote in 1947, 'the poet fails, quite deliberately, to satisfy one of the expectations of the contemporary audience. He does not depict individual character with psychological realism. For him, experience is universalized, and therefore character is a symbol.' At the Edinburgh Festival in 1949, however, he had a considerable success with his production of T. S. Eliot's new play *The Cocktail Party*, which was presented in America before opening in the West End in May 1950. In *The Cocktail Party* Eliot repeated the device he first used in *The Family Reunion* (1939) of working out a theme derived from Greek drama in terms of a conventional and naturalistic setting. *The Cocktail Party* has the outer forms of an upper middle-class comedy of manners; *The Confidential Clerk* (1953) elements of farce, and *The Elder Statesman* (1958) is a family melodrama. (Ronald Duncan used the same technique in his *Stratton* in 1950.) The conventional setting may have made Eliot's themes more acceptable to his audience, for they remain the essentially religious ones of the nature of self-knowledge, grace, martyrdom, and how to live a spiritual life in the materialist world. By writing in verse Eliot wished to raise the emotional intensity; but elevated speech conflicted with a naturalistic setting, and he progressively toned down the poetic element until it was so camouflaged that there seemed little to be gained from writing in verse at all.

The plays of Christopher Fry took the opposite course. Also a religious dramatist, his reputation was made by three serio-comedies, *A Phoenix Too Frequent, The Lady's Not For Burning* (1948) and *Venus Observed* (1950). *The Lady's Not For Burning*, with John Gielgud playing the life-weary soldier returning from the Hundred Years' War, transferred from the Arts Theatre to the Globe in 1949, showing that verse drama could have commercial success. This was confirmed in 1950 when Laurence Olivier presented the specially commissioned *Venus Observed* at the St James's Theatre. (Dennis Cannan's promising *Captain Carvallo* appeared in the same season.) The price of this success was a richer and richer verse evenly distributed among characters in flimsier and flimsier dramatic situations. While Eliot gradually reduced the poetic element in his plays, Fry supplied less and less of the convincingly dramatic, a tendency confirmed in 1954 by *The Dark is Light Enough*, where a more frugal use of verse exposed the underlying weakness of characterization and plot. Fry later moved to Hollywood.

At the beginning of the 1950s it did seem, however, that verse drama could successfully challenge the dominant naturalism. In January 1951 the *New Statesman*'s drama critic. T. C. Worsley, thought that public taste in general was changing towards a Theatre of Fantasy:

What we have seen is the development in the theatre-going public of a new hunger for the fantastic and the romantic, for the expanded vision and the stretched imagination, in short for the larger-than-life. This is easily explainable as a natural reaction from the sense of contraction which pervades at least the lives of the middle classes; and it is still the middle classes who make up the bulk of the theatre-going public. If they are finding that they can afford to do less and less, it at least costs no more to please the fantasy with extravagances than to discipline it with dry slices of real life.

81

But the escapism of plays like *Venus Observed* could easily cloy. By November 1952 the same critic was complaining at the Old Vic's 'prettification' of Eugène Labiche's *An Italian Straw Hat* as

an example of a now clearly recognizable theatrical mode which we may christen Arts Council *kitsch*. This has reared its pretty head on several occasions lately in the Waterloo Road, notably in recent productions of *Twelfth Night* and *Captain Brassbound's Conversion*. The principal ingredients are bags of good taste, a chorus of cavorting lasses and lads, and a great deal of self-conscious humour which ceaselessly proclaims: Isn't culture fun?

The same 'prettification' was at work in John Cranko's comedy-ballets, and the lyrical-romantic visions created by the Royal Ballet's chief choreographer Frederick Ashton. Peter Ustinov successfully exploited the taste for fantasy in *The Love of Four Colonels* (1951) and *Romanoff and Juliet* (1956), which managed to extract comedy from the Cold War; but in the end, fantasy was not enough.

In spite of the narrow range of its social reference, the 'well-made play' continued to give most satisfaction, although the tendency for a successful play to be kept running for a year or more reduced the opportunities for new work, and encouraged formulaic writing in the search for commercial success. Exceptionally, J. B. Priestley's *The Linden Tree* (1947) did confront the problem of middle-class response to post-war conditions, and Priestley continued his commentary on contemporary problems with *Home is Tomorrow* (1948), on the United Nations, and *Summer Day's Dream* (1949), which depicted the dangers of industrialization of a post-atomic-war future. He also sought to escape from naturalism in *Ever Since Paradise* (1947) and *The Dragon's Mouth* (with Jacquetta Hawkes, 1952). Further to the left, Ted Willis was building a reputation with his work for the Unity Theatre. Mainstream theatre however relied on workmanlike writers like Wynard Browne, Warren Chetham Strode and N. C. Hunter; Graham Greene was tempted into the theatre with *The Living Room* (1953) and *The Potting Shed* (New York, 1957; London, with the third act as originally written, 1958). The one generally acknowledged writer of promise to produce enough work to be judged on was John Whiting, whose *Saint's Day* was the controversial winner of the 1951 Festival Theatre prize. Neither this nor *A Penny for a Song* (1951), nor *Marching Song* (1954), was a commercial success, and when a further play *The Gates of Summer* failed to reach the West End in 1956, Whiting gave up playwriting altogether for film scripts, until commissioned by Peter Hall to write *The Devils*, successfully produced in 1961.

In this generally depressing climate Terence Rattigan's reputation as a sound commercial dramatist remained unchallenged, although his one attempt to produce something more epic, *Adventure Story* (1949), a study of Alexander the Great, was a failure. *The Winslow Boy* (1946) provided a series of satisfying theatrical moments, and a plea for the individual in the face of bureaucracy that gave a contemporary piquancy to the Edwardian setting. *Harlequinade* (1948) and *Who is Sylvia?* (1950) supplied light comedy, but Rattigan's chief concern was, in his own words, 'to transform my sense of theatre into sense of drama'. This he did in the one-act *The Browning Version*, which shared the bill with *Harlequinade*, and *The Deep Blue Sea* (1952). *The Deep Blue Sea* has an authentic sense of post-war difficulty and dissatisfaction. It is set, not in a drawing-room, but in a seedy flat where Hesther Collyer is living with her lover after leaving her husband, a judge. The play opens after her attempted suicide, which has failed because there is not enough money in the gas meter, a situation a long way from the 'butlers and antique-dealers' of most commercial theatre of the time. Hesther's relationship with her lover Freddie Page has failed, and Freddie is himself a failure, an ex-fighter pilot unable to settle down to peace. Hesther explains his callousness and drinking 'because his life stopped in 1940. He loved 1940, you know. There are some like that. He's never really been happy since he left the RAF.' For his part, Freddie Page concludes, 'It's been written in great bloody letters of fire over our heads – "You and I are death to each other."' A similar sentiment was to be expressed at the Royal Court in

May 1956. Rattigan does not offer a solution to Hesther's problem, except to go on living without husband or lover; his sense of drama resisted his sense of theatre, which told him that a fresh attempt at suicide would make a neater ending.

To understand the suddenness of the theatrical revival that began in 1956, it is important to appreciate the dearth that preceded it. In 1954 Kenneth Tynan concluded: 'The bare fact is that, apart from revivals and imports, there is nothing in the London theatre that one dares discuss with an intelligent man for more than five minutes.' In these circumstances the most important English playwright of the day was William Shakespeare, for productions of his plays at least kept the theatrical tradition alive. When the repaired Old Vic Theatre re-opened in 1950 it was the only one in London with a stage that could be thrust forward to break out of the picture frame of the proscenium arch. The rows and secessions of 1951 left the Old Vic at a low ebb (see p. 19) and although it received the largest Arts Council grant for the theatre, £26,000 a year, its resources were slender. The company pulled itself together however, and in 1953, under a new director, Michael Benthall, set out on a five-year plan to perform all thirty-six plays in Shakespeare's first folio. At the other centre of Shakespearian drama, the Memorial Theatre of Stratford, the directorships of Sir Barry Jackson from 1945 to 1948, and of Anthony Quayle until 1956 built a solid foundation for the theatre's future reputation.

In the absence of new English playwrights, the theatre was bound to look abroad. The Company of Four, for instance, was formed in 1945 at the Lyric Hammersmith as an enlightened alliance between the director Tyrone Guthrie, Glyndebourne Opera, The Arts Theatre Cambridge, and the non-profit subsidiary of H. M. Tennent, with the specific purpose of producing new and experimental plays by English writers; but it was quickly forced to fall back on translations and revivals. West End audiences were delighted by the romantic and fantastical plays of Jean Anouilh. From America, Arthur Miller and Tennessee Williams showed that it was possible to portray other than the middle classes, provided they lived in New York or New Orleans. Both ran into difficulties with the censor because of their sexual frankness. Their blunter social realism, in particular in Arthur Miller's *Death of a Salesman*, produced in London in 1949, gave actors a rare opportunity to break out of conventional English typecasting. In 1955 Campbell Williams took over the management of the Arts Theatre Club from Alec Clunes who had run it since 1942; to everyone's surprise he installed a young director just down from Cambridge, Peter Hall. Williams and Hall began with a policy of presenting the best of contemporary French drama, and had hits with Anouilh's *Waltz of the Toreadors* and Samuel Beckett's *Waiting for Godot*, both of which made successful West End transfers. During his brief period at the Arts, Peter Hall also directed the first Ionesco production in London, *The Lesson*. The success of *Waiting for Godot* showed that West End audiences were more flexible than most managements supposed. In 1956 Peter Daubeny, who specialized in presenting foreign companies, brought Bertolt Brecht's Berliner Ensemble to London.

1956 was the year when the ground began to shake beneath the country house, and by the end of the decade people were wondering what it could have been that made them so excited by the verse plays of Eliot and Fry. At the time, they seemed to offer a way out of the tired conventions of a theatre that had hardly changed since the 1930s, but the true drive of the theatre, as in all the arts, was towards a greater realism. The art of the theatre was weakened by the pressure of economics and the shortage of native writers who could burst the bounds of its conventions. In the novel, the Mandarin tradition flourished more strongly.

One of the points always made in Terence Rattigan's favour (and subsequently held against him) was that he was a sound theatrical craftsman. In the opening paragraph of *The Ordeal of Gilbert Pinfold* (1957), Evelyn Waugh made a similar claim for the novelists of his generation:

It may happen in the next hundred years that the English novelists of the present day will come to be valued as we now value the artists and craftsmen of the late eighteenth century. The originators, the exuberant men, are extinct and in their place subsists and modestly flourishes a generation notable for elegance and variety of contrivance. It may well happen that there are lean years ahead in which our posterity will look back hungrily to this period, when there was so much will and so much ability to please.

Waugh betrays both the strengths and the weaknesses of the established novelists who had first published in the 1930s, and who were now writing in a different world. Waugh himself, Ivy Compton-Burnett, Elizabeth Bowen, Rosamond Lehmann, Henry Green, Graham Greene, Joyce Cary, Anthony Powell and L. P. Hartley continued to write successfully and well, but it was an age without giants and without innovators. With the exception of Mervyn Peake's Gothic *Titus Groan* (1946), *Gormenghast* (1950) and *Titus Alone* (1959), and J. R. Tolkien's medievalizing *The Lord of the Rings* (1954, 1955), novelists were unaffected by the extremes of neo-romanticism of the 1940s, falling back instead, insofar as novel-writing was possible in wartime, on an examination of the recent past, with the period of the novelist's own childhood as a favourite setting. Childhood reminiscence remained a popular subject; Laurie Lee's *Cider With Rosie*, published in 1959, shows the durability of the theme. A lost childhood also implies a lost innocence, as L. P. Hartley demonstrated in *The Go-Between* (1953). In the case of Denton Welch, who died in 1948 and whose work is one of the few absolutely confined to the 1940s, one wonders whether childhood had ever been innocent in the first place.

The Go-Between, with a prologue and epilogue in the present but the action set in a country house in 1900, exactly exemplifies the use a skilful novelist could make of an encapsulated society distanced by time and social change. Ivy Compton-Burnett continued to produce her studies of family passion in a late Victorian setting whose increasing remoteness from contemporary society only served to emphasize the underlying abstraction of the moral dramas she portrayed. At a lower level of achievement, popular novelists like Nancy Mitford, Angela Thirkell, Howard Spring, Robert Henriques and Warwick Deeping exploited middle-class disenchantment with the post-war world by suggesting that nothing had changed.

The major novelists were fully aware of the reality of social change; their problem was in coming to terms with it. Evelyn Waugh's self-portrait in a distorting mirror, *The Ordeal of Gilbert Pinfold*, shows a man increasingly at odds with the times. *Brideshead Revisited* was a memorial to the recent past, *The Loved One* (1948) satirized the American present, and it was Waugh's satirical skills that sustained his final major work, the three novels of the *Sword of Honour* series, completed in 1961. The trilogy justifies Waugh's decision to become a soldier rather than sit the war out as he could have done, but it is an account of his disillusion with the army and the society that the war helped to create. Begun in 1952 with *Men at Arms*, and followed by *Officers and Gentlemen* in 1955, the series was interrupted, literally, by *The Ordeal of Gilbert Pinfold*. Although it is very funny, particularly in the earlier part of the trilogy, Waugh's Roman Catholic hero, Guy Crouchback, is more often victim than protagonist, and the image of defeat suggested by the title of the final volume, *Unconditional Surrender*, is not that of old nobility succumbing to new barbaric values; rather it is an internal loss of resistance. The resolution of the second novel and the turning-point of the trilogy takes place in 1941, when Germany attacked her former ally Russia and the seed of post-war discontents was sown. In Evelyn Waugh's words, it was 'a day of apocalypse for all the world for numberless generations':

It was just such a sunny, breezy Mediterranean day two years before when he [Guy Crouchback] read of the Russo-German alliance, when a decade of shame seemed to be ending in light and reason, when the Enemy was plain in view, huge and hateful, all disguise cast off; the modern age in arms.

Now that hallucination was dissolved, like the whales and turtles in the voyage from Crete, and he was back after less than two years' pilgrimage in a Holy Land of illusion in the old ambiguous world, where priests were spies and gallant friends proved traitors and his country was led blundering into dishonour.

The third part of the trilogy is spent in this ambiguous world, and Crouchback finds himself, as did Waugh, carrying out British policy in Yugoslavia that led to the establishment of a Communist regime. The trilogy ends with an epilogue set in 1951, ironically titled 'Festival of Britain'.

Politically of the opposite persuasion to Waugh, though also a Roman Catholic, Graham Greene continued to explore 'the old ambiguous world' that he had known since the 1930s. His political past, in the shape of a brief membership of the Oxford University Communist Club, kept him out of the United States for a time, and he took his revenge in *The Quiet American* (1956), set in Vietnam during the dying days of French rule, with America waiting in the wings. Greene's prescience of the consequences of the United States' conviction of its moral obligation to combat Communism gives the work a contemporary reference that masks the perennial nature of his themes. Greene avoided the provincialism of most English novelists by setting his stories abroad, often in locations that were about to become politically highly charged – Vietnam, Cuba (*Our Man in Havana*, 1958), the Congo (*A Burnt-Out Case*, 1961) – but the warring political interests and the suffering they cause in the real world are projections of the eternal struggle of the principles of good and evil, resolved, though only temporarily, by the working of grace achieved through suffering. Greene's fascination with the flawed personality who has some perception of absolute values yet who cannot live up to them, a deceiver who is also self-deceiving, reflects a period when nations were behaving with the same moral confusion.

Anthony Powell's confidence in the value of the Mandarin tradition is shown by his commitment to writing a novel in twelve self-contained volumes, *A Dance to the Music of Time*, published between 1951 and 1975, and covering the period between the First World War and the early 1970s. The series is concerned almost exclusively with the fate of a group of people whom the narrator first meets as a schoolboy at Eton, and it follows their careers through Oxford to the aristocratic and artistic circles of the London of the 1930s and then, with losses and additions, into the war and beyond. The milieu is upper-class, the occupations just those that the intellectual aristocracy would pursue in peace or war, although there is a distinction in the vast assembly of characters between those who are driven to seek power, and the more artistically minded. The seekers after power cause their own frustration, the artists decline to assert their will against fate. Always sceptical and ironic, Powell manipulates the inner-relationships of his characters in such a way as to suggest there is something mystical behind the surface of often comic events, and the occult is an important theme. Powell's approach, and his high style of prose, are summed up in the ruling image to which he commits himself in the opening pages of the first volume:

The image of Time brought thoughts of mortality: of human beings, facing outward like the Seasons, moving hand in hand in intricate measure: stepping slowly, methodically, sometimes a trifle awkwardly, in evolutions that take recognizable shape: or breaking into seemingly meaningless gyrations, while partners disappear only to reappear again, once more giving pattern to the spectacle: unable to control the melody, unable, perhaps, to control the steps of the dance.

The unavoidable comparison with *A Dance to the Music of Time* is C. P. Snow's sequence, *Strangers and Brothers*, eleven novels published between 1940 and 1970, and covering the same period in time as Powell's. Whereas Powell's narrative is linear, and his narrator Nicholas Jenkins is a constant, though self-effacing presence, Snow follows a complex pattern of overlapping periods, and his narrator Lewis Eliot varies in prominence, so that he is very much in the foreground in *Homecomings* (1956), much more an observer in *The Masters* (1951). The difference between the occupations of the two narrators marks an important difference in the style of the two sequences: Jenkins is himself a writer; Eliot is a lawyer, academic, and scientific civil servant. Jenkins represents the intellectual aristocracy as it existed before the war; Eliot is a product of the changes forced upon it. In *The New Men* (1954), in itself a significant title, the country house is the site of the development of a British atomic bomb, and Snow's chosen territory is the field of public affairs, the interlocking areas of academic science and government, represented by a Cambridge college and the offices of Whitehall. Lewis Eliot's ruling location is the corridors of power, a phrase first used in *Homecomings*, and the title of the novel of 1964.

Snow's interest in the pursuit of power caused him to write in a plain and naturalistic style that cannot match Powell's elegance and variety of contrivance. Superficially, the difference between Nicholas Jenkins and Lewis Eliot represents what Snow himself called 'the Two Cultures'. According to Snow, the older literary culture was in decline, while his new men belonged to the confident and expansive scientific culture that had no time for the Alexandrian intricacies of the *literati*. (Snow first floated the idea of the Two Cultures in the *New Statesman* in 1956; he expanded the theme with his Rede Lecture at Cambridge in 1959, and was taken to task for his philistinism by F. R. Leavis.) Snow's new men nonetheless operate in the old places, be they London club or Cambridge college, and though Lewis Eliot comes from lower middle-class stock, he takes on the necessary Mandarin coloration to achieve power. William Cooper's novel *The Struggles of Albert Woods* (1952) is almost a parody of the progress of Lewis Eliot; Cooper was Snow's ally in promoting the naturalistic novel, which Snow did with considerable force as a reviewer for the *Sunday Times*, and *Homecomings* is dedicated to Cooper.

Though he was a man of the Left, C. P. Snow's novels are about the pursuit of power in itself rather than in terms of a particular ideology; in *The Masters* it is portrayed in the almost laboratory-like conditions of a Cambridge college. Only occasionally is there any criticism of the system that exercises such fascination. In *Homecomings*, Lewis Eliot experiences a sense of post-war disillusion:

It had seemed to us all [in the 1930s] self-evident that society was loosening and that soon most people would be indifferent to class. We had turned out wrong. In our forties we had to recognize that English society had become more rigid, not less, since our youth. Its forms were crystallizing under our eyes into an elaborate and codified Byzantinism, decent enough, tolerable to live in, but not blown through by the winds of scepticism or individual protest or sense of outrage which were our native air. And those forms were not only too cut-and-dried for us: they would have seemed altogether too rigid for nineteenth-century Englishmen. The evidence was all about us, even at that wedding party: quite little things had, under our eyes, got fixed, and except for catastrophes, fixed for good.

With Ivy Compton-Burnett as a prime example, it is important to acknowledge that novelists do not have to confine their works to contemporary settings or contemporary issues, but the number of older novelists who avoided them tells us something about the difficulty of coming to terms with the post-war present. Writing in the *Listener* in 1954 Anthony Quinton accused post-war writers both old and new of refusing to face up to the changed circumstances:

the novels of the last decade have been singularly ineffective as purveyors of contemporary moral and social reality. They have made as poor an adjustment to the changes of the past twenty years as most writers on politics. Change is inescapable but change for the worse puts a special charge on our power of conforming with it. And the change for the worse I am talking about is merely the conventional decline in the standard of living of the middle-class. It is rather the more or less unacknowledged social redundancy of large sections of this class and its attendant moral dilemmas that constitute the analogue on the level of personal life of this country's international decline.

As evidence of the lack of social adjustment Anthony Quinton points to the novelist on what one might call the Evelyn Waugh–Nancy Mitford axis, who continued to write as though no social change had taken place: 'For all its linguistic and educational reinforcement the rigid class-stratification of English society is dissolving, but the fact is hardly noticed in most contemporary novels.' (On the subject of linguistic reinforcement, Nancy Mitford's *jeu d'esprit* for *Encounter* on the nuances of class reflected by U and non-U forms of speech was taken very seriously.)

Quinton's generalization must be qualified: he was perfectly aware that Kingsley Amis and John Wain had recently published novels that did take account of post-war change, but his criticism does apply to those of the older generation. One writer, however, then beginning a career of lasting significance, had found his material precisely in the problem of the social redundancy of sections of the middle class: Angus Wilson. Born in 1913, Angus Wilson's late arrival to literature at the age of thirty-four makes him an important figure in the transition between the pre-war and post-war worlds. He consciously identified himself with the pre-war, even Edwardian period (he is an admirer of Ivy Compton-Burnett); he could have been a member of the 'Auden generation', he could have been a figure of the 1940s, but instead he arrived on the scene just as the context that had framed the work of those generations was dissolving. He began as a short-story writer, and it should be noted that his first ever story, 'Raspberry Jam', is about the cruelty observed by a small boy – another loss of childhood innocence. The setting, however, is consciously contemporary, as Wilson himself has said:

Implicit in this first story also was the observation of the English social scene as it had changed since 1939. This social aspect coloured the larger part of the stories that I wrote for my first two books in 1949 and in 1950. I was struck then by the fact that a mild social revolution had taken place in England overnight, although its novelists had not yet noticed this. Readers and critics alike responded to this aspect of my stories. Indeed it earned me a reputation for being a 'social satirist', which seems to me only an aspect of my writing.

Angus Wilson began by observing the disappearing class from which he himself came, and its failure to adapt to post-war change; but as the outline of these changes became clearer he saw that the post-war generation of the politically active middle class was also becoming stranded. 'They had, I realized about

1950 or so, to share both in the triumph and the failure of Welfare England. It had also become quite clear that they were rapidly proving as much out of touch with the new post-war England as the more stupid middle-class "dodos" I had satirized in the earlier stories.' It is tempting to see Michael Frayn's Herbivores in this description, and certainly the plot of Wilson's first novel *Hemlock and After* (1952) involves a Herbivore scheme to establish a writers' retreat in a country-house. *Anglo-Saxon Attitudes* (1956) is similarly concentrated on the educated middle class; the process by which the protagonist, Professor Middleton, tracks down an archaeological fraud, and in so doing becomes reconciled to his responsibilities, is set against the carnivorous activities of his children and their contemporaries. A play, *The Mulberry Bush* (1955, revised 1956), is also set in the contemporary academic milieu.

Angus Wilson shows a confidence that most of his fellow writers did not, in that he was able to cope imaginatively with the changes that appeared such a threat to the Mandarin tradition. Wilson, while still identifying himself with the sources of that tradition, felt sure that what was taking place was development, not decay:

The English novel grew up with the emergence of a new social structure; the most serious novelists since James and Forster have reflected the decline of that structure in the very essence of their creation. Now that decline is complete, and the better novelists of today, who still belong to that vanished world, have been driven into the realms of childhood for their inspiration. But the new social structure has not come into being overnight. The new ruling class – that strange mixture of business experts, bureaucrats, social scientists and the rest of the Welfare set-up – are firmly in the saddle . . . a new generation is arising from the new ruling class who will accept the world they dominate. . . . It is from such new ruling classes, sure of themselves yet still vigorously believing in their future, that I believe the best of our novelists will come.

As the next chapter shows, it was the academic servants of this new class who found themselves in the best position to exploit the changes that Angus Wilson describes.

In the mid-1950s the intellectual aristocracy may have been showing no sign of dying out, but it was beginning to show signs of uncertainty about what it should do with its power. The defection of Burgess and Maclean to the Soviet Union in 1951 had shown that a public school, ancient university and Foreign Office career was not necessarily a guarantee of Mandarin incorruptibility; their success and that of their helpers had its roots in precisely those connections, relationships and institutions Mandarins trusted most, as the revelation that it was the distinguished art historian, Anthony Blunt, knighted for his services as Surveyor of the Queen's pictures, who abetted their escape, has shown. The intellectual aristocracy might have ensured that the educational and cultural institutions it had created were essentially unchanged by the post-war legislation, but a delight in Continental holidays and the connoisseurship of wine, though reflecting increasing affluence, was not in itself a totally satisfying intellectual pursuit. Introducing a feature on 'This New England' in June 1956, *Encounter* appeared to regret Edward Shils's 'more leisurely epochs':

> In an overcrowded country approaching the condition where the majority receive almost equal shares, there is little vivid variousness, a spreading grey of suburbs which make up in quantity of dimness for the more concentrated intense ugliness of nineteenth-century slums. Everywhere the price paid for diffused facilities is sacrifice of quality.

A month earlier the *London Magazine* confessed an uncertainty about its purpose: 'It is difficult not to feel that the present is a moment of peculiar confusion in literature, with the impulses of twenty, or even ten years ago fading out, and no new impulses of sufficient force and inspiration taking their place.'

It was this uncertainty that drove the *London Magazine* back on reminiscence, *Encounter* to the self-portrait. These tendencies combine in a book that is not usually recalled as one of the significant publications of 1956, *The Craft of Letters in England*. Edited by John Lehmann, it is a symposium published on the occasion of the first PEN international conference to be held in London for fifteen years. With the exception of the literary critic Paul Bloomfield and the *New Statesman*'s theatre critic T. C. Worsley, all the contributors wrote for either the *London Magazine* or *Encounter* or both, and they represented in the main the generation, with its roots in the 1930s, that emerged as survivors of the war. As a group self-portrait, *The Craft of Letters in England* shows a general lack of self-confidence, particularly as far as its creative powers are concerned. In the same mood as his editorial for the May *London Magazine*, John Lehmann introduced the collection with the admission that 'the outstanding figures of 1956 in creative literature have not the same stature as their predecessors of 1926'. At the same time the status of their craft was being eroded by contradictory forces that helped to undermine self-confidence:

in the English literary world, the *middle class* is now under increasing pressure from two sides, from those whose livelihood is bound up with the academic aspect of literature on the one side, and those who are occupied with the exploration of all that can appeal in literature to a mass, and mainly non-intellectual, audience. By middle class in this context I mean, not an income-bracket or standard of upbringing, but that body of intelligent readers who care for literature seriously as part of life, who can see through the specious appeal of four best-sellers out of five, whose opinions on the merits of books are not swayed by irrelevant 'social' considerations and are equally uninfluenced by the pretensions of an academic high-priesthood who have a vested interest in the esoteric and difficult.

John Lehmann's contributors provide a series of essays that reflect the unsatisfactory conditions that prevailed in the literary world. (J. I. M. Stewart on biography, Francis Wyndham on the novel, Philip Toynbee on the experimental novel, Roy Fuller and G. S. Fraser on aspects of poetry, T. C. Worsley on the theatre, Laurence Lerner on the New Criticism, Paul Bloomfield on the Bloomsbury school of criticism, Maurice

Cranston on the literature of ideas, Erik de Mauny on translation, and Veronica Wedgwood on history.) The liveliest contribution, and in this context the most apposite, is that of Alan Pryce-Jones on autobiography.

As editor of the *Times Literary Supplement* since 1948, Alan Pryce-Jones was in an excellent position to judge the mood of professional authors, and he chose to present a composite figure:

He is forty-five, let us say, and he has a job which gives him a certain amount of free time. Yes, he is paid £1,800 a year by the BBC. He has a wife and three children, and out of all four he is extremely fond of two – not always the same two. He has published ten books, of which eight are forgotten. Twice he has been asked to contribute to highbrow papers in America. The British Council has sent him on more than one occasion to Belgium. He is asked to an inordinate number of publisher's cocktail parties, several First Secretaries invite him to luncheon and at least one Ambassador to dine. He owns a post-war car and his shirts are cut to fit him, with the exception of one or two in a heavy green material which are reserved for addressing undergraduate clubs. In brief, he is a successful middle-aged writer who can pick his way through the world.

After spending the war in a secret bureaucratic job, and then finding a post at the BBC, our established writer, whose pre-war reputation was based on novels of personal relationships, wants to launch off again:

He cannot very well start with a novel, because personal relationships seem to be out of fashion in fiction, and they are all he knows about. He cannot write a Catholic novel, because he is not a Catholic, nor a satirical novel about life in a provincial university, because universities are already held in fee by a group of embattled dons who would certainly review him. There are travel books, of course, but the British Council has not sent him further than Belgium. Almost all other modern books seem to be about under-water fishing, mountain-climbing, the Esquimaux [sic], or theology. In short, there is nothing for it but an autobiography.

So the middle-aged author is driven back on the self-portrait, and Pryce-Jones's conclusion is devastating: 'The most important thing about him is that, by forty-five, he has lost faith in his art and so in himself. The one thing he can do, therefore, is to write about that loss – in other words to write autobiographically.'

In a sense, *The Craft of Letters in England* records that loss in a group autobiography, and other contributors underline the bleakness of the prospect. Entrusted with writing about 'Experiment and the Future of the Novel', Philip Toynbee, himself the author of two ill-received experiments, *Tea with Mrs Goodman* (1947) and *The Garden to the Sea* (1954), found it easier to write about the difficulties of the novelist than his achievements. The English novelist is 'on his own, struggling in a collapsed tradition, uncertain of his intractable medium and uncertain of his constantly changing material . . . the last quarter of a century has transformed his society, transformed his language, transformed his intellectual and emotional climate'. For Toynbee, this transformation meant that the novelist had lost his constituency, hence the confusion and lack of common impulse that Lehmann had noticed.

In these circumstances the writer turns back on himself and his past, to autobiography or fictionalized memories of childhood. Alternatively, he could seek security in religion or political conservatism. Those who might once have written novels turned instead to biography or academic literary criticism. The old 'man of letters' was being replaced by a specialist of some kind, usually with an academic post, who engaged in technical literary criticism, or was occupied with specific issues in psychology, economics or philosophy. The number of philosophers who took up literary issues is noteworthy: Stuart Hampshire, Richard Wollheim, Anthony Quinton, Isaiah Berlin, John Holloway, Iris Murdoch. But Iris Murdoch is the only major novelist, and John Holloway the only poet; and a craft of letters that does not have fiction, poetry or drama at its centre must feel as enfeebled as John Lehmann's symposium makes it appear.

The creative writers of the early 1950s were a few individualists whose talents enabled them to survive the decadence of a literary tradition that had lasted since the 1920s. That tradition survived as an institution (and in institutions) rather longer than it survived as a positive source of creative energy, and the generation that was already making itself felt, even as its seniors were deploring their own decay, was brought up in that tradition. This is why, while challenging their predecessors, the new men were also conservative in their outlook. The decadence of the older men was the result of social change and the excesses of Forties romanticism; the rising generation saw a need for a return to at least some of the values that its predecessors had neglected, and in that respect they too were to prove to be reactionaries. The vacuum left by the declining craftsmen of letters had a definite shape; the question was how the new writers would fill it.

CHAPTER FOUR

NEW LINES

*'the English literary scene is
peculiarly amenable to literary
history: it is savage with gang-
warfare which, at a distance, can
be dignified as disagreements
between schools of verse.'*

A. Alvarez *The New Poetry* (1962)

The styles and values described in the last chapter survived for
the longest in fiction and the theatre, where the lusher forms of
wartime romanticism were restrained by the prevailing naturalism. The culture of the Forties was challenged first where
romanticism was most extended, in poetry and painting. Here
the overthrow was complete almost before the theatrical revolution began. At the same time significant developments were
under way in fiction, and together these changes and the names
associated with them prepared the way for the general shift of
emphasis in the arts that took place after 1956.

In poetry the change has many of the features of the
imminent theatrical revolution, in that publicity and mass
media – in this case chiefly radio – played an important part in
making the change possible, at the same time underlining the
fact that it was taking place. Since many elements, including
names and dates, overlap with the better-known *coup d'état* in
the theatre, the poetic revolt can be treated as a dress rehearsal:

the Mandarin tradition was challenged by a group of younger writers who were the first to benefit from the post-war Welfare State. The poets were themselves chiefly academics; they were conscious of their privileged position, but dissatisfied by it; collectively, they became known as the Movement, a name not of their choosing, and they were wary of the distortions which acceptance of a popular label imposed. It is important to remember that – as some of its prime movers insist – the Movement did not exist.

The imagery of movements, revolution and *coup d'état* is appropriate to the well-established conspiracy theory of English literary politics. The conspiracy theory was being applied by the young Cambridge contributors to *Politics and Letters*, who denounced the Mandarins of Bloomsbury for keeping power over culture in their ageing hands. The fact that at the beginning of the 1950s an older generation *did* seem to control the universities, the literary pages of the Sunday newspapers and the weeklies, and the cultural departments of the BBC, gave the theory some weight. But, as V. S. Pritchett, an alleged arch-conspirator, wrote when the argument first blew up in 1953: 'The legend of the literary monopoly is a great consolation to that passion of envy which regularly visits the outskirts of literary society.'

The truth is that cliques are more apparent to those outside them than to those inside. However, it was not just young writers who subscribed to the conspiracy theory. In 1953 J. B. Priestley began a series of articles for the *New Statesman* whose title, 'Voice in the Wilderness', indicates the disillusion he was beginning to feel with post-war society. In his third article, which appeared in the same month as Pritchett's self-defence, Priestley expounded his theory of Blocks:

A writer solidly established in a Block can count on its support. At a time when critical standards are uncertain, when independent judgement is fast disappearing, when the prizes are few and so increasingly valuable, this Block support is almost worth a gold mine. Thus, there are some aesthetic enterprises that are hardly likely to succeed without some assistance from the Inverts' Block – called by a sardonic friend of mine 'the Girls' Friendly Society' – which enthusiastically gives its praise and patronage to whatever is decorative, 'amusing', 'good theatre', witty in the right way, and likely to make heterosexual relationships look ridiculous: all of which is probably the stiff price we are paying in London for our stupid laws against inversion.

The comment contrasts sadly with Priestley's criticism in 1948 of the persecution manias encouraged by the Cold War (see p. 31).

The editors of *Politics and Letters* could hardly avoid employing the conspiracy theory of English literature since their mentor was Leavis, who had long believed in the existence of a metropolitan plot against his ideas. But it is interesting that a version of the Cambridge view of London was also held in Oxford. In his autobiography, *Sprightly Running* (1962), John Wain has put the position very well:

the donnish writer, musing on the sad state of the world, has no difficulty in imagining a hotbed of super-intrigue in distant London; where the observer on the spot sees nothing but stupidity and shallowness he sees, or thinks he sees, a sinister and perfectly organized conspiracy.

This was the view of London held by the small group of dons centred on C. S. Lewis and J. R. Tolkien, known collectively as 'The Inklings', after the informal literary society which first heard Tolkien's *The Lord of the Rings* and C. S. Lewis's theological fiction. The irony is that the Inklings were themselves a conspiracy; according to Wain: 'This was a circle of instigators, almost of incendiaries, meeting to urge one another on in the task of redirecting the whole current of contemporary art and life.' Certainly the Inklings were very influential within the Oxford English Faculty; thanks to them the study of English literature stopped at 1830. Resentful of the twentieth century, they opposed Leavis, and until very late, the work of Eliot. Christian, highly conservative, they did much to create the right-wing atmosphere of post-war Oxford. And, though this refutes their view of a metropolitan monolith raised against them, C. S. Lewis and Dorothy Sayers (who associated herself with the Inklings if they did not associate themselves with her) had access to a much wider audience for their conservative Christian ideas through their talks for the BBC.

As must be expected, the Inklings denied having conspiratorial aims. C. S. Lewis wrote: 'Mr Wain has mistaken purely personal friendship for alliances.' If one analyses the separate positions of each member of the group, as Humphrey Carpenter has done so well in his book *The Inklings* (1978), then differences of opinion become quite plain. The most obvious example is John Wain himself who, as a Research Fellow of St John's College and a former pupil of C. S. Lewis, started going to the Inklings' meetings in 1946 and was a regular attender until they petered out towards the end of the decade. Wain disagreed with most of what the Inklings stood for, as *Sprightly Running* makes clear, although he did share their suspicion of the metropolis.

So the dangers of labels are demonstrated, but no one would deny the significance of connections, and Wain's are a case in point. An undergraduate at St John's during the war, he was friendly with fellow-undergraduate Philip Larkin and through him met Kingsley Amis. His membership of the Inklings linked him to one aspect of contemporary (though reactionary) literature in the 1940s; he also founded a poetry magazine, *Mandrake*, with Arthur Boyars, which ran from 1945 until 1956 and published some of the first work of the rising post-war generation. He also contributed to the last number of *Penguin New Writing*. His inclusion and the subject of his article, William Empson, create a link back to the 1930s, while the contact with John Lehmann was to have important consequences. This is not the demonstration of a conspiracy, but a question of historical fact. However, we should note that Wain also held to the conspiracy theory:

The danger is that when *every* book is reviewed by some charlatan whose only concern is to leave the reader with an impression of *his* cleverness, *his* personality, *his* graceful style, when *every* magazine is edited by someone whose object is to keep intact the network of social and political relationships that permitted his own rise to power, in short, when every genuine object is submerged in a general grabbing for plums and security – then the intellecual life of the country will be at a standstill.

It was as a member of a block of young provincial academics that Wain made his mark in the metropolis.

At the end of the 1940s it seemed that the poetic life of the country had already come to a standstill. Auden was in America, Eliot was writing plays, and other figures of the 1930s who might have been expected to give a lead were composing autobiographies which revised their views of the ideological commitments that had, at least in part, been the inspiration of their best work. In 1948 Louis MacNeice, depressed and drinking at the BBC, wrote, 'we are all conditioned by our times, and the times, it is quite likely, are against major poetry proper.' He had produced better work than most during the war, but now, as *Autumn Sequel* (1954) shows, he was beginning to think 'that the Muse has defaulted'. When C. Day Lewis published his *Poems 1943–47* in 1948, they contained lines which almost parody the frontier wireless-telegraphy of the 1930s aviator poet, lost in the wastes of the Cold War.

> Tonight, as flyers stranded
> On a mountain, the battery fading, we tap out
> Into a snow-capped void our weakening
> Vocations and desires.

George Barker, another poet of the 1930s, but one whose romantic bohemianism had found the 1940s quite congenial, also felt a chill. 'There is a perfectly serious prospect of a decline in the experimental writing of young poets for the simple reason that they can no longer write as they wish to write and eat at the same time. . . . It is already impossible for them to drink and write as they wish: the beer is no longer singing beer.'

Beery bohemianism, and the poetry that went with it, were going out of fashion. G. S. Fraser, a theoretician of the New Apocalypse ('The obscurity of our poetry, its air of something desperately snatched from dream or woven round a chime of words, are the results of disintegration not in ourselves, but in society'), has recorded that his generation of poets, 'the bohemian "out-group" of the 1940s', felt stranded. Fraser decided that poetry was taking a new direction, and in 1949 he followed it.

The 'New Romantics' have had a ten-years' innings; they have produced some fine individual poems but have left the tone, and the standards, of English poetry in general in a state of confusion. There can be no harm, anyway, in asking the coming poets of the 1950s to aim, in their diction, at closeness to natural feeling, at relevance, at restraint.

Wrey Gardiner's Grey Walls Press published a final *New Romantic Anthology*, edited by Stefan Schimanski and Henry Treece, in 1949, before going to the wall itself shortly afterwards.

The death of Dylan Thomas in 1953, the year after the publication of his *Collected Poems* 1934–1952, might be taken as an end to the romantic movement he had helped to launch in the 1930s, were it not for the fact that the sordid circumstances of his death could not prevent the growth of a Dylan Thomas legend.

He was in every sense a bard – a minstrel-poet whose verse was written to be chanted, whose chant was intended to move us, to reach us, before everything, through those feelings which spring from nature and which modern civilization is calculated to deaden and kill. His poetry speaks to those Homeric emotions that folk-tale and folk-song call into play . . .

mourned Kathleen Raine in the *New Statesman*.

The romantic strain in English verse, one characterized by a greater concern for the poet's emotional than for his intellectual responses, a concern reflected in a more violent imagery and looser metrical structure than that of the stricter verse that was to dominate the 1950s, by no means disappeared, any more than the Audenesque had excluded it in the 1930s. John Heath-Stubbs, George Barker, Vernon Watkins, Norman Nicholson, Kathleen Raine, were still writing, and could find publication in Howard Sergeant's magazine *Outposts*, or John Heath-Stubbs's 1953 anthology *Images of Tomorrow*, while Heath-Stubbs's and David Wright's joint selection for the *Faber Book of Twentieth Century Verse* (1953) emphasized the romantic continuity. There were also young poets of the post-war generation who respected the work of Dylan Thomas and Sidney Keyes; in 1952 Dannie Abse launched *Poetry and Poverty*, a magazine intended to inaugurate 'The Second Phase of Romanticism'.

Nobody wants to save the corpse of *The New Apocalypse* . . . rather the time has come for poetry to move into a new and second phase of Neo-Romanticism. What should be discarded are its faults alone: there is no need to throw the whole apparatus of Romantic expression overboard, particularly as the present alternative mode of writing appears to be so trivial and so precious.

Poetry and Poverty ran for only seven numbers, but in 1953 it was able to hand on the flame to Jon Silkin's *Stand*, which maintained an alternative position to the dominant poetry of the 1950s, and which was to come into its own in the 1960s.

The problem at the beginning of the new decade was not dominance of one approach over another, but a general exhaustion. Alan Ross wrote, as the 1950s opened:

The present is a time of disenchantment for the writer. Religious, political and psycho-analytical formulas have lost both their novelty and practical effectiveness. Marxism has deteriorated into a cliché. Western civilization, dead ground between the United States and the totalitarian State, threatens to become a bog. Poets, not unnaturally, have become increasingly reluctant to acknowledge any specific descriptive label. The bridges have given way too often, the signposts proved misleading. At the moment there is neither a single major influence over modern poetry nor a contemporary movement.

With no obvious leaders in their own generation, younger poets turned back to the examples of Robert Graves, Edwin Muir and William Empson, senior poets who remained individualists and escaped the limitations of a group label. Graves justified the poet's perennial concern for his craft and his relationship with his muse and with Muir upheld the validity of myth; the knotted references and strict forms of William Empson presented a challenge to university poets trained in the discipline of critical explication of I. A. Richards, Leavis, and Empson himself.

Should a poet choose to write in imitation of any individual master, there was still the problem of publication. Alan Pryce-Jones wrote in the *Listener* in 1949:

> If you talk to any modern poet he will tell you – and rightly – that he has very few outlets for his work. Publishers and editors are wary of poetry, little reviews are few in number and they do not pay their contributors a living wage simply because they cannot. In the end the poet finds himself elbowed into a corner of some established weekly (if he is lucky) – sandwiched between an article on agrarian reform in Southern Italy and an argument in favour of raising the bank rate. Under such conditions it is naturally the little poems which get published. Like small pictures and short concertos they squeeze their way into a public showing while the bigger works wait in obscurity – perhaps for ever.

A major handicap to the development of fresh approaches to poetry was the lack of any strong critical magazine. The old established literary magazines had folded (even *Scrutiny* closed in 1953), and such new ventures as there were had such small circulations that their influence was slight. *Essays in Criticism*, launched in 1951, published some of the Movement's poets, but this was chiefly an academic journal. It was in order to provide *some* outlet for new poetry that the Arts Council founded the Poetry Book Society in 1954, and that PEN launched its annual anthologies, *New Poems*, in 1953. Roy Fuller, an editor of PEN's first volume, has recorded the difficulty of finding any contributors.

In these circumstances poets were forced back on their own resources. When John Wain moved to Reading University in 1947 to take up a teaching post he was able to persuade the School of Art to publish small collections by himself and Kingsley Amis, financed by subscription. Philip Larkin privately published his second collection, *XX Poems*, in Belfast in 1952. Erica Marx's Hand and Flower Press provided another outlet. The most fruitful association between poets and a small press was the Oxford University Poetry Society's link-up with Oscar Mellor's Fantasy Press. The Fantasy Press was very small indeed; there was only enough type to set up four pages of poetry at a time. Mellor was a painter who operated a hand press in his small cottage in the village of Eynsham, just outside Oxford. In 1952 the press began to produce a series of ninepenny pamphlets for the Poetry Society under the title 'Fantasy Poets', and from these very small beginnings grew much of the poetic progress of the 1950s.

There were in all thirty-five Fantasy Poets in the series that ran from 1952 to 1957; at the same time, the Press took on publication of an annual Oxford Poetry anthology, a magazine *New Poems* (six numbers 1951–1953) and a number of individual collections. Oxford poets dominated, but there were also important contributions from Cambridge and from slightly senior Oxbridge graduates, including Larkin, Amis, Donald Davie and Wain. With such a spread of contributors there was no uniformity of style (Fantasy Poet No. 29 was Daibhidh Michell – a misprint for Mitchell – who wrote in Scots), and the collection was the seedbed for both the Movement and its slightly later successor, the Group. However, as Eric Homberger has pointed out in his study *The Art of the Real* (1977), an important critical stiffening was provided by American postgraduates studying in Oxford, and in particular by Donald Hall.

Hall was a graduate of Harvard, where he had studied with the poet Richard Wilbur, and this connection is one of the sources of the return to poetic order after the romantic indulgences of the 1940s. According to Homberger, 'formalism was, if not invented, at least perfected by Wilbur.' In 1951 his pupil brought the discipline to Oxford:

all the time that technical matters have seemed to bear the major part of my activity, an intellectual structure has been growing out of this preoccupation to spread itself over all human activity. I have come to think that all human action is formal; all personality is an aesthetic structure, a making something exist by statement: like saying a word. Symmetry becomes the root of morality, conduct and judgment, and reality is a terrifying chaos outside form glimpsed only occasionally, and never, of course, understood without a translation into form.

Donald Hall was in a position to impress and influence his English colleagues; he edited the first eight of the Fantasy Poets and the first five numbers of *New Poems*. He won the Newdigate Prize in 1953 and edited the 1953 *Oxford Poetry*.

Hall, however, was by no means the only practising poet who felt that there should be a return to disciplined techniques and a formal style. In 1952 Donald Davie, then teaching at Dublin University, published *Purity of Diction in English Verse*. His topic was eighteenth-century English verse, the denigrated period between the death of Pope and the publication of Wordsworth and Coleridge's *Lyrical Ballads*, but it was 'to the would-be poet of today that I should like to address myself'. When the volume was reprinted in 1966 Davie added a postscript which revealed that if the Movement had ever had a manifesto, he hoped that this would have been it. His starting-point was T. S. Eliot's project to purify the language of the tribe, but Davie found himself attacking Eliot and Ezra Pound for breaking the tradition of English verse with the invention of modernism, the post-symbolist language of *The Waste Land* and the *Cantos*. Eliot and Pound made their meaning by a collage of symbols, allusions and quotations that was not dependent on ordinary syntax or the regularity of metre and rhyme, and Davie saw sinister consequences proceeding from this attack on the rational structure of language. As a reform it was necessary to return to the regular relationships of meaning, metaphor and metre, to a purer diction based on eighteenth-

1. Rodrigo Moynihan
*Portrait Group
(The Teaching
Staff of the
Painting School,
Royal College
of Art)*
1951

2. Rodrigo Moynihan
Grey and Violet
1955

3. Ceramic mural by Victor Pasmore at the Regatta Restaurant
for the Festival of Britain 1951

4. Lucian Freud
*Interior Near
Paddington* 1951

5. Alan Davie
*Entrance to a
Paradise* 1949

6. John Bratby *Window, Self Portrait, Jean and Hands* 1957

7. Francis Bacon *Study after Velasquez's Portrait of Pope Innocent X* 1953

8. Jack Smith *Mother Bathing Child* 1953

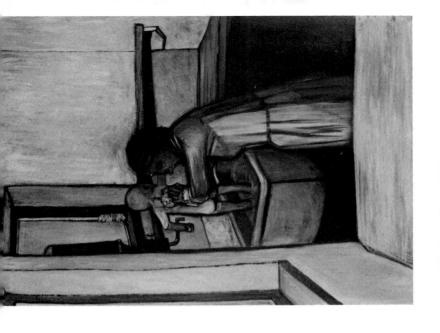

9. Frank Auerbach
*Head of
E. O. W. VIII*
1956

10. Robyn Denny
7/1960

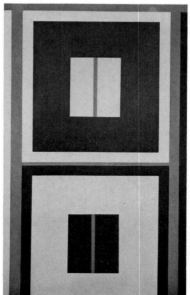

11. The original maquette for *The Monument to the Unknown Political Prisoner* by Reg Butler

12. Richard Hamilton *Just What is it that Makes Today's Homes so Different, so Appealing?* 1956

century models. There was something essentially conservative in this turning back: 'the distinguishing excellence of pure diction [is] the practice of refurbishing old metaphors gone dead, rather than hunting out of new ones.'

Again, Donald Davie was not alone in reacting against the experiments of Eliot and Pound and, more especially, against the poetic permissiveness that these experiments had appeared to sanction in the 1940s. James Devaney's *Poetry in Our Time* (1953) and Marjorie Boulton's *The Anatomy of Poetry* (1953) are both critical of the results of modernism. Reviewing poetry collections by James Kirkup (*A Correct Compassion*) and Francis King (*Rod of Incantation*), Richard Church commented in the *Listener* in 1952: 'Neither of these poets shows much regard, at least technically, for the fashion which has dominated English poetry since the 1920s, what one might call the Boston–Mont Parnasse mode, which hung a sparse body of thought and emotion with tags from foreign tongues, cribs from other authors and learned references.' Neither Kirkup nor King had links with the Movement, although Kirkup's title *A Correct Compassion* would be very suitable for a Movement poem.

The progress of formalism by 1953 was registered by G. S. Fraser in his introduction to the anthology *Springtime*.

On a purely technical plane, poetry seems to be going through a period of consolidation and simplification – of reaction against experiment for its own sake. The literary ideal today, of young poets, is possibly not novelty, but decorum . . . The tendency seems to be towards a somewhat chaste diction that may be used with a level conversational tone of voice, but is not conversational itself.

While this process of consolidation and simplification was going on, there remained the problem of finding an outlet for the results. For the first time a mass medium – radio – provided the answer. It is ironic, considering the contempt in which the post-war generation held their fading seniors, that it should be that key figure of the 1930s, John Lehmann, who was responsible for the breakthrough.

As we saw in the last chapter, the firm of John Lehmann Ltd

was wound up against his wishes at the end of 1952. Protests in the press and the sympathy of literary London were small consolations for Lehmann, but as he records in his memoir *The Ample Proposition*, the stresses of 1952 were somewhat compensated for by the BBC Third Programme's invitation to be the editor and presenter of the first ever literary magazine of the air. The first edition of *New Soundings*, produced by the novelist P. H. Newby (who was later to become a Head of the Third), was broadcast on 9 January 1952. The experiment was judged a success and further editions followed monthly from March.

Although the BBC had clearly played safe in trusting the programme to Lehmann, he went out of his way to find new young contributors, as far out of his way as Oxford and Cambridge, that is. As a result, besides presenting established *New Writing* figures like Henry Green, Louis MacNeice and Christopher Isherwood, as well as the better of the post-romantics like George Barker and Vernon Watkins, Lehmann broadcast many of the Fantasy Poets, among them Elizabeth Jennings, John Holloway, Thom Gunn, Donald Davie and John Wain. Publication in the *Listener* was a further bonus. Unfortunately for Lehmann, there was another shock in store for him. *New Soundings* was such a success that in mid-1952 it was given another six months' run. At the beginning of 1953 Lehmann was told that the programme would continue – but without him. While the BBC will tolerate any amount of empire-building by members of its staff, it lives in fear of power being wielded by outsiders like Lehmann. To Lehmann it seemed that he was being sacked for his success: 'to dismiss an editor completely because the magazine he had created, organized and kept going had been a resounding success, seemed to me, well, out of a looking-glass world.'

The removal of Lehmann left a space. His replacement was one of the young contributors to *New Soundings*, John Wain. It is here that the difficulty of writing justly about the conspiracy theory becomes acute. Wain has written that his programme *First Reading* produced 'some pretty brutal in-fighting; the literary world is full of people who, if they can't knock you out in the ring itself, will wait till you are going home afterwards, and then follow you down an alley with a broken bottle', which suggests that vested interests conspired against the programme. But Wain in the same breath admits his own policy in taking on the programme: 'This was a chance to move a few of the established reputations gently to one side and allow new people their turn, people whose view of what should be attempted was roughly the same as my own, and I took it.'

Certainly Wain made no bones about what his intentions were. He opened the first programme on 26 April 1953 with the statement that he did not possess John Lehmann's 'broad impartiality', and that he was going to use the programme 'as a means of putting over a certain point of view about contemporary letters'. A period of expansion, he said, had to be followed by 'a period of consolidation'. His script then continued with a passage that was cut from the broadcast. 'The virtues of courage and enterprise give place to the virtues of sanity, detachment, clear-headedness, judgment; the typical virtues of the administrator.' Wain was using the metaphor of territorial expansion; the pioneers of twentieth-century literature had carved out new areas it was now necessary to civilize, but the virtues of the administrator are not necessarily creative, particularly as far as poetry is concerned, and the detachment and judgment of Movement poetry can also be read as emotional coldness and intellectual caution. Wain's first item, however, fitted neither category, indeed it was positively aggressive, for it was an extract from Kingsley Amis's as yet unpublished novel *Lucky Jim*, the farcical scene of burning the bedclothes during Dixon's 'cultural' weekend at Professor Welch's. The first programme also included poetry by Wain's *Mandrake* colleague Arthur Boyars (Fantasy Poet No. 18), and Bernard Bergonzi (editor of Fantasy Poets 30–350).

The following monthly programmes included A. Alvarez, 'with a case against much of the poetry written today', attacking George Barker and Stephen Spender and protesting that there was 'almost no poetry being written today that presents any genuine intellectual difficulty'. (Alvarez has subsequently developed and modified his critical position.) There were also poems by G. S. Fraser, Hilary Corke, Philip Larkin, Donald Davie and Geoffrey Hill, but *First Reading* did not seem to be having the controversial effect intended. In the fourth programme, on 30 July 1953, noting of his initial remarks that 'no manifesto had ever cut less ice', Wain reissued his call for discipline, in stronger terms:

The kind of poetry I think we should encourage is the kind that is poetry first and something else afterwards. That sounds trite, but the fact is that for the last twenty years it has been possible to become a well-known poet in this country being something else first and a poet second. In the Thirties it was enough to be the right kind of sophisticated sociological observer, with the proper political reflexes; you were that first, and a poet second; and it was good enough. In the Forties it was sufficient merely to react against what you called the aridity of the Thirties into a loose romanticism which expressed itself in a slipshod vagueness and a generally high emotional temperature.

Meanwhile, the old guard had in fact been stirring. The novelist Hugh Massingham, writing one of the few interesting radio and television columns of the period for the *New Statesman*, had interpreted Wain's talk of 'consolidation' as 'the old fogies can be led off to the slaughterhouse after being festooned with the usual sacrificial garlands. After that Mr Wain and his fledglings can move in and establish the new dispensation.' Massingham was of course in favour of encouraging the young, and so had considered ignoring 'Mr Wain's deplorable broadcasts'; but the standard of contribution was so low and the poetry so hard to follow that it was necessary to speak up – which Massingham accordingly did, continuing his attack in the following week. This was the signal for a general engagement on the letters page of the *New Statesman*, and the first entertaining literary controversy since the war. Wain and G. S. Fraser rose in defence, John Lehmann developed a side issue with Fraser over the merits and meaning of 'provincialism', while Albert Hunt (who was to become an art school impresario in the 1960s) attacked 'young dons' of his own generation 'who amuse themselves by dabbling in literature'. This in turn led to dispute as to whether you could be a 'don' at a provincial university, and whether or not they were paid as well as bus drivers. The arguments broke out of the letters page into the *New Statesman*'s editorial column, and finally into V. S. Pritchett's opening article for the Autumn Books number, where he made the remark quoted earlier about the envious outskirts of literary society. He also discussed Amis's still unpublished *Lucky Jim* as 'a successful and quite new piece of observation of the caddish and pushing provincial young man', thus providing his opponents with more publicity.

Wain's editorship of *First Reading* was scheduled to run for six months, and it was not extended. In what looks like an attempt by the BBC to show cultural balance, the second series of *First Reading* was presented by Ludovic Kennedy, who matched Wain's choice of *Lucky Jim* with an extract from Evelyn Waugh's forthcoming *Men at Arms*. In the *New Statesman* William Salter (for Hugh Massingham had also been replaced as radio critic) commented, 'in fairness to Mr Kennedy it must be said that his comments were no more infuriating than Mr Wain's . . . they merely infuriated in a different way.' The BBC seems to have regretted its attempts to found a literary magazine of the air, for *First Reading* was killed off in 1954, and the cause of literature had to be served by duller and less dangerous programmes such as *New Poetry* – 'half an hour of readings from recently published volumes'.

The arguments over *First Reading* were more useful in dramatizing a growing conflict between generations than in deciding any issues about poetry. They help to show the process by which the carnivorous young men of 1951 were growing into the angry young men of 1956. And broadcasting made a significant contribution to the process. Wain wrote in 1956, 'it is a fact that the very people who are now dominant were unknown before they became the centre of controversy in these six programmes, and the reviewers laughed at me for bringing forward exactly those writers whose boots they are now licking.'

113

If the Movement poets had a rough handling from the citadel of Bloomsbury Socialism, the *New Statesman*, they were considerably assisted by the Liberal–Conservative *Spectator*. (To be fair, several Movement poets were published in the *New Statesman*, and the regular poetry reviewer G. S. Fraser was obviously sympathetic.) The promoter at the *Spectator* was Anthony Hartley, who began to publish poetry in the *Spectator* in 1952, and who contributed a short story to Wain's *First Reading* No 4. Hartley gradually took on the poetry reviewing for the *Spectator*, and by 1954 was also a regular theatre critic. In 1953 Amis, Larkin, Davie and Elizabeth Jennings all had poems published in the magazine. In 1954 Kingsley Amis became a regular monthly fiction reviewer, and Wain also contributed reviews; Thom Gunn, John Holloway and Robert Conquest joined the list of poetry contributors. In his reviews, Anthony Hartley pushed the idea that there was a new generation of poets, 'the University Wits', who 'call themselves *ironic, intellectual, rigorous, witty*. They are called by others *cynical, clever, arid*, and *facetious*.' (This article of January 1954 included an attack on Edith Sitwell's *Gardeners and Astronomers* which provoked a telegram from the poetess suggesting the *Spectator* should have Hartley stuffed.)

At regular intervals Hartley promoted the University Wits. In August 1954, reviewing a batch of Fantasy Press publications, Thom Gunn's *Fighting Terms*, George Macbeth's *A Form of Words*, Donald Davie as Fantasy Poet No. 19 and Jonathan Price as Fantasy Poet No. 20, he declared:

New names in the reviews, a fresh atmosphere of controversy, a new spirit of criticism – there are signs that some other group of poets is appearing on the horizon. . . . Of course, it has its roots in the Thirties. The attempt at a return to romanticism which came between was essentially a sport. In the poems of William Empson and, to a lesser extent, those of Auden, the present generation of under or just over thirties have found their masters, a development which first became evident in Mr John Wain's essay on Mr Empson's poetry in *Penguin New Writing*. The common influence is, no doubt, one of the main reasons for the impression of unity given by their work.

114

Hartley's article concluded, 'we are now in the presence of the only considerable movement in English poetry since the Thirties.'

It was not until October 1954, however, that this new flowering of English poetry was graced with a capital letter. In 1953 Wilson Harris, who had edited the *Spectator* since 1933, was forced to retire by his fellow directors at the age of sixty-nine. He was replaced by the former assistant editor, Walter Taplin, who gradually introduced new features into the paper. In October 1954, as a stimulus to circulation, the *Spectator* launched the first of what it called occasional 'literary editorials'. It was titled 'In the Movement', and its anonymous author was the literary editor J. D. Scott, who repeated Hartley's previous assessments of 'this new Movement of the Fifties – its metaphysical wit, its glittering intellectuality, its rich Empsonian ambiguities', and so on in similar vein. At last the new generation had a label.

The vagueness of the phrase 'the Movement' underlines the dangers of all labels. (It must be noted in passing that two of Hartley's poets in his August 1954 review, Jonathan Price and George Macbeth, are not normally considered Movement poets.) Conventionally, a new movement would be expected to have a manifesto, a little magazine and at least one group anthology. By the end of 1954 all the Movement could show was a number of statements from Hartley and Wain, a brief run of the Third Programme and a scatter of small press publications. There was no Movement magazine as such, although George Hartley's *Listen*, launched in 1954 from Hessle, East Yorkshire, did publish many of the new poets. What was lacking was any definitive group publication.

In 1955 that need was supplied in, of all places, Japan. In 1953 D. J. Enright, a wartime pupil of Leavis's at Cambridge, became a lecturer at Kouan University. (Previously he had taught at Alexandria University in Egypt and as an extra-mural lecturer in Birmingham. A collection of poems, *Laughing Hyena*, was published in 1953.) In Japan, Enright found it difficult to demonstrate that there was more to contemporary

English poetry than T. S. Eliot and Dylan Thomas, and accordingly put together a small collection of poems that he liked, calling it *Poets of the 1950s*. It was published in Tokyo in 1955. Enright, away from the literary politics of England, had educational rather than polemical intentions, but besides making a significant selection of contributors, he persuaded each poet to make a short statement of his principles, statements which have been quoted, usually against their authors, ever since.

Enright's choice as the *Poets of the 1950s* comprised himself, Kingsley Amis, Robert Conquest, Donald Davie, John Holloway, Elizabeth Jennings, Philip Larkin and John Wain. The volume was hardly seen in England but, with the addition of Thom Gunn, it is exactly the same selection of names (and a similar choice of poems) as that made by Robert Conquest when he edited the anthology *New Lines* for Macmillan in 1956.

New Lines represents the moment of the Movement. It has no individual statements as in Enright's collection, but an introduction by Robert Conquest firmly places it in the tradition of group anthologies claiming to stand for the poetry of their decade. (The title links it with the *New Signatures* and *New Country* anthologies of the 1930s.) 'It is in the belief that a general tendency has once again set in, and that a genuine and healthy poetry of the new period has established itself, that this collection has been made.' *New Lines* was to reform poetry following the collapse of taste for which the 1940s were responsible. It was then that

the debilitating theory that poetry *must* be metaphorical gained wide acceptance. Poets were encouraged to produce diffuse and sentimental verbiage, or hollow technical pirouettes: praise even went to writers whose verse seemed to have been put together from the snippets in the 'Towards More Picturesque Speech' page of the *Reader's Digest*. Residual nuisances like the Social-realists, the Lallans-mongers, the church-furnishers and the neo-Georgians were able to maintain themselves. In these circumstances it became more plain than is usually the case that without integrity and judgment enough to prevent surrender to subjective moods or social pressures all the technical and emotional gifts are almost worthless.

Given its aggressive stance, it is not surprising that *New Lines* ran into opposition. At the very moment when these poets gained their objective, they became the target for all the accusations they had made against their seniors. *New Lines* immediately provoked a counter-anthology, *Mavericks* (1957), edited by Dannie Abse and Howard Sergeant. The romantic strain in English poetry surfaced again.

Whatever the merits or demerits of 'The Movement' as such, we are of the opinion that, due to the intensive methods of publicity which have been adopted, there is real danger that it may serve to distract attention from these young poets outside 'The Movement' who are making a valid attempt to grapple with problems beyond those of mere technique and to communicate, lucidly and honestly, what they feel to be significant experience.

The 'Mavericks', mainly contributors to *Poetry and Poverty* and *Outposts*, were J. C. Hall, David Wright, Vernon Scannell, Dannie Abse, Michael Hamburger, John Smith, Anthony Cronin, W. Price Turner and Jon Silkin – all poets, according to Abse, who were not afraid of the 'primary Dionysian excitement'.

Mavericks did not have the circulation of *New Lines*, but one of its contributors, David Wright, as a senior survivor of the 1940s, was able to maintain the counter-attack in *Encounter*:

Nobody who has read the correspondence columns of the English literary periodicals over the past three or four years can possibly be unaware that we are in the presence of an impalpable and ambiguous phenomenon generally referred to as 'The Movement', whose existence is affirmed and disavowed – sometimes in consecutive sentences – by its adherents, victims, and bandwagon-masters. It all began, as far as I can remember, with some young provincial dons exclaiming at the iniquity of the London literary racket in the tone of awed horror that Sunday papers adopt in those articles they have about the razor gangs and street women of Soho. Almost simultaneously – at the drop, as it were, of a cocktail glass – the voices of these same young men

117

were heard wafted on Third programmes, their verse and opinions presented weekly on Fridays and Sundays in the booksy periodicals and newspapers, while the London critics mustered their most impressive jargon to inform the nation in leading articles that a poetic renaissance unparalleled since the Thirties was at hand. . . . In no time whatsoever, the London literary racket, if it ever existed, was bust wide open.

This is no more than the common assault of literary controversy, a repetition of the row over *First Reading*, and one might expect the editor of *New Lines* to take up the challenge. But this is Robert Conquest's answer to Wright:

> half the time, he seems to be reviewing not what is actually there but a preconceived idea: that imaginary, or at least irrelevant, bugbear – 'The Movement'. This word was originally applied some years ago in the *Spectator*, I think, to a group of poets who were then going in for what was then described as 'rich Empsonian ambiguities' and paying a lot of respect to Dr Leavis. Two or three of the nine poets in *New Lines* certainly started out this way, but even they have pulled free, and are no more to be blamed than Yeats is for once having been a Pre-Raphaelite. And I should have thought that most of us pretty obviously had no dealings at all with Empson or Leavis or any of it. There are two pages in my introduction notably hostile to the movement (which I disassociate the rest of us from to the extent of referring to it as 'that group') and to its formulae, but conceding that it had been of some slight help in teaching a few poets one of many necessary lessons.

For one Movement poet, then, the Movement very definitely did not exist.

Putting aside the razors and broken bottles of literary gang-warfare, *New Lines* has to be taken at face value. Under whatever label, the anthology was presented as evidence that 'a general tendency' had 'once again set in'. That was the view of its editor, and there is every reason to suppose that he meant what he said. The problem is to find the right description for what was setting in. Writing before *New Lines* appeared, Anthony Hartley had been eager to prescribe what that general tendency – he called it a 'similarity of tone rather than of subject-matter' – should be:

A liberalism distrustful of too much richness or too much fanaticism, austere and sceptical. A liberalism egalitarian and anti-aristocratic. A liberalism profoundly opposed to fashion in the metropolitan sense of the word and in this and other ways displaying strong connections with F. R. Leavis and *Scrutiny*.

Hartley's propaganda for the Movement was not, it should be noted, rewarded by the inclusion of his own poetry in *New Lines*, and when Conquest himself came to define the general tendency, distrust of fanaticism revealed itself in extreme caution:

these poets do not have as much in common as they would if they were a group of doctrine-saddled writers forming a definite school complete with programmes and rules. What they do have in common is perhaps, at its lowest, little more than a negative determination to avoid bad principles.

This caution seems justified when the contributors are looked at individually. D. J. Enright, editor of *Poets of the 1950s*, shows few of the characteristics of his colleagues. His forms are irregular, and his work as a teacher in Egypt and Japan has given him a range of exotic, unprovincial reference. Robert Conquest's forms are more regular than Enright's, but there is a similarity in that both use exotic locations. Conquest had served in the army throughout the war, and then travelled as a Foreign Office official. His sequence 'Reflections in Landscapes' had won a Festival of Britain poetry prize in 1951. Both Enright and Conquest are critical of the deliberate difficulties and ambiguities of poetry imitating Empson: 'almost as much a vehicle for unpleasant exhibitionism and sentimentality as the trends it was designed to correct,' wrote Conquest in his introduction to *New Lines*. He is nonetheless intellectual and critical in his approach in that at least six of his eight poems in *New Lines* are concentrated on the problem of poetry and the imagination.

A preoccupation with perception, a theme common to several *New Lines* poets, is a prominent feature of the selection from Elizabeth Jennings (Fantasy Poet No. 1). In his introduction, Conquest was happy to link this to contemporary fashion in linguistic philosophy: 'Post-war poetry has often been criticized for dealing too much with language, and with the poetic process itself, as though these were in some way illegitimate subjects. This seems a rather superficial misconception: the nature of art and of the whole problem of communications has in recent years been seen to be at the centre of philosophy and human life.'

Paradoxically, the one *New Lines* poet who had actually trained and practised as a linguistic philosopher, John Holloway, is the one nearest to being a 'romantic'. The author of *Language and Intelligence* (1951), Holloway had shifted from his earlier philosophic interests to English literature, and in 1953 published *The Victorian Sage*, a study reflecting the growing interest in the nineteenth century. (Unfortunately, Holloway's pioneering study ignores John Ruskin.) In his poetry, he is concerned with the observation of emotional states and relationships, while a poem like 'The Minute' – a moment of epiphany experienced on a country walk – would fit easily into a collection of romantic landscape poetry. By contrast, Thom Gunn, a young Cambridge poet (Fantasy Poet No. 16) not included in *Poets of the 1950s*, is the most 'philosophical' of the *New Lines* poets – philosophical in the then unfashionable sense of a metaphysical probing into the nature of things.

So far Robert Conquest's definition of a unity of 'negative determination' seems all too accurate; none of the poets are quite what they might be expected to be. Donald Davie, as a polemicist on behalf of regular metre and purified diction, does at least follow his own principles, and in 'Rejoinder to a Critic' we do find a metaphysical conceit in the Empsonian scientistic manner (in this case, Donne plus the Atom Bomb. The poem is quoted on p. 143). But a conversational tone masks an ambiguity which seems to conflict with his call for direct statement. Davie's technical practice – regularity of metre, urbanity of tone – acts to control emotions which he distrusts but has to acknowledge within himself, as in 'Cherry Ripe', or within others, as in 'Remembering the Thirties'.

The Empsonian is even criticized by Empson's promoter, John Wain, who in his comment in *Poets of the 1950s* admits that he has done himself no service by praising Empson and Robert Graves. In *New Lines* the acknowledgement to Empson is there in 'Eighth Type of Ambiguity', and there is a quantity of *terza rima*, but the verse is far less clotted than the master's. That is appropriate, for a major theme is the difficulties that lie in the way of communication, as in the sequence 'Who Speaks My Language?'

The most negative of determinations was expressed by Philip Larkin in a rare comment on his own work for *Poets of the 1950s*: 'I believe that every poem must be its own sole freshly created universe, and therefore have no belief in "tradition" or a common myth-kitty or casual allusions in poems to other poems or poets, which last I find unpleasantly like the talk of literary understrappers letting you see they know the right people.' Taking all of Larkin's work from *The North Ship* (1945), through *XX Poems* (1951), to *The Less Deceived* (1955), two kinds of poems emerge, one a very closely wrought and more or less private expression of agony, the other a more public utterance, as in 'Church Going', which is almost a sour version of John Betjeman. This second voice has an 'oh-now-come-off-it' tone also heard in Kingsley Amis (to whom Larkin dedicated *XX Poems*).

Kingsley Amis (who dedicated *Lucky Jim* to Larkin) made the most notorious statement of the supposed rough, tough, no-nonsense attitude of the Movement in *Poets of the 1950s*, but at the same time he managed to depreciate his and others' efforts.

The trouble with the newer poets, including myself, is that they often are lucid and nothing else – except arid and bald, and that, on the other hand, the strict forms seem to give some of them the idea that they can be as sentimental and trite as they please provided they do it in *terza rima*. But their great deficiency is meagreness and triviality of subject-matter: nobody wants any more poems on the grander themes for a few years, but at the same time nobody wants any more poems about philosophers or paintings or novelists or art galleries or mythology or foreign cities or other poems. At least I hope nobody wants them.

In fact, quite a number of the *New Lines* poems are precisely about these subjects, and in his own work Amis showed himself very concerned about attitudes to poetry, as in 'Against Romanticism'. His themes are perennially poetic, protesting against the mutability of emotion and experience through time and memory, and the distortions of emotion itself; even in lines aggressively expressed there is a sense of regret:

> We men have got love well weighed up; our stuff
> Can get by without it.

Robert Conquest, then, was right to be cautious about defining the principles of *New Lines* – and that very caution is one of the collection's unifying themes. To begin with, there was caution about the actual craft of poetry, following the experiments of the 1920s and 1930s, and the excesses of the 1940s. *New Lines* was a response to the general call to order, for a return to tradition away from modernism, that had gone out on all fronts in the early 1950s. In *Mavericks* Dannie Abse wrote, 'I'm certainly not opposed to discipline and form and style.' The formalism of the Movement poets presented problems for the slightly later 'Group' poets, who followed even stricter critical procedures, in that they existed specifically to hold regular meetings to discuss their work in almost seminar-like conditions. (The history of the Group begins with the meetings arranged by Philip Hobsbaum in Cambridge from 1952 to 1955, when they moved to London; Edward Lucie-Smith took over as chairman in 1959. *A Group Anthology* was published in 1963.) Several of the Group poets were published by the Fantasy Press: Adrian Mitchell (No. 24), Lucie-Smith (No. 25); George Macbeth edited Nos. 19 to 24, and the Press published his collection *A Form of Words* in 1954. From 1952 to 1954 George Macbeth and Anthony Thwaite helped to edit *Trio*, an undergraduate Oxford poetry magazine favouring 'strictness of form'. By the time *New Lines* appeared in 1956, formalism had become so much the dominant mode that it was necessary to reassert the emotional content of poetry, and this the Group began to do, although their technical preference was formalist. It was not until a new generation began to emerge at the end of the decade that a reaction against the conservative principles of the Movement set in, although its leading members maintained their influence into the 1970s.

It would be over-simplistic to expect developments in one art form to parallel precisely those in another, but there are comparisons to be drawn between the state of poetry and the state of painting in Britain in the late 1940s, and some of the strategies adopted to change those states have illuminating similarities. The vital difference between poetry and painting is that while British poets have always been able to draw on a vigorous native tradition, painters have had to look abroad: in the 1930s to Paris, in the 1950s to New York.

For the brief period of the war years British artists were cut off from both the waning influence of Paris and the growing influence of America. All artists, of whatever severity of abstract principles, were touched in those years by one or other of the twin sources of English Neo-Romantic painting: Surrealism and the traditional English landscape feeling. The Surrealist Graham Sutherland and the picturesque John Piper were the leaders of a school of younger Neo-Romantic painters which blossomed in the artificial conditions of wartime. Two more isolated artists, Ivon Hitchens and Henry Moore, combined abstraction with a sense of landscape that informs even the ostensibly figure-derived reclining sculptures of Moore. The landscape feeling also penetrated the previously puritanically constructivist abstracts of Ben Nicholson and the standing forms of Barbara Hepworth, both of them responding to the Cornish landscape of St Ives to which they had withdrawn in 1939. The circle of Surrealism and abstraction was squared by Francis Bacon who, uninterested in

123

landscape, combined the most violently expressive and surreal images with a concern for the traditional preoccupations of painting, explored through the traditional materials of oil and canvas, and indeed using traditional formats – for instance his series of screaming Popes derived from Velasquez (Plate 7).

All these were separated and independent painters, and remained so, rather like those senior surviving poets of the 1930s admired by the Movement. That is not to say that they were unsuccessful or unrewarded. Bacon's career flourished throughout the 1950s, Henry Moore was given a major retrospective in the Festival year of 1951, Graham Sutherland in the Coronation year of 1953, and these three, Barbara Hepworth and Ben Nicholson acquired international reputations in the 1950s which they have not lost. But the fact remains that they were isolated by their reputations and personalities. Of the two artists more likely to lead a school – Nicholson and Sutherland – Graham Sutherland rather lost his way after 1945, his landscape paraphrases giving place to spiky forms and harsh colours derived from the Mediterranean landscape that was once more accessible to him. The thorn trees of the south fed the imagery of his religious commissions, notably the tapestry designed for Coventry Cathedral, completed in 1957. He also took up portrait painting, his status reflected by that of his sitters, who did not always appreciate the results. His portrait of Winston Churchill (1954) was secretly burnt.

One of the causes of Graham Sutherland's difficulties was the reconnection of London to the mainstream of Continental painting, symbolized by the immediate post-war shows of new work by Picasso, Braque and Matisse. The London-based group of Neo-Romantic painters he had inspired broke up of its own accord. The romantic atmospherics of their wartime work always had a tendency towards picturesque superficiality, which is most clearly evident in the work of John Piper, and most now tried to discipline themselves by adopting a post-Cubist lineality that derives from Picasso, mediated by the direct example of the Polish refugee artist Jankel Adler, who died in London in 1949. John Craxton and John Minton (who committed suicide in 1957) travelled to Italy and Greece, and came back with brighter palettes as a result. The Glasgow painters Robert MacBryde and Robert Colquhoun kept to the murkier tones of Cubism, as did Prunella Clough, who chose more down-to-earth subjects than the crying clowns and gypsy women of the two Roberts. Keith Vaughan evolved his own personal – and restricted – theme of nude figures in landscape. Michael Ayrton, always the most literary of the group, moved towards a form of realism and extended his activities from art criticism into novels. Ayrton, his Neo-Romantic phase over, became an isolated figure; Lucian Freud, though closely linked by friendship with this group, always had been independent in his work because of his highly individual expressionist deformation of careful draughtmanship (Plate 4). The broader touch of his paintings in the early 1950s owed something to his friend Francis Bacon; an agonized view of the world underlies their superficially different techniques (Plate 7).

The Neo-Romantic movement in painting faded almost precisely at the same moment as it did in poetry, and its survivors did not satisfactorily resolve the problem of adjusting their styles to the ideas of the School of Paris, still regarded as the authentic source of the avant-garde in art. That the School of Paris was itself about to be supplanted by the School of New York had something to do with this loss of direction. But for once the metropolis did not have a monopoly on the means of production and exchange of ideas. An alternative centre of activity existed in the Penwith peninsula of Cornwall, based on the fishing villages of Newlyn and St Ives.

The Penwith peninsula had attracted artists by the distinctive qualities of its landscape and light since the 1880s, and many artists rented or owned studios there. In the 1930s the dominant St Ives style had been academic naturalism, although the area was known to modernists like John Tunnard and Ben Nicholson. At the beginning of the war Nicholson moved with Barbara Hepworth to a house in St Ives owned by the painter and art critic Adrian Stokes. The Russian-born Constructivist Naum

Gabo also spent the war there as a refugee, and as a result a small group of artists representing the Constructivist branch of European Modernism preserved the abstract tradition intact throughout the war years. This tradition was, as was pointed out earlier, somewhat modified by the magical properties of the Cornish landscape, but the avant-garde continuity remained, and a number of abstract and semi-abstract painters – Patrick Heron, John Wells, Peter Lanyon, Bryan Winter and Terry Frost among them – lived and worked in the area in the post-war period. In 1949 there was a belated battle of the moderns when Nicholson, Hepworth and others broke away from the St Ives Society of Artists to form the Penwith Society of Arts, and it was the Penwith Society that held the first post-war exhibition of exclusively abstract paintings in 1950.

The most decisive break with Neo-Romanticism, as opposed to a modification or slipping away, was made by an artist whose previous work in the 1940s epitomized the soft, appealing qualities of late romantic impressionism: Victor Pasmore. During the war Pasmore had modified the intended social realism of the Euston Road School to produce poetic misty evocations of the riverscape of London. In 1948 he made a break so decisive that the selectors of the Festival of Britain show *British Painting 1925–1950* had to include him in both the anthology featuring the traditionalists and the anthology of the avant-garde. Between 1948 and 1951 he made a series of experiments with degrees of abstraction (Plate 3), including collage, that was almost a crash course in modernism, before settling on a series of abstract low-relief constructions which became his customary mode of expression throughout the 1950s, and which extended into architecture with his designs for Peterlee New Town. Abstract reliefs have an obvious connection with Ben Nicholson's pre- and post-war work, and Pasmore exhibited with the Penwith Society. The examples of Pasmore and Nicholson encouraged a group of younger abstract painters, principally Kenneth and Mary Martin, Anthony Hill, Terry Frost and Adrian Heath, to persevere with a linear abstraction that gradually came under the influence of Abstract Expressionism.

The little that has been written about British post-war art is so dominated by the arrival of Abstract Expressionism from America in the mid-1950s that it is difficult to appreciate that there was a period between the decline of Neo-Romanticism and the rise of Abstract Expressionism when attempts were made to steer painting in another direction. (This lacuna was partially filled by an exhibition in 1984, *The Forgotten Fifties*. It revealed, incidentally, how drab the visual environment of the Fifties was, in comparison with later decades.) Abstract Expressionism constituted such a radical development that it was bound to have the impact that post-Cubism or late Constructivism did not have; it restored the idea of an avant-garde just as the whole concept of Modernism seemed to be fading. But before American painting swept all before it, experiments were made with a different solution. M. H. Middleton described the problem, and the solution, as they appeared in 1952:

Pasmore becomes constructivist; Sutherland turns to portraiture. There seems to be no glance of recognition as the two files of ants pass one another in opposite directions, intent upon their unseen destinations. The perennial ambivalence of art – in the last analysis its mainspring – is as marked as ever. Nevertheless, as the formal discoveries of the great pioneers of the first thirty years of this century become dispersed throughout the world and settle slowly into a new academicism, disenchantment spreads. An increasing number of painters retreat from the impasse towards a new form of realism, and one may note the beginnings of a new, though non-impressionist, return to the object. Nothing now remains to be discovered except the painter's own soul.

Middleton was reviewing an exhibition at the Institute of Contemporary Arts, *Recent Trends in Realist Painting*. The word 'naturalism' having been freely used in the previous chapter, some distinction – at least in terms of painting – must be made between naturalism and realism. The distinction is not always easy to make, but it becomes clear if qualifying terms such as 'academic' naturalism and 'social' realism are added. The realist is interested in natural appearances, but he is not concerned to render them in the customary and conventional terms – which by 1950 meant a subdued impressionism. Rather, he is anxious to convey the expressive qualities of things by re-sensitizing their images; the subject-matter can be as ordinary and banal as everyday life, the painter tries to renew our perception of it. It is often an academic convention that some things are not fit subjects for painting – chip friers or kitchen sinks – so it is precisely towards these everyday objects that the realist is drawn. The qualifying term 'social' implies a political dimension, for it is the Mandarins who define the proper subject for art, to paint what is conceived of as social reality and to imply that conditions are not what they should be is to challenge the Mandarin view of the world.

The drive towards realist painting in the early 1950s was largely conducted by one man, John Berger, whose political views over-emphasized the ideological aspects of realism and probably did the movement some harm. Berger, a painter turned critic and later novelist, was a member of the Communist Party, at least before 1956, and his calls for realism were confused in people's minds with the Russian form of Social Realism approved by Stalin. Bright-eyed, big-chested Stakhanovites painted in essentially nineteenth-century academic style were not what Berger meant at all, and under attack in 1953 he protested: 'Far from dragging politics into art, art has dragged me into politics.' But the confusion persisted. Berger wrote art criticism for the *New Statesman*, and used his position to welcome realism wherever he saw it. In January 1952 he wrote enthusiastically about the *Young Contemporaries* exhibition, an annual event begun in 1949 which featured work from British art schools. Berger claimed that 'slowly but quite certainly something is happening to British painting: something which had previously been suspected – and hoped for – but which is now actually proved.' Students were choosing representational themes, abandoning subjectivity for communication. Interestingly, Berger compares the young painters to the neo-realist cinema of Italian directors like de Sica and Rossellini, rather than drawing on the more obvious example of the Italian painter Renato Guttuso.

In September 1952 Berger was given an opportunity to demonstrate 'his thesis that 'there are now two academic dangers: on the one side Royal Academy naturalism, on the other over-formalization and abstraction. Only those who steer between them – along the middle of the road – will progress beyond either.' The Whitechapel Art Gallery invited him to mount a selection of contemporary realist paintings which, characteristically, he called *Looking Forward*. Forty artists were represented, and whether Berger intended it or not, the breadth of selection demonstrates the imprecision of the 'realist' label. The academic naturalists were represented by Rodrigo Moynihan and Claude Rogers, former members of the Euston Road School which had begun in the 1930s as a response to the political tensions of that decade, but whose impressionism was now chiefly concerned with austere problems of rendering subject and atmosphere in paint. Ruskin Spear's cityscapes were in the same naturalistic vein. An alternative conception of realism among older artists was represented by L. S. Lowry's painting of the industrial North, and the melancholy pictures of South Wales miners by the Polish refugee artist Josef Herman. Carel Weight's obsessive depictions of ordinary suburban streets and houses pressed close to surrealism.

All these artists offered versions of realism that had been in existence since before the war; the main interest of *Looking Forward* is in the younger painters Berger selected: Derrick Greaves, Jack Smith, Edward Middleditch and Euan Uglow. All these were still students at the Royal College of Art in 1952, and the 'Royal College realists' (among them another student not included in Berger's show, John Bratby) began to be thought of as a distinct group. Berger was not the only one to promote them. The director of the Beaux Arts Gallery in Bruton Street, Mrs Helen Lessore, mounted a series of one-man shows of these artists from 1953 onwards – the Gallery also showed Michael Fussell and Michael Andrews; associated with them were John Eyles and Michael Tothill, while Euan Uglow rather held back until the 1960s – which gave the movement an appearance of cohesion. It received something like official recognition in 1956 when Derrick Greaves, John Bratby, Edward Middleditch and Jack Smith were selected for the British pavilion at the Venice Biennale.

The cohesion of the group was short-lived, and like that of the Movement poets it was to a certain extent an external creation that obscured the distinctions within it. Jack Smith's *Mother Bathing Child* (1953), for instance, has a symbolist melancholy very different from John Bratby's enthusiastic visual autobiography (Plates 6 and 8). By the end of the 1950s these artists were no longer occupied with 'realist' concerns, with the exception of John Bratby, whose personal success had encouraged a kind of self-parody. And even at the height of the group's popularity other painters, notably Leon Kossoff and Frank Auerbach, had been attacking the problem of realism from a different angle. Both Kossoff and Auerbach were at one time pupils of David Bomberg (who died in 1957), a Vorticist before the First World War who had settled on a form of expressionism that made vigorous use of the actual qualities of paint itself. Bomberg's evening classes at the Borough Polytechnic in London led to the emergence of the 'Borough Bottega' – the title of a show at the Walker's Galleries in 1955 – with a style that rejected ideas of painterly elegance by building up the picture surface with coarse lumps of paint that are representational in intention, but unavoidably real shapes and texture (Plate 9). (The Beaux Arts Gallery gave Leon Kossoff and Frank Auerbach their first one-man shows in 1956 and 1957.) The thickness of their paint gave this branch of realism affinities with the 'matter' painters influenced by Jean Dubuffet.

What unity there was among realist painters of the 1950s came from the Beaux Arts Gallery connection and John Berger's pen – rather as Anthony Hartley had helped to drum up interest in the Movement. Like the Movement poets, the realists ran into opposition, notably from the senior avant-garde art critic Herbert Read, who resented Berger's attack on the sculpture competition organized in 1952–3 by the Institute of Contemporary Arts to design a memorial for 'The Unknown Political Prisoner'. (Read was Chairman of the ICA and on the international jury of the competition.) The competition had obvious Cold War overtones, confirmed by the refusal of Russia to take part, but Berger's objections were more to the abstract bias shown in the choice of prize-winners. The first prize went to the rising British sculptor Reg Butler (Plate 11), and others to Barbara Hepworth, Alexander Calder, Naum Gabo and Lyn Chadwick, another member of a group of successful semi-abstract contemporary British sculptors. Always looking forward, John Berger denounced the competition as a failure 'because it has encouraged the most hapless, aimless, and therefore inevitably reactionary type of work. Only one thing can now justify the competition: if it really forces us to draw the necessary conclusion that beyond all the qualifying, fragmentary arguments, the "official" modern art of the West is now bankrupt.' Herbert Read replied in Cold War terms. 'If we tear aside Mr Berger's camouflage, we find him saying quite bluntly, like his colleagues in Russia, that art must be illustrative.' The *New Statesman*'s other critic, the abstract painter Patrick Heron, joined in the debate and accused Berger of promoting a fiction, arguing that most people were not interested in art, and never would be. For several weeks readers of the *New Statesman* were entertained by the sight of their two art critics battling out the contrary views of art-for-itself – and so for the élite – and art-for-the-people – and so for propaganda.

The debate was muddled and inconclusive, for neither side managed to make its point sufficiently in the terms of the other. Berger himself later became disenchanted with the painters he had promoted, particularly Bratby, but his campaign for realism illustrates the difficulty artists had in finding a way forward from a tradition of modernism that was already thirty years old. Literary and picturesque Neo-Romanticism had proved regressive and self-indulgent; realism became entangled with unpopular political attitudes; but abstraction – until the American example was assimilated – offered little more than arid intellectualism and a reworking of old problems. Realism, with its challenge to the Mandarin conception of the purpose of art, encouraged a coarseness and vigour that most painting of the early 1950s lacked. It was the vigour and emotionalism of Abstract Expressionism that led to its dominance after 1956. In 1957 the Tate Gallery re-hung its collection from the modern British school, and David Sylvester seized the opportunity to make a re-assessment of contemporary British painting:

What it adds up to is something as remote from the rest of modern painting as British films are from real films. This is largely because it has an absence of attack and earthiness, a sort of stiff-upper-lipped air. So that when we arrive at the far end of Gallery XVIII and come upon two Bratbys, which have not got this atmosphere of doing the done thing and please do not spit and gentlemen lift the seat, we feel for the first time that we are looking at paintings, paintings in the ordinary sense of the word.

Writing in 1957, Sylvester consciously or unconsciously had taken with him into Gallery XVIII ideas and criticisms of gentility that derive from contemporary literature, especially drama. Conversely, the ungenteel realist painters and their spokesmen suggest ideas about the state of literature in the years of the Movement.

'The only thing shared by all Realists,' wrote John Berger in *Permanent Red* (1960), 'is the nature of their relationship to the art tradition they inherit. They are Realists in so far as they bring into art aspects of nature and life ignored or forbidden by the rule makers.' The poets and painters of the 1950s stood in an uncomfortable position to the traditions they inherited. The decayed romanticism of the 1940s represented the furthest extension of the great developments of Modernism that began in the second decade of the twentieth century. In particular,

Surrealism, which equally influenced Neo-Romantic painting and Apocalyptic poetry, seemed played out. In a period of political and economic constriction, the idea of an ever-progressing avant-garde was no longer valid, and the only way forward was back, to some point before the great experiments of the twentieth century had led to the current confusion and loss of direction. Roy Fuller in *The Craft of Letters in England* noted the 'neutralism' of the Movement poets but appreciated their problem, particularly in the face of W. H. Auden, who represented the continuity of the tradition from the early moderns, T. S. Eliot and Ezra Pound. Auden

by ransacking the past of his art – as Picasso and Stravinsky ransacked theirs – so brilliantly and so completely for his own purposes has added to the difficulty. Perhaps for young poets one way round this immense father-figure – who seems to some to have already said everything worth saying about the contemporary situation – is by a return to realism, as for painters I suppose that is one way round Picasso.

Not only is the cross-reference illuminating, Fuller's comment shows the extent to which poets and painters were forced to adopt a negative attitude to the work of their predecessors. This was being conservative in the best sense, that of trying to rescue their art from indulgence and to restore discipline; but in the end the negative attitude proved the most significant – and debilitating – aspect of their work. The positive contribution, on the other hand, was the bringing into art of aspects of life previously ignored or forbidden. In poetry, for all of Kingsley Amis's pose of philistinism ('nobody wants any more poems on the grander themes for a few years'), the subject-matter tended to be the traditional preoccupations of poets; but members of the Movement also showed an interest in art forms without any appeal to Mandarin taste: jazz and science fiction. These have both always tended to be cult interests, but their rise to popularity in the late 1940s were the first examples of the reversal of the normal process of the communication of style. Previously, aristocratic tastes had been fed downwards through the social classes, but science fiction, and particularly jazz, travelled in the opposite direction, establishing a pattern that radically altered the culture of the 1960s.

There had long been jazz fans in Britain, but the wartime American forces radio network had introduced many young people to a form of music not available on the BBC. This tended to emphasize the cult aspect of jazz, and the New Orleans jazzmen whose style became the subject of such earnest revival in Britain in the late 1940s would have been bemused by the intellectual respect with which their entertainment-music was treated. But jazz, especially traditional jazz, had an earthiness, a rawness, that was definitely, to use Nancy Mitford's phrase, non-U, and it had a proletarian, non-Mandarin vigour. There was a slight shift in popularity towards the more sophisticated modern jazz in the mid-1950s, partly as a result of greater availability through long-playing records, and the use of jazz in films, but a taste for jazz remained one of the touchstones of contemporaneity, and John Wain, Kingsley Amis and Philip Larkin developed a side-line as jazz critics. The critical conservatism of their poetry coloured their preference for traditional jazz. Philip Larkin, quoting Benny Green's *The Reluctant Art* (1962), has written, '"After Parker you had to be something of a musician to follow the best jazz of the day." Of course! After Picasso! After Pound! There could hardly have been a conciser summary of what I don't believe about art.'

Science fiction and jazz had the same un-institutionalized appeal that offended Mandarin susceptibilities. In 1955 Angus Wilson wrote that 'it is dangerous to praise science fiction publicly, as I have once before found to my cost'. Kingsley Amis claimed that magazines such as *Amazing Science Fiction* 'will, at least in a good month, contain as much that is genuinely imaginative and coherent as, say, what is averagely available in the *London Magazine*', which was really kicking the Mandarin where it hurt. Science fiction, like jazz, acquired a kind of intellectual chic that its originators did not intend it to have, and an enthusiasm among painters for science fiction in pulp magazines prepared the way for the Pop imagery of the early 1960s.

By taking an interest in jazz and science fiction the members of the Movement were by-passing the customary channels of taste, and showed that they had not lost touch with their lower middle-class, as opposed to gentry, roots. They were bringing into art aspects of life ignored by the Mandarins, and nowhere is this more evident than in their novels. As the last chapter showed, there was something of a feeling of despair about the state of contemporary fiction in the early 1950s. With the exception of Angus Wilson – whose distinctive contribution was to introduce a greater frankness about homosexuality – there appeared to be no signs of development at all from new writers. The post-war period was a difficult time to begin a career, and it was not until 1953 that a new generation of novelists could be said to have established itself, among them P. H. Newby, William Sansom, J. D. Scott, Thomas Hinde, John Mortimer, Doris Lessing, Olivia Manning, Elizabeth Taylor, Muriel Spark and Nigel Dennis, and the reviewers were beginning to show more confidence that the novel might not be dying after all. But it was the first novels of John Wain, Kingsley Amis and Iris Murdoch that suggested that a different kind of novel was evolving.

In fact there is nothing particularly new about the form these novels take. Wain's *Hurry on Down* (1953), Amis's *Lucky Jim* (1954) and Murdoch's *Under the Net* (1954) are all concerned with the picaresque adventures of a young man, a plot as old as the novel itself. (Iris Murdoch's association with the Movement novelists was restricted more or less to her first novel, and was probably the result of coincidence. By the time her fourth book, *The Bell*, was published in 1958 the moral and philosophical concerns of her fiction had made the distinction clear.) It was not surprising that the new novelists of the 1950s should be resolutely unexperimental; the achievements of modernism in the novel had been in the Twenties and Thirties and that impulse seemed exhausted. It was also difficult to get published against the prevailing taste for naturalism. Malcolm Lowry's *Under the Volcano* (1947) was the only addition to the brief list of successful experimentalists since Joyce, and although William Golding's *Pincher Martin* (1956) and *Free Fall* (1959) have been labelled experimental, his first novel. *Lord of the Flies* (1954), conceals its symbolic conflicts within a naturalistic story. Between 1957 and 1960 Lawrence Durrell published the four novels of his *Alexandria Quartet*, which he described as a 'four-decker novel whose form is based on the relativity proposition'. The series enjoyed considerable success, but its 'experimentalism' is really a throwback to the Neo-Romantic poeticizing of the 1940s.

Apart from the difficulty of sustaining an experimental style, be it in terms of language, streams of consciousness, elaborate symbolism or tricks of time-scale – as Lawrence Durrell proves – the refusal to experiment reflects the negative attitude of the rising generation to the modernist work of their predecessors. Instead, the new writers confronted their surroundings as they actually were, where people did not live in country houses, and where there was a strong pressure to conform to mediocre cultural values and spurious social ones. The trio of picaresque novels which set the style for this new realism adopted a fresh attitude to the world in which their adventures took place. John Wain's *Hurry on Down* and Kingsley Amis's *Lucky Jim*, published so closely together by two writers already linked by their poetry, seemed to crystallize what that attitude was:

A new hero has risen among us. Is he the intellectual tough, or the tough intellectual? He is consciously, even conscientiously, graceless. His face, when not dead-pan, is set in a snarl of exasperation. He has one skin too few, but his is not the sensitiveness of the young man in earlier twentieth-century fiction: it is the phoney to which his nerve-ends are tremblingly exposed, and at the least suspicion of the phoney he gets tough. He is at odds with his conventional university education, though he comes generally from a famous university: he has seen through the academic racket as he sees through all the others. A racket is phoneyness organized, and in contact with phoneyness he turns red just as litmus paper does in contact with an acid. In life he

136

has been among us for some little time. One may speculate whence he derives. The Services, certainly, helped to make him; but George Orwell, Dr Leavis and the Logical Positivists – or, rather, the attitudes these represent – all contributed to his genesis. In fiction I think he first arrived last year, as the central character of Mr John Wain's novel *Hurry on Down*. He turns up again in Mr Amis's *Lucky Jim*.

Walter Allen's review in the *New Statesman* helped to guarantee *Lucky Jim*'s success, and success always brings with it a certain distortion. It is important to remember, as Kingsley Amis has pointed out, that 'Jim is a man in a book, not a "generation"'. But Amis's Jim Dixon, Wain's Charles Lumley and Iris Murdoch's Jake Donoghue, did seem to view the post-war world as one in which the individual – the hero – was entirely dependent on his own moral resources to make his way. Charles Lumley and Jim Dixon succeed by rejecting the conventional paths suggested to them by their education; Jake Donoghue holds on to his artistic integrity against commercial pressure. All three books imply a criticism of the cultural values that had been passed on to post-war society – most comically expressed by Jim Dixon's hatred of Professor Welch and his artist son Bernard. Naturally this criticism caused resentment: by 1956 *Lucky Jim* had become so established as a reference point that the *Listener's* anonymous reviewer of Philip Larkin's collection *The Less Deceived* could link Larkin to 'the "Lucky Jim" poets, with all that implies of self-consciously middle-class and anti-intellectual attitudes, the laudation of the mediocre and *gemütlich*, the frightened snigger at the excellent'.

In fiction as in poetry a gap was opening up between the generations, and the younger was turning against the older. The fact that the man of letters was being ousted by the academic critic was just one more sign of the middle class. G. S. Fraser sadly records in *The Craft of Letters in England*:

I once had the pleasure, in the Caves de France in Soho, in introducing a poet of the 1950s, Mr Donald Davie, who teaches English in Dublin, to Mr Wrey Gardiner, who edited *Poetry Quarterly* and helped to run the Grey Walls Press in the 1940s, and to Mr

Randall Swingler, who has vivid memories of the political excitements of the 1930s. It was an amiable occasion, but one was aware, at the same time, very vividly, of the invisible roadblocks that hampered any real communication. Not only the poet as a type, but the concept of poetry, suffers change.

The arrival of *Look Back in Anger* and *The Outsider* in 1956 made the gap appear complete.

Walter Allen had identified two important features in his review of *Lucky Jim* in 1954: the new works tended to approach the world from the point of view of an individual – a hero, or anti-hero as it became fashionable to describe him; secondly, these heroes were the complete opposite of the conforming intellectual described in the last chapter by Shils and Noel Annan. A common factor is the rejection of the roles imposed on the hero by a university education. In a forerunner to the type of novel we are discussing, William Cooper's *Scenes from Provincial Life* (1950), Joe Lunn is freed from provincial schoolmastering by the outbreak of war. In Wain's *Hurry on Down*, Charles Lumley's adventures begin when he leaves university and refuses to take a conventional job. Amis's Jim Dixon has gone so far as to become a provincial university lecturer himself before stepping aside. Thomas Hinde's Larry Vincent in *Happy as Larry* (1957) is a much more extreme example of the alienated intellectual, a hero lacking all heroic qualities, an ex-schoolmaster and failed writer with an unsure grip on reality that suggests a prototype for a character by Harold Pinter. The bohemian underworld Larry Vincent inhabits in London has affinities with the Dublin of J. P. Donleavy's *The Ginger Man* (published in Paris in 1955 and in a bowdlerized version in England in 1956), in which Sebastian Dangerfield is studying law on a GI scholarship at Trinity College. All these characters are middle-class in origin, and literary or academic in aspiration, but the disaffected hero who rejects the conventions imposed upon him by his upbringing also appears in other settings: Peter Forster's Edward Primrose abandons stockbroking in *The Primrose Path* (1955) and, in novels relating to the Suez affair, Hugh Thomas's Simon Smith in *The World's Game* (1957) abandons the Foreign Office, while Andrew Sinclair's Bumbo Bailey in *The Breaking of Bumbo* (1957) is dismissed from the Brigade of Guards. Without wishing to impose a Freudian reading, it would appear that the intellectual children of the Welfare State were rejecting their parents.

The hostility of the new writers of the 1950s to both the aesthetic and social attitudes of the 1930s demonstrates this rejection. The abandonment of avant-garde approaches to art and literature in favour of a form of realism has already been discussed, but when John Wain wrote in 1949, 'The Thirties are dead at Oxford', he was speaking in more than a technical sense about poetry, just as when Anthony Hartley dismissed C. Day Lewis's *Collected Poems 1954*, Spender's *Collected Poems 1928–1953* (1955) and MacNeice's *Autumn Sequel* (1954) as 'A Georgian, a Neo-Romantic, and an Irishman'. Auden was still respected, but he had abandoned Communism for Christianity. The one figure of the 1930s to whom general acknowledgement was made was George Orwell. Robert Conquest claimed in *New Lines*, 'One might, without stretching matters too far, say that George Orwell with his principle of real, rather than ideological honesty, exerted, even though indirectly, one of the major influences on modern poetry.' The Movement's Orwell was the Orwell of his 1946 essay, 'The Prevention of Literature'; his exposure of the political hypocrisies of the 1930s certainly helped to turn the Movement against that generation; but the Movement poets hardly show the passionate and uncompromising commitment to Socialist principles upheld by Orwell. Commitment of any kind was considered dubious. Reviewing Philip Toynbee's memoir of the 1930s, *Friends Apart* (1954), Wain commented that *joining* something had then been thought the answer to the problem of influencing events: 'Since 1946 nobody above the Jehovah's Witness level has taken this attitude; are we right, or will the Sixties think us as silly as we think the Thirties?'

Critical and political caution went hand in hand. 'Remembering the Thirties,' wrote Donald Davie in his poem of that title, 'A neutral tone is nowadays preferred.' But there were other factors besides a negative reaction to the ideas of the earlier generation that encouraged a less committed stance. Economic factors meant that it was virtually impossible to live by one's art alone; as a result it was necessary to make some accommodation with the institutions of the Welfare State. In spite of the novelists' fictional rejection of ordinary jobs, of the Movement poets two were librarians, six were academics and one a civil servant who later became an academic. (To be fair, Wain gave up his academic post in 1955, Amis gave up his in 1963.) John Holloway has made an important point about the consequences of social functions:

The two social lodgments for the poet in our society seem to be poet as Minority – rebel, bohemian, aspiring seer, these are all versions of the spiritual nomad that an advanced society can accommodate and even (while carefully preserving the sense of rebellion) use; and the second, an age-old status, the poet as *clericus*, clerk. The second kind gravitates to the universities, or kindred things – schools, libraries, the law, the BBC. The teaching profession, anyhow, is flexible and tolerant enough to find a light harness occasionally for a nomad. But that aside, one can see in this kind of social accommodation a standing invitation to something like the second language of poetry: its claim to be relaxed, yet mature, its dryness and intelligence, its decorous reticence.

New Lines is poetry conceived in this second language. G. S. Fraser described the rise of its practitioners to pre-eminence in the 1950s as 'an ousting of the bohemians by the pedants'.

John Holloway pointed out that 'the *clericus* has the stronger position in society and his language wins', but for the poets of *New Lines* this was not entirely without a struggle. The fact that many of the poets were also critics was a point made against them time and time again. *Mavericks* contributor Anthony Cronin's attack in *Encounter* is typical:

we seem to be entering on a period when the younger academics, spotting maybe the flaw in [F. R. Leavis's] logic, should go a step further and devote their subsidized leisure to proving that the critic who has learned the trade can with the same industry and lack of concern for the importance of a personal vision supply the poems as well.

There was of course some truth in this; Philip Larkin noted 'the cunning merger between poet, literary critic and academic critic (three classes now notoriously indistinguishable): it is hardly an exaggeration to say that the poet has gained the happy position wherein he can praise his own poetry in the press and explain it in the classroom'. But one can hardly expect a salaried teacher to resign on the publication (usually unpaid) of a book of poems. Donald Davie had no conscience about being a *clericus*: 'Academic is no bad thing to be, and in any case becomes inescapable, as the philistinism of Anglo-American society forces all artists – not just writers – back into the campus as the last stronghold.'

Because so many of the Movement poets happened to be teaching in provincial universities, the argument over academicism became confused with the question of provincialism. 'Provincial' does not mean very much, except as a term of abuse, and clearly the Movement poets were only provincial in a geographical sense by reasons of chance. Their poetry is certainly not regional – the principal regional poetry of the 1950s was written in Scotland, where there was a revival of writing in the lowland Scots dialect Lallans, stimulated by Hugh MacDiarmid's *A Drunk Man Looks at the Thistle* (1926). Sidney Goodsir Smith (who happened to have been born in New Zealand) ran the magazine *Lines*, and his own Lallans poems occasionally appeared in the London weeklies or on the BBC.

The only sense in which the Movement poets were provincial is that they were anti-metropolitan, that is, against the old guard of the 1930s and 1940s. Donald Davie gave a hostile review to G. S. Fraser's *The Modern Writer and his World* (1953):

London may soon be the most provincial of our cities. At any rate, many young writers now prize the approval of Dr Leavis or Mr Bateson beyond the accolade of Mr Raymond Mortimer or Mr

141

Connolly or Sir Harold Nicolson; and they may be right to do so. Mr Fraser seems to look for 'the generally accepted view' in the conversations of Hampstead and Notting Hill, in the literary pages of the Sunday papers, or among what few survive of the occasional literary magazines. He might come nearer to it in the common-rooms of provincial universities.

The irony is that the Movement poets were indeed becoming, as Davie suggests, the source of a generally accepted view, and they were finding that their opinions were being increasingly sought – and increasingly challenged. By 1957 Bernard Bergonzi, only a few years younger than the *New Lines* poets, was asking: 'Is it possible that, already, the new establishment in criticism (and in verse, and the novel) has arrived?' The aggressive attitude shown by the rising generation to their seniors gave the impression of being progressive – and one can thank John Wain for wishing to 'move a few of the established reputations gently to one side' – but once the process that Bergonzi was questioning was complete, the conservative aspects of their radicalism began to show through.

In the wider context of the period, beyond the institutional pressures on the *clericus* to conform, the early 1950s were not years which encouraged very much optimism. The attitudes of the Movement poets reflect the restrictive conditions of the Cold War. Eric Homberger has written of the contemporaneous rise of formalism in the United States: 'An increasingly isolated and defensive intelligentsia, which saw the abandonment of its traditional adversary function as a tempting though dangerous opportunity to affect a *rapprochement* with America in the post-war period, managed to praise a dominant style in poetry which turned its back on the new "reality" of the Cold War.' Since, unlike their American counterparts, British intellectuals were not harrassed by loyalty oaths or Congressional enquiries, their response was less extreme; indeed it tended to be neutral – but in that neutrality was a caution, and a self-limitation. The Cold War tended to freeze public attitudes, and counselled silence about private ones. It recommended a guarded private life, in which only small gestures were possible, gestures chiefly about the difficulty of making a gesture. Hence the concern of the Movement poets with the problems of perception and expression. There is a comparison here with the attitude displayed by Second World War poets like Keith Douglas or Roy Fuller who, against the mainstream of romanticism, adopted a laconic, self-protective style. This is Donald Davie's 'Rejoinder to a Critic':

> 'Alas, alas, who's injured by my love?'
> And recent history answers: Half Japan!
> Not love, but hate? Well, both are versions of
> The 'feeling' that you dare me to . . . Be dumb!
> Appear concerned only to make it scan!
> How dare we now be anything but numb?

In 1957 the Fabian Society published an essay by Kingsley Amis, *Socialism and the Intellectuals*, which must be the most apolitical pamphlet ever produced for that body. Amis identifies himself as 'an elderly young intellectual, perhaps, with connections in the educational and literary world and left-wing sympathies' who will probably vote Labour until the end of his days. But the main thrust of his argument is to show how difficult it is for the intellectual to have any political convictions at all, even after 1956, with the absurdities of Suez and the feeling of impotence in the face of the failure of the Hungarian uprising. There is a strong flavour of Jimmy Porter's claim in *Look Back in Anger*, 'there aren't any good, brave causes left', in Amis's comparison of the issues of 1937 and 1957. Although what Amis calls the 'sociological academic' university teacher remains active, 'the decline in political activity among intellectuals as a whole must, I think, be taken as a fact in the perspective of the last twenty years, and it is particularly noticeable among our younger novelists and poets'. Amis notes that many young intellectuals have moved to the right since 1945, and that there tends to be a re-assertion of tradition (the Roman Catholic Church, or Dr Leavis) against the New Barbarism which used to mean Hitlerism, but now it means the Welfare State and commercial television. The Welfare State, indeed, is notoriously unpopular with intellectuals. It was all very well to press for higher working-class wages in the old days, but now that the wages have risen the picture is less attractive; why, some of them are actually better off than we ourselves.

Amis concludes by doubting whether intellectuals really had anything to offer the Labour Party. It would seem that the Labour Party had little to offer him, for he admits that he has no respectable motive for being politically active at all.

Kingsley Amis voted Labour for the last time in 1964. The decline in educational standards, the European Economic Community and Vietnam caused him to switch his allegiance to the Conservative Party, though, to judge from the corresponding pamphlet, *Lucky Jim's Politics* (1968), with scarcely more conviction than he felt for Labour in 1957. But the inherent conservatism, especially in cultural matters, of men like Amis was already apparent to the philosopher-critic Richard Wollheim in 1956. He wrote in *Encounter* that 'it seems as if there is a certain move back to the old nineteenth-century standards. Certain young novelists have discovered what can only be called a new kind of innocence in ambition. A man, they seem to be saying, is more likely to be harmlessly employed in looking after himself than in crusading for the large generalized slogans of liberal doctrine.' Like Amis, Wollheim argues that the establishment of the Welfare State has changed the political climate, with consequences for literature.

The typical figure of the intellectual left, the 'progressive man', the *homme de gauche*, who for the last thirty years or so has been such a stock feature both of English life and of English letters, is on his way out. Who is to take his place as the contemporary type? One of the most likely candidates is this new hero. If he does, if he assumes the vacant place, he will sit there, I am sure, as something quite new in this country's society and literature, as the *homme de droite*.

A case history in the evolution of this new right-wing intelligentsia was made available in 1956 by the publication of George Scott's interim memoir, *Time and Place*. George Scott went up to Oxford from grammar school in the immediate post-war period, when the university was rapidly expanding to cope with the dual pressure of returning ex-servicemen and the Butler Education Act. He shared the editorship of the undergraduate magazine *Cherwell* with Kenneth Tynan, and among his contemporaries names Maurice Cranston, Anthony Wedgwood Benn, Edward Boyle and Ludovic Kennedy, with whom he shared tutorials from Lord David Cecil. A combination of literary and journalistic interests got him a job on the *Daily Express* in 1948. The advantageous position given by an Oxford education does not seem to have made him particularly grateful.

It is true enough that by various designs or accidents we have been given our ration of the rich man's education and given a smell of his ancient privileges. It is true that this education, combined with the breaking down of old barriers, has enabled us to win our places in the professions, in the civil service, in politics. But now we are there, as someone remarked in other circumstances, where are we? Either we are classless, cut off from our roots, but not yet integrated into new environments, or else we are considered members of that vast and amorphous middle-class. And it is as the latter that our fortune is most dubious.

It is the rhetoric of the Angry Young Man, and from a right-wing stance.

The society that Scott opposes is that created by the Labour government of 1945: 'whether they know it or not, and I fancy they do not, the revolutionaries have bred a generation of counter-revolutionaries.' In George Scott's case his educational advantages led him to a profound admiration of his employer Lord Beaverbrook, both for his 'true intellectual status' and for his ruthless appetite for power. In May 1954, Scott became editor of the weekly *Truth*, which he revived in the style of a more right-wing *Spectator*. *Time and Place* conveys the aggression bred by post-war dissatisfactions, an aggression that is as much between generations as between Left and Right. The book opens with a cruel portrait of Stephen Spender on his way to the launching party for the *London Magazine*, and Scott is happy to point out the irony of the 1930s generation's own dissatisfaction with the way things had turned out. 'So many of the contemporaries of Lehmann and Spender are becalmed on what they regard as the dead sea of the Welfare State. The curious thing is that whether they realize it or not this is very like the world – though retaining more human instincts – to which all their pre-war volumes of propaganda were directing them.' In its polemical attitude *Time and Place* is as much of 1956 as *Look Back in Anger*.

Reference to *Look Back in Anger* leads forward into the next chapter, but it is important to appreciate the degree to which the ground had been prepared for Osborne. It is also important to appreciate the limitations of the new developments. In cultural terms, the Movement was reactionary and conservative, and since it actively rejected the idea of the avant-garde it could not progress, any more than realist painters could develop their art beyond a certain point. Even John Berger had to admit that 'a realist work of art deepens rather than extends the experience of the painter. It does not present him with a rare, strange or exotic vision, but with a vision that will make him more aware of the meaning and significance of familiar ordinary experience.' The Movement's emphasis on discipline and accuracy was a useful service to poetry after the Apocalyptics, and a positive contribution to the general drive towards realism, just as the painters' return to the object was a necessary correction to Neo-Romantic vagueness. The novels at last began to take stock of the changed circumstances of post-war Britain, but the difficulty about being realistic in the 1950s was that, calmly considered, reality was bleak.

The worst of the caution of the Movement was the caution about itself, the disclaiming of any responsibility for what it was doing. The saddest example of this is Conquest's second anthology *New Lines 2* (1963), which necessarily dilutes the effect of the original *New Lines* by including twenty-four poets instead of nine. But Conquest seems anxious to pretend that there had never been any intention in assembling the nine in the first place: '*New Lines* was not produced *a priori* on the grounds that a change of taste was needed, let alone to launch a "Movement".'

At least one *New Lines* contributor, Donald Davie, has bitterly disagreed with this attitude:

> We ridiculed and depreciated 'the Movement' even as we kept it going. I don't know, but I should imagine that this would have been the most baffling thing about us, to any Frenchman (say) or American, who got into company with two or three of us. For in their countries, as far as I can see, writers who set out in concert to write a chapter of literary history don't have to pretend elaborately to be doing something else. Why should they? We in the Movement did so, for the same reasons which brought the whole thing to a halt and broke it up before it was under way – out of pusillanimity; from the unforgivable literary sin of going much further than half way to meet our readers, forestalling their objections, trying to keep in their good books.

Significantly, Davie describes the readers they were supposedly trying to please not as the middlebrow public but the self-conscious élite, 'the readers of *Essays in Criticism* and the ex-readers of *Scrutiny*', whose sophisticated knowledge of the manoeuvres of literary politics meant that the Movement felt itself obliged to pretend that it was not doing what it had in fact undertaken. Once the Mandarins of poetry were overthrown, the Movement was in a position to deny its conspiratorial origins, while the misunderstandings attending the arrival of the Angry Young Men made the University Wits doubly cautious about accepting labels of any kind.

CHAPTER FIVE

DECLARATION

'You're hurt because everything is
changed. Jimmy is hurt because
everything is the same. And neither
of you can face it. Something's
gone wrong somewhere, hasn't it?'

Alison to her father
in *Look Back in Anger*

Retrospectively, 1956 has become an *annus mirabilis*. The
1950s do not have the convenient end-stops of dates and events
that encapsulate the Second World War. Instead, the decade
works towards a climacteric of change, and is then carried
forward by the energies that change released. If the 1950s *are*
focused in this way, then the point of focus is 1956. It is the
first moment of history after the Second World War about
which there is anything like a persistent myth, and like the
myths of wartime, it is a combination of historical truths and
popular distortion. The pattern for the myth is provided by the
coincidence of political events and cultural shift: crudely, Suez
and *Look Back in Anger* seem part of the same event, although
Look Back in Anger was first performed in May and the
landings at Suez did not take place until the beginning of
November.

The political events surrounding the British decision to join
with France in an invasion of Egypt have taken on a symbolic

significance in Britain's post-war history: it was the moment when Britain had to come to terms with her second-class status in the world, though this truth was only gradually appreciated. In restrospect 'Suez' became an even more divisive issue than it was at the time. The government's handling of Nasser's nationalization of the Suez Canal raised the political temperature, and the decision to use force angered the Left and caused dissension among the Tories, although neither objections to the policy nor its subsequent failure were serious threats to the government's position. The Prime Minister, Sir Anthony Eden, resigned afterwards, but on the grounds of genuine ill health, and the Conservative Party stayed in power until 1964. Many people in Britain supported the government's attempt to reassert a lost imperial power: their only regret was that it was a failure, and that the United States ensured that it would be.

Suez had most effect on the intelligentsia, because it summed up all their dissatisfactions with the way the country was being run; the protests over Suez – and the awareness of nuclear danger that it provoked – were the starting-point for the Campaign for Nuclear Disarmament which got under way at the beginning of 1958. Kingsley Amis's Fabian pamphlet *Socialism and the Intellectuals* appeared in January 1957, only a few months after the crisis, and suggested that intellectuals were not as perturbed by Suez as they had been in the 1930s by the Spanish Civil War. This claim was fiercely attacked in the *New Statesman*. Amis's attacker wrote:

I suspect – in fact I am sure – that Lucky Jim, at least in his political context, is dead, killed on the afternoon of 30 October, 1956, by Sir Anthony Eden; and that what Mr Amis has written in this pamphlet is merely Jim's last will and testament. It may be that Mr Amis was not inflamed by the Suez issue; but in that case he is the one intellectual who was not. The London air, at least, is loud with lamentations of intellectuals who now regret having failed to do their fair share at the last election to keep the Tories out. Nobody who attended the great Suez demonstration in Trafalgar Square feels the need for another Spain. The rumpus has even invaded the Athenaeum. Never in modern history has the intellectual element in a nation been so united, militant and, I submit, successful. After all, Messrs Auden, Spender and Co. lost their battle; we won.

The writer is Paul Johnson, then a member of the *New Statesman* staff, who was about to publish a book on the Suez affair. Johnson has since exchanged his left-wing views for those of the right, as have a significant number of 1950s radicals, including Amis and the historian Hugh Thomas, who claimed to have been converted from his original conservative position by the Suez débâcle and resigned from the Foreign Office as a result.

Suez was probably more disturbing for already-committed right-wing intellectuals than for those on the left, whose opinions of the government were only confirmed. Both the *Spectator* and *Truth* were against the government; for *Truth* the policy was fatal, as the magazine's proprietor Ronald Staples was a friend of Eden's and objected to his editor George Scott's attacks. Staples died at the end of 1956; *Truth* was killed off without warning a year later when his estate was wound up, for Staples had decided that the magazine should not continue.

The effect of the Suez affair was complicated by its coincidence with the uprising in Hungary. The Western powers were not able to assist the revolt, and Britain and France were not even in a position to protest about the brutal Russian suppression of opposition, since their own forces were attacking Egypt at the very moment when the Russian tanks moved back into Budapest. Politically, it showed that the slight thaw in the Cold War that followed Stalin's death in 1953 had not made any fundamental difference to the hostility between East and West. As we shall see, it did contribute to the disillusionment of British Communists and fellow-travellers, although the disputes resulting from Khrushchev's attack on Stalin's memory at the Twentieth Party Congress in 1956 had begun before the Hungarian rising took place.

The timing of Suez and Hungary was coincidental, but their combined effect was to exacerbate dissatisfactions and tensions. Some of these dissatisfactions had been voiced in the novels of

Amis and Wain, but there was nothing that gave them particular focus. What was needed was a myth, and in 1956 there appeared the myth of the Angry Young Man.

When writing about what are known as the Angry Young Men, it is tempting to adapt Leavis's remark about the Sitwells: 'They belong to the history of publicity rather than poetry.' Publicity has handed us the phrase Angry Young Man, but no one knows from where, and even the briefest examination of the careers of those to whom the label has been attached shows that some of them were not very angry, and some of them were not very young. In 1951 the phrase was used by the Christian apologist Leslie Paul as the title of his autobiography, but the book had nothing to do with the phenomenon that appeared five years later, except that it is an account of disillusion with the *'isms* of the 1930s. The label, with its connotations of group association, was quickly pushed away by those who were supposed to wear it. In 1957 John Osborne declared 'I have only met Mr Amis once briefly, and I have never met Mr Wain, nor any of the rest of these poor successful freaks.' But a label has its uses, if only as a means of drawing attention to oneself by denying the applicability of the description. John Wain's publishers advertised his books with the display card, 'JOHN WAIN IS *NOT* AN ANGRY YOUNG MAN'.

The Angry Young Man is a myth: yet myths are imaginative versions of the truth, and advertisers know that the best way to present a product is to exaggerate its novel – and truthful – qualities. It is also appropriate that publicity should play an important part in creating and confusing this particular issue. The 1950s are a central period in the history of publicity itself; 1956 was the first full year of commercial television, and in the same year restrictions on newsprint finally came to an end. Newspapers and radio had of course been operating as mass media since before the war, but the addition of a second channel, particularly one entirely dependent on advertising revenue, marked a significant alteration in the way ideas were, literally, transmitted. Accurate or not, Angry Young Man was a compelling slogan.

The most immediate sources of the myth of the Angry Young Man are John Osborne's play *Look Back in Anger* and Colin Wilson's book *The Outsider*. Both appeared at almost the same time – the play was launched on 8 May 1956, the book was published on 26 May. Both could be discussed in the same breath, as J. B. Priestley did in an article for the *New Statesman* that is one of the first to use the phrase. The reviews in the Sunday papers gave the signal that something was happening, and the popular press followed. Kenneth Tynan in the *Observer* and Harold Hobson in the *Sunday Times* praised Osborne; Philip Toynbee and Cyril Connolly, in like manner, praised Wilson. But if the argument about romanticism and realism is correct, then *Look Back in Anger* and *The Outsider* represented opposite tendencies, for it is unlikely that the Mandarin Connolly would discover the same virtues as the carnivorous Tynan.

On the surface, Colin Wilson's *The Outsider* is in tune with the theme of the alienated intellectual that underlies much mid-1950s writing. Wilson had no university education at all, he left school at sixteen and spent the next eight years doing the variety of menial jobs that feature in, for instance, *Hurry on Down,* including the almost obligatory period as a hospital porter. During his wanderings he made two visits to Paris, the second time coming into contact with the latest of a long line of American exile magazines, the *Paris Review*, and finding in Existentialism a philosophical framework for his ideas on the unappreciated artist. Throughout this time he was trying to write fiction, but in 1954 an encounter with Angus Wilson, then assistant superintendent of the British Museum Reading Room, turned his ideas towards the study that emerged as *The Outsider.* (The book is gratefully dedicated to Angus Wilson.) Colin Wilson sent an outline of the book to Victor Gollancz under the title *The Pain Threshold*, but a wise decision by

Gollancz's reader, Jon Evans, gave it the name that did so much towards the book's sudden success.

Gollancz's eager acceptance of the proposal when it arrived out of the blue is another pointer to the true significance of Wilson's book. Gollancz's Left Book Club commitments were behind him; now his main preoccupations were philosophy and religion, and Wilson supplied a quasi-mystical mixture of the two. Drawing on a wide variety of quotations (and misquotations) from nineteenth- and twentieth-century European literature, Wilson portrays the Outsider as the man, almost always an artist or intellectual, who has perceived the unreality of everyday life. While the common man remains unaware of his bondage, the Outsider rejects conventional thought and so becomes free. But this is only the first stage, for having freed himself of his shackles, the Outsider must move forward onto a higher plane of thought, beyond philosophy into religion. Just as it is a mystical moment which first makes the Outsider aware of his Outsidership, Wilson's religion relies on a transcendental vision that has nothing to do with the formal rituals or civilizing values of an established church. It also has nothing to do, it must be added, with Christian charity or love:

As the Outsider's insight becomes deeper, so that he no longer sees men as a million million individuals, but instead sees the world-will that drives them all like ants in a formicary, he knows that they will never escape their stupidity and delusions, that no amount of logic and knowledge can make man any more than an insect; the most irritating of the human lice is the humanist with his puffed-up pride in Reason and his ignorance of his own silliness.

Instead, the Outsider must 'find his way back into daylight where he can know a single undivided Will, Nietzsche's "pure will without the troubles of intellect"'. Far from being a fresh development, Wilson's book is a throw-back to the home-grown existentialism of the war years, the so-called 'personalism' that had its roots in the Anarchist movement, and which provided a philosophical justification for Neo-Romanticism. Colin Wilson's portrayal of the unhappy artist is in direct line of descent from Cyril Connolly's *The Unquiet Grave*, which may be why Connolly praised Wilson's book (see *Under Siege* pp. 105–6).

All this is a far cry from the comedy of *Lucky Jim*; indeed, reviewing Wilson's book, Kingsley Amis chilled the rhetoric of *The Outsider* with university wit: 'One of the prime indications of the sickness of mankind in the mid-twentieth century is that so much excited attention is paid to books about the sickness of mankind in the mid-twentieth century.' But although Wilson's ideas are more derivative than was realized, his book emphasized the decay of conventionally-held cultural values, and stirred the emotions of those who felt divided from the society in which they lived. Above all, the title of his book and his treatment of its theme in terms of a personality added a new and easily identified character to the chorus of disenchanted fictional personalities who were voicing their dissatisfaction with the way society had developed. It was this, rather than his reactionary views, that contributed so powerfully to the myth. Many more people knew about the book than had actually read it.

It must be conceded, also, that there were romantic over-tones to *Look Back in Anger,* however realistic the setting. How the English Stage Company came into being is described later, but the fact that this fresh protest against the times was made from the stage, when English theatre was at its blandest, gave added impetus to Osborne's message. The protesting individual was no longer a character in a book but a walking, and endlessly talking, figure on the stage.

Although his leading character was educated at a post-war provincial university, John Osborne was not. By origin lower middle-class, he left school at eighteen, was turned down for National Service and worked briefly in the lower reaches of journalism before becoming an actor in the lower reaches of provincial repertory. While in the provinces, Osborne wrote two plays which are now lost, and a third, *Epitaph for George Dillon* (in collaboration with Anthony Creighton), that was produced after *Look Back in Anger*. Like *The Outsider, Look*

Declaration

Back in Anger arrived out of the blue, when the English Stage Company advertised for scripts. It was the only one of some 750 submissions to reach the stage.

The play focuses the moment of what it is impossible to avoid calling the Angry Young Man. It is a portrait of a dissatisfied, unpleasant but articulate young man with 'one skin too few'. It is possible to find him in fictional representations, and it is possible to find him in real life.

We fought in that last war. Now we are clerks, teachers, script-writers, even bus conductors. At the moment, I personally am selling glacé cherries by the ten-ton lot. If I could see my way to get by until a week on Tuesday, it would be something of a shock. Friday evening and the type-writer is what I aim at. I have in my circuit of professionals encountered one or two other young writers and the odd mid-thirty-year-old novelist. So far, society, our society, has shovelled us about much as it cared to. We are offered up as cannon-fodder, then sent off to University. Now we can remain as peaceful form-fillers, income-tax payers, semi-private individuals, pending some other State idiocy or perhaps hydrogen obliteration. Against all this, in the art we interest ourselves about, what do we face? Victoriana; fringe-haired twenties; 'young poets' of the sports-car '30s. Mr Priestley striding the Yorkshire tea-parties of good old Edwardia. In this age of TV and mach numbers, the *New Statesman* panning Science Fiction.

The quotation is from a letter to the *New Statesman* in 1954 from the novelist Peter Crowcroft, whose first book, *The Fallen Sky*, appeared in that year. It is not so far from Crowcroft's actual glacé cherries to Jimmy Porter's fictional sweet-stall, and both make a concatenation of political and cultural protest – in Jimmy Porter's case against the Bomb, Sunday newspapers, marriage, T. S. Eliot, the Church and 'Mummy'.

Jimmy Porter had a forerunner on the English stage, Terence Rattigan's Freddie Page in *The Deep Blue Sea;* but whereas Freddie Page's problem is that he had known the excitement of action, Jimmy Porter's is that he has not even known that. There is a negative, retrogressive bitterness in looking back in anger; the text stresses that Jimmy was born out of his time, not just within the twentieth century but out of his appropriate period in history, the Romantic revolutionary years of Shelley, with whom he is specifically compared. His wife, Alison, and his temporary mistress, Helena, are agreed on his romantic redundancy:

Helena: There's no place for people like that any longer in sex, or politics, or anything. That's why he's so futile. Sometimes when I listen to him, I feel he thinks he's still in the middle of the French Revolution. And that's where he ought to be, of course. He doesn't know where he is, or where he's going. He'll never do anything, and he'll never amount to anything.

Alison: I suppose he's what you'd call an Eminent Victorian. Slightly comic – in a way . . .

Jimmy Porter appears to agree with them in his nostalgia for working-class virtues and even the faded glories of the Edwardian Empire, represented in the play by Alison's father. There are overtones of George Orwell in this, although Jimmy Porter does not seem to share his disillusion with the Spanish Civil War. But then (unlike his fictional father, who died as a result of his wounds), Jimmy Porter was not there.

I suppose people of our generation aren't able to die for good causes any longer. We had all that done for us, in the Thirties and the Forties, when we were still kids. (*In his familiar, semi-serious mood*) There aren't any good, brave causes left. If the big bang does come, and we all get killed off, it won't be in aid of the old-fashioned grand design. It'll just be for the Brave New-nothing-very-much-thank-you. About as pointless and inglorious as stepping in front of a bus.

This is a despairing view, and accounts for the play's unsatisfactory ending with its squirrels and bears. But it was the negative aspect of Osborne's egocentric tirades that conveyed the anger of his generation. The play is set a long way from the shires, in an attic flat in a Midlands town. It is a minor detail, but the utterly realistic setting (at one point Jimmy bangs on the water-tank in search of 'Mummy', which must give Freudians a feast day) has no kitchen sink; the Porters must go out to the bathroom to fill a kettle. Jimmy Porter also finds some release in playing jazz. His sexual irritation with the conventions of marriage, his annoyance at the 'posh' Sunday papers, which he nonetheless reads, his interest in Vaughan Williams whom he at least pretends to listen to on the BBC, show that he is trapped by the values he rejects, just as he is married to – and loves – a girl whose values he despises. It is no wonder that Kenneth Tynan treated Jimmy as though he were a real person:

One cannot imagine Porter listening with a straight face to speeches about our inalienable right to flog Cypriot schoolboys. You could never mobilize him and his kind into a lynching mob, since the art he lives for, jazz, was invented by Negroes; and if you gave him a razor, he would do nothing with it but shave. The Porters of our time deplore the tyranny of 'good taste' and refuse to accept 'emotional' as a term of abuse; they are classless, and they are also leaderless. Mr Osborne is their first spokesman in the London theatre.

The realism of *Look Back in Anger* does not lie in its conventional three-act, one-set, small-cast treatment, but in the fact that people were prepared to accept Osborne's fiction as real.

Amis and Wain prepared the stage for the Angry Young Man, Colin Wilson gave him an identity as the Outsider, John Osborne gave him a voice. John Braine proceeded to demonstrate that he had absorbed the materialistic morality of his times. There is a certain amount of jealous anger in Jimmy Porter, but some of his fellow characters were ready to improve their position. Both Amis's Jim Dixon and Wain's Charles Lumley end up better off than when they started – Dixon as personal assistant to a wealthy man, Lumley as a script-writer. In 1957 John Braine's novel, *Room at the Top*, presented Joe Lampton as the Ambitious Young Man.

John Braine had similar lower middle-class roots to Osborne's, though with a Yorkshire as opposed to London background. He did not go to university either, and after a variety of jobs became a librarian. In 1951 he decided to become a writer, and during a brief period in London before tuberculosis forced him into hospital for eighteen months, wrote a piece for the *New Statesman* on the clientele of a roadhouse that foreshadows the materialistic observations of *Room at the Top*, 'money and lust and pride of the eye'. (Only Ian Fleming's James Bond stories are as brand conscious as Braine's novel.) Joe Lampton is disaffected only because of his origins as a working-class Yorkshire lad who spent his time as a prisoner of war taking his accountancy exams rather than trying to escape. He escapes his origins by gradually adopting the uniform and ruthlessness of the commercial world. His ambitions are 'an Aston-Martin, 3-guinea linen shirts, a girl with a Riviera suntan', and in the course of the novel he places himself in reach of them by abandoning romance with a mistress, who dies violently, and by impregnating the daughter of the local textile magnate. Braine has said, 'in the Welfare State the young man on the make has to be a bit tougher and learn how to fiddle more cleverly. My job in writing about Joe Lampton was to look at him clearly. It's not the job of a novelist to pass moral judgements.' In the moral world of Logical Positivism, it might be added, such judgements are meaningless.

It is pleasing to report literary success, and if the Angry Young Men did possess a streak of ambition, then their chief spokesmen at least were well rewarded. Colin Wilson made £20,000 in the first year of *The Outsider*'s publication, Osborne was reported to have made the same amount from *Look Back in Anger*, John Braine made £12,000 from *Room at the Top* by 1958, Kingsley Amis's *Lucky Jim* went through twenty impressions between 1954 and 1957. The last three books received a further boost by being made into films for their authors. The price of this success was to be saddled with a label they individually rejected: Angry Young Man.

In 1957, MacGibbon and Kee published a volume that offers an opposing mirror to *The Craft of Letters in England* – *Declaration*. The aggressive title contrasts with the retiring good manners of its predecessor; unlike the despairing chorus of *The Craft of Letters*, the voices of *Declaration* speak against each other, the personalities of the eight contributors are promoted with portrait photographs and biographical details, and although the editor Tom Maschler is quick to denounce the 'lower level of journalism' that produced the phrase 'Angry Young Man', *Declaration* also exists to exploit this non-existent person's success.

As the account of the Movement tried to show, the historian is hamstrung by disclaimers. What makes *Declaration* so typical of the new generation, whose arrival it proclaims, is its internal dissent – and the outright refusal of one of its principal spokesmen to be included at all. Kingsley Amis refused to participate, with the words 'I hate all this pharisaical twittering about the "state of our civilization" and I suspect anyone who wants to buttonhole me about my "role in society"', thus remaining consistent with 1950s caution about joining anything. Those who did join – Doris Lessing, Colin Wilson, John Osborne, John Wain, Kenneth Tynan, Bill Hopkins, Lindsay Anderson and Stuart Holroyd – represented a spectrum far broader than that of *The Craft of Letters in England*, both socially and politically. But where *Declaration is* a mirror-image of its predecessor of 1956 is that it too believes that there has been some kind of cultural collapse. Doris Lessing: 'If there is one thing which distinguishes our literature, it is a confusion of standards and the uncertainty of values.' Colin Wilson: 'I believe that our civilization is in decline, and the Outsiders are a symptom of that decline.' On this the contributors were all agreed, and they were also generally agreed on the causes of this decline, causes already identified by George Scott – the moral and political failure of the older generation – and by Kingsley Amis – the New Barbarism.

Hostility to the previous generation, and the state in which it had left culture, is urgently expressed by Wain's protest at the log-rolling of reputations in 'the smart magazines' of the literary world, and in Tynan's complaint that in British drama 'plays continue to be written on the assumption that there are still people who live in awe of the Crown, the Empire, the established Church, the public schools and upper classes'. Lindsay Anderson focuses on the failure of the British cinema – or, as he puts it more accurately, the '*English* cinema (and Southern English at that), metropolitan in attitude, and entirely middle-class' – to reflect any social change since 1945, preferring to reinforce through endless war films the myth of British greatness and the mutual cohesion of the class system. At the same time Anderson, dealing with a mass medium, attacks the banalities of the new barbarism of newspaper and television. For other contributors, the 'Outsider' group of Wilson, Holroyd and Hopkins, these are only part of the greater barbarism of the twentieth century. Osborne's essay, which manages to include the British H bomb, Suez, the newspapers' idolatry of royalty and the 'self-conscious literary mob people who write sneering, parochial stuff in the weekend reviews', sums up *Declaration*'s hostility, in gross and in detail, to the world its contributors inherited.

The contributors are also agreed that is still possible for the artist to do something about the crisis. Bill Hopkins: 'writers must become the pathfinders to a new civilization'; John Wain: 'it is in order for [an artist] to marshall his thoughts, from time to time, about what would broadly be called "social issues".' But, as these two quotations suggest, disagreement begins with the question of what the artist should actually do about the crisis, and how far this is a directly political task. It is here that the spectrum begins to divide.

Both Doris Lessing and Lindsay Anderson are in favour of political commitment, a view consistent with their left-wing opinions. (Doris Lessing had only just left the Communist Party when *Declaration* was published.) Lessing stands a little apart from the other contributors, in that at thirty-eight she was somewhat older, her first novel, *The Grass is Singing*, having been published in 1949. She welcomes the vitality of the new writers, but at the same time condemns them as parochial:

Rejecting 'propaganda', for this is what they believe they are doing, they reject an imaginative understanding of what I am convinced is the basic conflict of our time. The mental climate created by the Cold War has produced a generation of young intellectuals who totally reject everything communism stands for; they cut themselves off imaginatively from a third of mankind, and impoverish themselves by doing so.

Lindsay Anderson, at the age of thirty-four a film critic and rising documentary film-maker, represents the 'New' rather than the 'Old' Left. He points to the contradiction in the association in the public imagination of Osborne with Amis and Wain, 'who are fashionable precisely because they express the directly opposite attitude to his own . . . basically they are both of anti-idealist, anti-emotional, and tepid or evasive in their social commitments . . . they are so depressingly representative in all this of what we may call the *Liberal* establishment'.

As the man who hailed Osborne as the spokesman of the under-thirties, and who yet had one foot in the coterie world of the unreformed intelligentsia that Anderson attacks, Kenneth Tynan is more cautious. 'I want drama to be vocal in protest; and I frankly do not see whence the voices will come if not from the Left,' he writes; but he manages to put a space between himself and 'the flourishing bunch, worth more than a passing word' of young Leftists. He manages a certain nostalgia for the period 1945–50, but he is doubtful that Socialism can be transferred directly to the stage. Socialist plays are *meant* to be angry, but 'fun, in the theatre at least, has become very nearly a Tory monopoly'; hence the need for a truly international theatre like the Royal Court, that will both protest and entertain. Tynan however is cynical about the chances of Socialism providing a rallying-point for the post-war young; it is clear that he believes they are more likely to be seduced by journalism, advertising and affluence.

Over against the varieties of commitment to the left are set the views of three writers who reject politics in all its forms: Colin Wilson, Bill Hopkins and Stuart Holroyd. In 1957 Hopkins and Holroyd were riding on the coat-tails of Wilson's reputation. Hopkins's first novel, *The Divine and the Decay*, was awaiting publication; Holroyd's study of poetry and religion, *Emergence from Chaos*, had just appeared. The trio rehearse the arguments of *The Outsider* for a spiritual as opposed to materialist freedom. Holroyd: 'One of the great mistakes of this century has been our persistence in seeking freedom on the political level. *Freedom is an inner condition*.' Without actually saying so, Holroyd, Hopkins and Wilson would be glad to abandon democracy altogether. Wilson's emphasis in *The Outsider* on Nietzsche's Will to Power suggests that Fascism would give more scope for the prophetic writer-mystic.

Between these two opposing groups stand John Osborne and John Wain. Though they write in contrasting styles – Osborne untidy and splenetic, Wain academic and cautious – they are both careful to protect their craft from the demands of political commitment. One could not describe Osborne as neutral, but he specifically avoids formal ideology:

I am not going to define my socialism. Socialism is an experimental idea, not a dogma; an attitude to truth and liberty, the way people should live and treat each other. Individual definitions are unimportant. The difference between Socialist and Tory values should have been made clear enough by this time. I am a writer and my own contribution to a socialist society is to demonstrate those values in my own medium, not to discover the best ways of implementing them.

Wain is even more cautious; he admits that the writer must be socially aware: 'the chief danger is that he may be pushed too often into the role of social prophet. The public at the moment is in an alarmingly eager mood . . . The minute any kind of artist attracts attention, he is treated as a spokesman for his generation, his nation, his class, and what not.' Instead, as with Osborne, 'all I can do is to go on trying to tackle the problems of contemporary life as they confront me personally: "tackle" them by seeking to give them adequate literary expression, rather than "solve" them.'

Wain's disclaimer brings us full circle, not just to the mutual squabbling that takes place within *Declaration*, but to the whole idea of the Angry Young Man as nothing more than a literary stunt. Allowances must be made for coincidence and the distortions of publicity, yet something did happen in 1956 to change people's perceptions of their culture and their society. This change took place at the cultural rather than political level precisely because the political life of the mid-1950s had reached a state of consensus, something that even the Suez crisis did not shake. Since the 1930s people looked to the Left to generate cultural change, but the Left was in disarray. Isolated by the Cold War, the Communist Party was passing through its own internal crisis, and the Hungarian uprising weakened its position still further. The Labour Party was still uncertain as to what had gone wrong in 1951, or what to do about it. Thus, while there was considerable emotional support for the sort of criticisms of society that came from the Left, there was little formal commitment; instead, there was the general distrust of practical politics that led to the incipient Fascism of Colin Wilson.

The Angry Young Men were constantly sniped at for their lack of commitment, which must have been exasperating for a group of writers who did not consider themselves a group at all. Kenneth Allsop's *The Angry Decade*, published in 1958, well before the decade was over, is ostensibly a survey of the phenomenon, but is more a contribution to the debate. Allsop points out that the cultural developments of the mid-1950s have a direct relation to the creation of the Welfare State:

the ingrates do not think a great deal of the new deal. They display neither enthusiasm for their elevation nor comradeship towards the idealists who put them where they are. One point of view seems to be that the education and the opportunity have been spread too thinly, like prole margarine of the bad old days. The larger result is that the dissentients feel unassimilated. They are a new rootless, faithless, classless class – and consequently, because of a feeling of being misplaced and misprized, also often charmless – who are becalmed in the social sea . . . They feel a mixture of guilt about renegading from their hereditary background and contempt for the oafish orthodoxy of their families. Success, meaning money, is judged to be the safest measure – and there doesn't seem enough of that to go round.

The reply to this kind of attack, as we have seen in Wain and Osborne's contributions to *Declaration*, is that the primary responsibility is to one's craft. And it is interesting to see how the myth of the Angry Young Man looks as if it is based on the contributors' *second* production rather than their first. Kingsley Amis's *That Uncertain Feeling* (1955) satirizes the mores of a small Welsh town, but the hero specifically chooses modest circumstances and domesticity against ambition. John Wain's *Living in the Present* (1955) rejects ennui in favour of romantic love. Osborne's *The Entertainer* (1957), with its background of Suez and the metaphor of a crumbling theatre for British society, does continue in Jimmy Porter's vein. Colin Wilson's *Religion and the Rebel* (1957) develops the Nietzschean themes of *The Outsider*. The pattern shifts, widening the gap between the novelists and Osborne. And the myth as publicly perceived also changes, for *Religion and the Rebel* was greeted with an execration almost as universal as the praise that greeted *The Outsider*. Wilson had already retired to Cornwall, and it was not until he published the novel *Ritual in the Dark* in 1960 that his reputation revived. In the 1960s a new generation turned to Wilson in search of meaning in mysticism and the occult.

The Angry Young Man, then, was a composite figure, and it is right to discuss him in terms of a personality rather than of a school of writers. Personality, after all, is what attracts publicity. The 'University Wits' provided him with an education, courtesy of the 1944 Education Act; his working-class or lower middle-class origins gave him a view of the world that made him resentful of those who continued to enjoy the privileges from which he felt excluded. The political and literary values of the older generation of intellectuals offered him little except targets for his criticism, to the extent that 'intellectual' was liable to be used as a term of abuse. A combination of youth, ambition and dissatisfaction with the *status quo* generated a creative energy that was to make itself felt particularly in the theatre and cinema. 1956 was a kind of explosion created by the focusing of opposing forces. And after an explosion the fragments disperse in opposite directions.

* * *

Declaration

George Devine, artistic director of the English Stage Company, had long dreamed of creating a Writers' Theatre. As early as 1946 he drafted an appeal to writers on behalf of the Young Vic:

Most of you have turned your backs on the theatre. We don't blame you. In the last thirty years we have offered you little; our means of expression have been thin, our willingness to co-operate non-existent. But here and now we are ready to do something new . . . If you have any discarded ideas, rake them up again. If you have none, think about it. We'll play with anyone who is honest.

Ten years later, the division between drama and literature was even deeper; one of the remarkable changes in cultural life after 1956 was the shift of emphasis that brought theatrical writing back into the mainstream.

George Devine's persistence did a lot to bring about the change. The story of the formation of the English Stage Company has been told in Irving Wardle's excellent biography, *The Theatres of George Devine* (1978). After the collapse of the Young Vic in 1951 Devine survived as a freelance director and actor, but he was still eager to put into practice his theories about how a permanent company should be created and run. In 1952 he met a young post-war Oxford graduate, Tony Richardson, who was then working for the BBC as a television director, and the two joined forces. At the same time the verse-playwright Ronald Duncan, who lived in Devon and had founded the local Taw and Torridge Festival in 1953, was trying to interest his friends – Lord Harewood, then working at the Royal Opera House, Covent Garden, among them – in forming a theatrical group that would supply local festivals with plays, rather as the English Opera Group provided operas. (Ronald Duncan was the librettist of Benjamin Britten's *The Rape of Lucretia*, 1946.) The arrival of a rich retired businessman, Neville Blond, on the scene in 1954 put the venture on a commercial footing and the two interests came together, although the festival idea disappeared, and it was decided to establish a permanent theatre in London. George Devine

165

became Artistic Director and Tony Richardson his assistant. After complex negotiations in search of a suitable site, the lease was taken of the Royal Court Theatre in Sloane Square, and following repairs and modifications, the English Stage Company opened its doors on 2 April 1956.

It is ironic that Ronald Duncan should have been instrumental in setting up the English Stage Company, for George Devine disliked verse drama and all that it stood for. In the early years of the Court the artistic director was often at loggerheads with his board of management, especially Duncan. Their first season included two one-act verse plays by Duncan, with décor by John Minton, which shows what compromises it is sometimes necessary to make. Devine announced that 'ours is not to be a producer's theatre, or an actor's theatre; it is a writer's theatre', but the fact remained that there were few writers who wrote what Devine was looking for. The first season, then, had to have a judicious stiffening of import and translation besides new plays, and this remained Devine's policy until his retirement at the beginning of 1966. Osborne being an unknown quantity, Devine's main hopes for the first season were Nigel Dennis's adaptation of his novel *Cards of Identity*, and a revised version of Angus Wilson's *The Mulberry Bush*, first staged by the Bristol Old Vic in 1955. *The Mulberry Bush* began the season in repertory with Arthur Miller's Cold War allegory, *The Crucible*. *Look Back in Anger* followed for a short run, before Duncan's two plays and *Cards of Identity*. *Look Back in Anger*'s reputation developed only slowly, but after Dennis's play proved a failure, it was brought back for a longer run. A brief extract was shown on television, and from that moment on interest really began to grow. The crown of the season was supposed to be Brecht's *Good Woman of Setzuan*, but it was played during the Hungarian crisis and its aftermath, and was unpopular in the way that the success of *Look Back in Anger* was helped by Suez. Those in the know could feel easier about the future of British theatre at the end of 1956, but the Royal Court's first year was a financial disaster, and Devine had to mount a production of Wycherley's Restoration comedy, *The*

Country Wife, to save the company's finances. In the long run, though, the Court's financial future was more assured, for *Look Back in Anger* was to generate £50,000 worth of royalties which allowed the Court to continue to experiment.

The theatrical revolution of 1956 might have been less impressive if it had not coincided with the success in the West End of a very different approach to theatre, Joan Littlewood's Theatre Workshop production of Brendan Behan's *The Quare Fellow*. This was not the first of her productions to reach the West End – *The Good Soldier Schweyk* had done so in 1954 – but *The Quare Fellow*, and the drunken behaviour of its author, gave people something to talk about. Joan Littlewood had founded Theatre Workshop with Ewan MacColl in 1945, and for years it struggled as a small touring company in the North of England, with occasional visits to Eastern Europe. It had very strong Communist sympathies in its early days, which did not help it get the recognition it deserved. Ewan MacColl's *Uranium 235* got as far as the Embassy Theatre, Swiss Cottage after the 1951 Edinburgh Festival, but the critics resented its propagandist aims. In 1953, however, Theatre Workshop found a permanent home in a dilapidated former music-hall at Strat-ford-atte-Bowe in London's East End, and in these particularly difficult circumstances Joan Littlewood created a team of actors and a style of playing that was to be as important in subverting country-house theatre as Devine's new playwrights. All theat-rical directors have to be autocrats, and both Devine and Littlewood ran benevolent dictatorships. The co-operative nature of Theatre Workshop stemmed from ideological motives and the economic necessity that had led its founders to pool their demobilization grants, and it came out in the vigorous ensemble playing that was the Workshop's distinctive style. Joan Littlewood's productions up to 1956 were mainly of classics, and writers, some of them already members of the company, were absorbed in the same way as the actors. Brendan Behan's *The Hostage* (1958) began life as a romantic tragedy in Gaelic, but it was completely transformed into a feisty quasi-musical by the time it reached the West End.

167

The change in the theatrical atmosphere began only slowly, but a number of technical developments helped it along. In March 1957 the Chancellor of the Exchequer freed live theatre of Entertainment Tax, favourably widening the narrow margins on which the progressive theatre operated. The Arts Council also began to increase its aid to the theatre, essential for an organization like the Royal Court. In 1956, £55,682 went on drama; by 1960 the sum was £84,660. This does not compare with the much greater increase in state patronage after 1964 but, to quote John Elsom in *Post-War British Theatre*, 'the foundations of the current British theatre system were laid during this middle phase. What started out by being a rescue operation turned into a major reconstruction'; and this was particularly true with the Arts Council's help to the provincial repertory system.

The official benevolence of the Arts Council was rather reluctantly followed by the Lord Chamberlain's office. In 1956, irritated by the Lord Chamberlain's refusal to license anything that dealt even remotely with homosexuality, members of the 'Group' commercial managements, including Binkie Beaumont and Ian Hunter, took over a moribund theatre club, the Watergate, and ran the Comedy Theatre as the New Watergate, opening with Arthur Miller's *A View from the Bridge*, directed by Peter Brook, and following with Robert Anderson's *Tea and Sympathy* and Tennessee Williams's *Cat on a Hot Tin Roof*. This West End theatre ran successfully as a club for two years and attracted 60,000 members until, in 1958, the Lord Chamberlain announced that he was officially dropping his ban on homosexual topics, and censorship generally became a little more relaxed. There were other embarrassing absurdities. Sartre's *Huis Clos* was performed without cuts on television, but had trouble with a theatrical licence. In April 1957 the Royal Court gave a home to Roger Blin's production in French of Beckett's *Fin de Partie* without getting into trouble; but when in the following year, the Court applied for a licence to produce the English translation as *Endgame*, the censor stepped in, and there was a six-month delay while the two sides haggled. Hamm's line referring to God as 'The Bastard! He doesn't exist' had to be modified to 'The Swine!'

Beckett's minimalism and Ionesco's surrealism were not the only foreign influences that made themselves felt in the period 1956–58; the new ideas were a challenge to the realist mode in which English theatre was developing. Bertolt Brecht's Berliner Ensemble played in London in 1956 just after Brecht's death, and sparked off a rare theoretical debate over his use of 'alienating' production devices that discouraged the audience from being seduced into bourgeois sentiment by emphasizing that the play is a performance, and not pretended naturalism. The technique was particuarly appropriate to Brecht's brand of Epic Theatre – the other term, besides alienation, that he contributed to the theatrical vocabulary. Epic Theatre engaged didactically in the larger moral and political issues that could only be referred to obliquely in Jimmy Porter's attic flat. Another version of non-naturalistic, non-realist drama presented in London was Jean Genet's *The Balcony*, performed at the Arts Theatre Club in 1957. The play's mixture of politics and brothel-fantasies was sensational; Genet quarrelled with both the management and the director Peter Zadek, who was banned by Genet from the first night. Zadek, however, did not lose faith in Genet's expressionism as a result:

The Balcony seems to me to point to a more profitable line of development for *new* and adventurous experiment in the theatre than the pseudo-avant-garde writing of post-war English dramatists. *Cards of Identity*, which unfortunately lost itself in intellectual tomfoolery, was the only play produced by the English Stage Company that tried, imaginatively to find new form for new content. Whereas our 'angry young man' lacks precisely that quality which he spends so much time in publicizing: anger, violence. He has quickly become respectable and therefore – a little boring?

Finally, a new approach to the business of acting itself was becoming popular, the so-called Method. Method-acting derived from the teaching of Stanislavsky, and used improvisation to help the actor *feel* his way into the inside of his part, rather than simply putting the character on with his make-up. Method methods varied. For instance, Joan Littlewood used her own at the Theatre Workshop, making her actors rehearse in a well on the roof of the theatre to experience the architectural bleakness of a prison yard; but the characteristic Method style was created by Lee Strasberg's teaching at the Actors' Studio in New York. The Actors' Studio opened in 1947, and created a new type of actor, the most famous of whom in English eyes, thanks to his screen performances, was Marlon Brando. From 1956 onwards Method classes became popular in London, with the London Studio, and Charles Marowitz's Method Workshop, which opened in September 1957. Whatever was done to achieve the effect, Method acting was intended to produce a greater emotional conviction; it was a physical style of acting at complete odds with the conventional good manners demanded in country-house plays.

As actors changed their style so, slowly, did their audiences. They remained middle-class, but the excitement generated at the Royal Court attracted young people who until then had found their main satisfaction and entertainment in the cinema – and the foreign cinema at that. Derek Granger commented in December 1956:

It is a matter for special remark that Mr Osborne alone should have captured the young imagination and with it the fisher-sweatered noctambules from Espresso-land, the *jeunes-mariés* from Knightbridge, the bed-sitter *avant-garde* from Bayswater and Notting Hill. Almost the worst thing about the English theatre is that it has lacked for so long the support of the young intelligentsia. Audiences are apt to look as discreetly silver-haired as if they had been furnished by a casting agency themselves.

For many theatres that last comment remained true, but the prospect of a new audience, and a new-found freedom to treat things as they really were, helped to attract the new writers for whom George Devine was looking. In April 1958, T. C. Worsley wrote, 'if my grapevine reports rightly . . . the theatre as a medium is now at the forefront of their minds. Every young aspirant before the war was writing a novel; today he or she may equally as likely be writing a play. That is the Court's achievement and it is an important one.'

The Royal Court's major find was, of course, John Osborne, who followed up in April 1957 with *The Entertainer*, a commercial success at the Royal Court and then at the Palace Theatre, thanks to the astute combination of Osborne's topicality with a rich part for Sir Laurence Olivier as Archie Rice. A production of his earlier play *Epitaph for George Dillon* followed in 1958, but the musical, *The World of Paul Slickey*, directed by Osborne himself at the Palace Theatre in May 1959, was taken off after only six weeks, and Osborne did not have a new play produced until *Luther* in 1961. One author does not make a Writers' Theatre. In May 1957 the Royal Court staged the first of a series of rehearsed readings of new plays, given on Sunday nights – an inexpensive way of giving writers a chance to see their work come off the page. In 1958 a writers' group began to meet privately for discussions and workshop sessions. Some of the Royal Court writers were not precisely its discoveries. They were novelists like Nigel Dennis, whose original play *The Making of Moo* was in the 1957 season, and Doris Lessing, whose *Each His Own Wilderness* was produced in 1958. Others had worked elsewhere. Michael Hastings's *Don't Destroy Me* was at the New Lindsay Club in 1956 before *Yes – And After* was at the Court in 1957; Willis Hall's *The Long and the Short and the Tall*, at the Court in 1959, began life as *The Disciplines of War* for the Oxford University Theatre Group at the Edinburgh Festival in 1958. But the commitment to a Writers' Theatre made the Royal Court the focus for the 'first wave' of dramatists that began to break in 1958.

Two playwrights began with Sunday night productions. John Arden's *The Waters of Babylon* in 1957 was followed by full-scale productions of *Live Like Pigs* in 1958 and *Serjeant Musgrave's Dance* in 1959. N. F. Simpson's *A Resounding Tinkle* was tried out in 1957, before being severely pruned and staged as a one-acter with *The Hole* in 1958. The full-length *One-Way Pendulum* followed in 1959 and proved a commercial success, which Arden's plays had certainly not been. N. F. Simpson came to the Court via a competition for new plays organized by the *Observer* in 1957; the same competition produced Ann Jellicoe's *The Sport of My Mad Mother* at the Court in 1958, and Errol John's *Moon on a Rainbow Shawl*, produced in 1959. John was a West Indian writer, as was Barry Reckford whose *Flesh to a Tiger* had been presented in 1958. The Nigerian novelist Wole Soyinka was a member of the writers' group and took part in the topical improvisation *Eleven Men Dead at Hola Camp* in 1959. The poet Christopher Logue contributed a Sunday night production, *The Trial of Cob and Leach*, in 1959, and the lyrics to Harry Cookson's musical *The Lily White Boys* in 1960.

Besides giving others the courage to follow, in one case the Royal Court managed to launch a writer through a different theatre. In 1958, Arts Council finance made it possible to mount a special season of four new productions from provincial companies, but Devine had doubts about the quality of the plays that were available. Anxious to ensure that at least one would be a success in London, he sent the script of Arnold Wesker's *Chicken Soup With Barley*, which had been under consideration for a Sunday night performance at the Court, to the Belgrade Theatre, Coventry. The Belgrade was the first new theatre to be built after the war, and had only just opened under its director Bryan Bailey who, like Devine, was committed to encouraging new writers. Not only was the script sent, a Royal Court director, John Dexter, was loaned as well, and *Chicken Soup With Barley* had a brief run in Coventry before duly appearing at the Royal Court. In 1959 Wesker's earlier play, *The Kitchen*, was given two Sunday night performances at the Court, and the Belgrade Theatre premièred *Roots*, the second play in Wesker's trilogy with *Chicken Soup* and *I'm Talking About Jerusalem*, which followed in 1960. In both cases the Royal Court presented the play in London, with a special production of the entire trilogy in 1960.

Theatre Workshop's contribution to the growing number of new writers was nineteen-year-old Shelagh Delaney, whose first play, *A Taste of Honey* (1958), had a long West End run. The Belgrade Coventry launched her second, *The Lion in Love*, in 1960. Theatre Workshop exploited its communitarian, working-class tradition with Stephen Lewis's *Sparrers Can't Sing* (1960), Wolf Mankowitz's *Make Me an Offer*, and Frank Norman's *Fings Ain't Wot They Used T'be*, both launched in 1959. Another working-class writer with roots in the East End, Bernard Kops, had his first play, *The Hamlet of Stepney Green*, produced by the Oxford Playhouse in 1958; *Goodbye World* followed in 1959, produced at Guildford, and *Change for the Angel* at the Arts Theatre Club in 1960. The Oxford Playhouse presented Robert Bolt's *The Critic and the Heart* in 1957, and in the same year the Royal Court, Liverpool presented his *Flowering Cherry*, which transferred to the West End. These provincial theatres, together with the Arts Theatre at Cambridge and the Royal at Brighton, provided a nursery for productions that could be brought to London, and there were signs that commercial managements were waking up to the possibilities of the new drama.

An early indication was impresario Michael Codron's brief season at the Lyric Hammersmith in May 1958, which launched both John Mortimer and Harold Pinter. (Pinter had had a one-act play, *The Room*, performed by students in Bristol in 1957.) Mortimer's two one-act plays, *Dock Brief* – originally a radio play – and *What Shall We Tell Caroline?*, afterwards found a home at the Garrick, but Pinter's *The Birthday Party*, first seen at the Arts Cambridge, was greeted with blank incomprehension. In January 1960 *The Dumb Waiter* and *The Room* were put on at the newly opened Hampstead Theatre Club, and later moved to the Royal Court; in May *The Caretaker* opened at the Arts Theatre Club and subsequently transferred to the Duchess. Peter Shaffer's *Five-Finger Exercise* had a successful West End transfer from Cambridge in 1958; in 1960 Keith Waterhouse's adaptation with Willis Hall of his book *Billy Liar* was a sound commercial hit, as was Robert Bolt's *A Man for All Seasons*, though John Mortimer's first full-length play *The Wrong Side of the Park* was a more modest success.

John Mortimer's shift from writing novels to plays shows the new consideration writers were giving the theatre. The fact that *Dock Brief* began life as a radio play is a reminder of the contribution of radio and television to the change. John Mortimer, Robert Bolt, Giles Cooper, Harold Pinter, Alun Owen, N. F. Simpson, John Arden, Stan Barstow, Keith Waterhouse and Willis Hall all had their first work produced on the radio. The expansion of television following the opening of a commercial channel in September 1955 greatly increased the demand for new plays, for there was a limit to the number of adaptations possible from the stage. By 1959, with seven or eight plays a week on the commercial and BBC channels, there was a need for some 400 self-contained plays a year, besides serials, and the importance of the writer to television was recognized when film and television writers combined in that year to form the Writers' Guild of Great Britain.

The commercial companies took the lead in developing television drama. In 1958 ABC TV brought in Sydney Newman from Canada to run their Sunday night Armchair Theatre. He boldly commissioned original plays from writers like Harold Pinter, Giles Cooper, Ted Willis, Alun Owen and Clive Exton (one of the first writers to establish his reputation entirely through television). Granada TV and Associated-Rediffusion also made important contributions, and the competition stimulated the BBC to commission work from writers like Osborne, Mortimer, Arden and John Whiting. John Russell Taylor argues in his study, *Anger and After*, that Pinter's two original television plays, *Night School* and *A Night Out*, and a television production of *The Birthday Party* did much to familiarize people with his style, and so prepared the way for the commercial success of *The Caretaker* in 1960.

Between 1950 and 1960 the number of television licences issued increased from a quarter of a million to ten million, the most rapid expansion coinciding with the arrival of commercial television. In itself, the acquisition of television sets showed the rise in working-class prosperity; the consequence of television ownership was a massive change in the way the working classes entertained themselves. The shift accelerated the decline of the old provincial repertory and touring theatres (compensating actors and writers by the new opportunities in television), and the cinema was badly affected. The rise of a 'new wave' of British film-makers, closely associated with the Royal Court, has to be seen against a background of general decline.

As Chapter 1 showed, the British film industry entered the 1950s in a very weak state, dominated as it was by American money and influence. In 1951 a third form of protection was added to the quota system and funding from the National Film Finance Corporation: a scheme devised by Sir William Eady by which film exhibitors paid a fraction of the price of every cinema ticket sold into a fund that was re-distributed to the makers of British films, in proportion to their own receipts at the box office. Eady money, as it became known, was a help, but it was impossible to distinguish between films made in the United Kingdom by genuine British companies and those made by American companies in order to use up blocked royalties and avoid the restriction of the quota. A lot of Eady money went to cheaply produced second features and bland documentary shorts. The number of first feature films produced in Britain was seventy-eight in 1950 and seventy-five in 1960, having risen slightly and then fallen back again in the interim period. The National Film Finance Corporation lost £3 million when Alexander Korda's production company, British Lion, went bankrupt in 1954. (A British Lion distribution company survived.) Although the NFFC was kept afloat by the government it lost money steadily.

The one bright spot in the late 1940s and early 1950s was provided by the productions of Michael Balcon's Ealing Studios. Balcon had started producing films at Ealing in 1938, and during the war the studios made the appropriate dramas and semi-documentaries such as *Next of Kin* (1942) and *San Demetrio London* (1943) to assist the war effort. After the war the dramas continued, including *Hue and Cry* (1947) and *The Blue Lamp* (1950), but in 1949, the same year as Anthony

Asquith's almost expressionist portrayal of post-war Vienna in Graham Greene's *The Third Man*, three remarkable comedies, all unmistakably British, established Ealing's post-war reputation. They were *Kind Hearts and Coronets, Whisky Galore* and *Passport to Pimlico*. Their 'Britishness', however, was a rather cosy view of the community, more ideal than real. *The Man in the White Suit* (1951) did take a rare look at British industry, but managed to avoid being too critical by balancing the faults of the industrialists with those of the trade unions. The last Ealing film was released in 1959, but the company's fortunes had begun to decline in 1954, and in 1955 the studios themselves were sold – to BBC Television.

In 1955 the ownership of television sets was increasing rapidly, and the cinema audience shrinking correspondingly. In the peak year of 1946 the audience was 30 million; by 1960 it was down by almost two-thirds. The decline in audience was accelerated by the closure of cinemas; of the 4,500 cinemas operating in 1950, 1,550 had closed by 1960. As if in anticipation, Anglo-American film production had already begun to decline, and there were complaints of a shortage of films from 1954 onwards. There were enough to go round, but the choice was severely restricted. Independent cinemas in the so-called 'National' distribution circuit suffered the most, but the major distribution chains of ABC and Rank were also squeezed. In 1958 Rank amalgamated its two distribution circuits, Odeon and Gaumont, which until then had been in competition with each other, and closed its redundant cinemas. Faced with this alarming decline, American producers responded by concentrating their resources on block-busters in the new wide-screen techniques, which the British could not afford to make, or turned out cheap horror and teen-quickies to exploit the surviving youth market. With little chance of competing with the American films that monopolized the two profitable distribution chains, an independent producer had small chance of getting his money back.

The statistics make the economic decline of the British cinema seem inevitable, but the films that were produced had become fixed in a mould that was as out of date as the country-house play; indeed their worlds were very similar. Writing in the British Film Institute's magazine *Sight and Sound* in 1955, Penelope Houston described contemporary Britain as 'The Undiscovered Country':

Tolerance and trust in compromise, the hallmarks of the English character, work against the 'engaged' artist in any medium; so does that celebrated English custom of ignoring a disagreeable fact, on the assumption that if left alone it may quietly go away. All this means that many areas of experience are closed off to the British film-maker. A no less significant issue, and one affecting the whole picture of life that we are given on the screen, is the intriguing and unmentionable subject of class.

During the war the image of a socially cohesive and purposeful nation had been acceptable, but the post-war portrayal of a society of bumbling amateurs successfully defeating 'authority', as in *Passport to Pimlico*, the comic 'museum' view of a Britain of vintage cars (*Genevieve*, 1953) and steam trains (*The Titfield Thunderbolt*, Ealing 1953) was comforting – and illusory. Costume dramas, literary adaptations and social comedies sustained a cinematic tradition of sorts, but the film-makers did not care to look at their world with their own eyes, turning instead to stage plays and novels. And as the 1950s progressed, they turned increasingly to books about the war.

In the 1950s, the actual horrors being far enough behind them, British film-makers began to fight the Second World War all over again, looking for the social cohesion that some films made in wartime had helped to create: *Appointment with Venus* (1951), *The Wooden Horse* (1952), *The Cruel Sea* (1953), *The Dam Busters* (1954), *Cockleshell Heroes* (1955), *The Battle of the River Plate* (1956), *The Bridge on the River Kwai* (1957), *Above Us the Waves* (1958), *Yesterday's Enemy* (1959) and *Sink the Bismarck* (1960). One of the last Ealing films to be made was *Dunkirk* in 1958, which in its context reflected a nostalgia not only for the better days of Britain when it was possible to make defeat look like victory, but also the better

177

days of Ealing itself, before it too was defeated. George Stonier, under his *New Statesman* pseudonym of William Whitebait, read the significance of this concentration on a period when issues appeared retrospectively clear cut:

A dozen years after the Second World War we find ourselves in the really quite desperate situation of being, not sick of war, but hideously in love with it. Not actively fighting, we aren't at peace. The H-Bomb looms ahead, and we daren't look at it; so we creep back to the lacerating comfort of 'last time' . . . while we 'adventure' at Suez, in the cinemas we are still thrashing Rommel – and discovering he was a gentleman! – sweeping the Atlantic of submarines, sending the few to scatter Goering's many. The more we lose face in the world's counsels, the grander, in our excessively modest way, we swell in this illusionary mirror held up by the screen. It is less a spur to morale than a salve to wounded pride; and as art or entertainment, dreadfully dull.

Those who wished to challenge the anodyne or regressive views of the world offered by British films had, for purely practical reasons, to restrict themselves to film criticism, chiefly in *Sight and Sound*, several of whose contributors had begun by writing for the more aggressive *Sequence*, launched by the Oxford University Film Society in 1947 and, after two Oxford issues, leading a precarious independent existence until 1952. Among its founders were Penelope Houston and Lindsay Anderson – Anderson editing all fourteen numbers of *Sequence* that managed to appear. His final co-editor was Karel Reisz, a Cambridge graduate who in 1952 went to work for the British Film Institute planning the programmes for the National Film Theatre, which had begun as the Telekinema for the Festival of Britain. Anderson, meanwhile, was teaching himself filmmaking with short documentaries, including a brief personal view of a crowd at a fun-fair, *O Dreamland*, made in 1953. In 1955 the British Film Institute set aside £12,500 to help experimental film-makers, and Karel Reisz and Tony Richardson were given help to make a short film about a dance hall, *Momma Don't Allow*. This was one of the first serious-though-entertaining acknowledgements of the growing 'sub-culture' of jazz clubs and Teddy Boys. The fund also helped Lorenza Mazzetti and Denis Horne complete a film about two deaf mutes, *Together*. These three films, whose production had been interdependent in terms of personnel – particularly in the cameraman Walter Lassally and Lindsay Anderson's help with the editing of *Together* – formed the first programme at the National Film Theatre of what Karel Reisz dubbed Free Cinema.

Free Cinema No. 1 was shown in February of the pivotal year of 1956. Between 1956 and 1959 six programmes of avant-garde short films were shown, only three of them British. Other film-makers in the British programme were Claude Goretta and Alain Tanner with *Nice Time* in 1957 and Robert Vas with *Refuge England* in 1959. 'Free Cinema' was a rallying-cry, and Lindsay Anderson in particular gave it a left-wing slant. 'An attitude means a style. A style means an attitude. Implicit in our attitude is a belief in freedom, in the importance of people and in the significance of the everyday.' The introduction of Free Cinema No. 3 in 1957 stated:

We ask you to view it not as critics, not as a diversion, but in direct relation to a British cinema still obstinately class-bound; still rejecting the stimulus of contemporary life, as well as the responsibility to criticize; still reflecting a metropolitan Southern English culture which excludes the rich diversity of tradition and personality which is the whole of Britain.

By concentrating in particular on work and the working class, notably with *Everyday Except Christmas* (1957), a film about Covent Garden market directed by Anderson and produced by Reisz, Free Cinema was heir to the pre-war school of documentary founded by John Grierson; but Grierson was hostile to Free Cinema because it made far more personal statements than the sociological neutrality of the Grierson school. The most overtly political film associated with Free Cinema was the collective film made for the Campaign for Nuclear Disarmament in 1958, *March to Aldermaston*.

Anderson's success with *Everyday Except Christmas*, which

won a *Grand Prix* at the Venice Film Festival, did not lead to work in the commercial cinema (apart from some episodes of *Robin Hood* for television); instead, like Tony Richardson, he went to work for the Royal Court, directing Willis Hall's *The Long and the Short and the Tall*. (It was Anderson who introduced Arnold Wesker to the Royal Court, Wesker having met him on a course at the London Film School.) When the final Free Cinema programme was announced in 1959, Anderson said the movement had been a failure because it had not attracted sufficient support from the younger generation. Be that as it may, three British film directors, Anderson, Reisz and Richardson, cut their teeth in the movement, and their first feature films – when at last they were able to make them, in Anderson's case not until *This Sporting Life* in 1963 – show precisely the realist concern for the significance of everyday working-class life that Anderson had demanded.

Free Cinema provided valuable experience, but it is fair to say that the impetus for a change of attitude in feature films came more from the theatre and the novel. It was too late to prevent *Lucky Jim* from being made into a harmless farce, and although there was an element of social realism in two films scripted by Ted Willis – *Woman in a Dressing Gown*, made in 1957, and *No Trees in the Street*, made in 1958 – the first firm indication of a change came with the release in January 1959 of Jack Clayton's film version of *Room at the Top*. The film had a mixed reception. G. W. Stonier called it 'all front and no back', but here was a film with a sense of attack sadly lacking from most British efforts. In *Sight and Sound* Penelope Houston wrote, 'this seems a film which can only be summed up in the special context of our present-day cinema. Firstly, it has the impact of genuine innovation: a new subject, a new setting, a new talent. More significantly, it shows what can be achieved in spite of compromise.' It was one of the first British films to be explicit about sexual passion.

By the time *Room at the Top* was released, most the playwrights launched since 1956 had had their work taken up with a view to being made into films. The first to appear was

180

Declaration

Look Back in Anger, released in June 1959. Compromise was evident in the casting of Richard Burton as Jimmy Porter and the damping down of his tirades by the screen adaptor Nigel Kneale, the television writer who wrote the *Quatermass* series. But the significance of the film was that it was the first production of Woodfall Films, formed by John Osborne and Tony Richardson with the American producer Harry Saltzman (Associated British Pictures also backed the production, which guaranteed a proper circuit release.) Richardson directed *Look Back in Anger*, *The Entertainer* (released in 1960) and *A Taste of Honey* (released in 1961). He also produced Karel Reisz's first feature, *Saturday Night and Sunday Morning*, released in 1960. Other writers, directors and actors to form production companies were Richard Attenborough and Bryan Forbes, who made *The Angry Silence* (1959); Joseph Losey and Stanley Baker, who made *The Criminal* (1960) with a script by Alun Owen; and Wolf Mankowitz.

If *Room at the Top* was the first sign of a new approach in the cinema, *Saturday Night and Sunday Morning* confirmed it. Adapted from Alan Sillitoe's novel of working-class life in Nottingham, the challenge to the Ealing Comedy view of the world is summed up in the conclusion to the pre-credit opening sequence: 'What I'm out for is a good time. All the rest is propaganda.' People and their circumstances were not presented as comics or caricatures, sex was treated frankly, and the hero, played by Albert Finney, was even allowed to get away with his womanizing and contempt for authority. In 1959 Isabel Quigley had written in the *Spectator*, 'for years and years we have known that the British film picture of ourselves was phoney. Everyone in the country knew it, it was one of the big national lies that everyone concurred in.' *Saturday Night and Sunday Morning* broke with that form of propaganda.

It is possible, however, to exaggerate the overall importance of such films. The British cinema remained in thrall to America, and the war films continued to march across the screen. 1960 marks a moment of potential. The Free Cinema cameraman Walter Lassally commented in *Sight and Sound*, 'if I had to

181

summarize in one phrase what a potential British new wave would be up against, I would say: the Dead Hand. The Dead Hand of apathy, of complacency and convention, whose grip is felt on all sides of the industry.' In spite of sporadic revivals the indigenous British cinema is still only fitfully alive.

1960 was a similar point of potential for the theatre, and the writers, actors and directors of the first wave have been joined by fresh talent, while continuing to develop their own. The launching of the English Stage Company was not the exclusive cause of the shift of emphasis within the arts after 1956, but the idea of a Writers' Theatre encouraged talents that might have been trapped in other forms or stifled by the commercial stage. Because the risks that were taken paid off, the more conservative dared to follow – Terence Rattigan began to unbend in his later plays, though he got little thanks for it. There is no rigid unity to the Writers' Theatre that emerged, which is as it should be, but a new realism links the early work of Osborne, Arden, Wesker, Delaney and, in their settings and subject matter, Ann Jellicoe and Harold Pinter. The phrase 'kitchen sink' was first applied to the realist painters of the previous chapter; the playwrights were following the same strategy in bringing in material and language that was previously unacceptable. Alan Brien caught the new mood in the *Spectator* in September 1959:

fresh and provocative theatrical entertainment has begun to sprout on our stages in the last few years. It has displayed two significant innovations. The settings have been unfamiliar – a Midlands attic, an Irish brothel, a new housing estate, a Soho gambling-shop, a Bayswater basement. The characters have been misfits and outcasts exiled in the no-man's-land between the working class and the middle class. The dialogue has also been eloquent, bawdy, witty and concrete. The basic kick of the whole movement has been the feeling that the play was written last weekend, the exhilaration of listening to talk alive with images from the newspapers, the advertisements, the entertainments of today.

The new plays and playwrights successfully broke the power of the country-house formula, but the fact that the change of location from middle class to lower-class and working class was still perceived in just these terms shows that English culture remained as class-bound as ever. T. C. Worsley complained in the *New Statesman* in February 1959: 'The research begun at the Royal Court – four years ago was it? has finally been perfected. The English play can now break through the class barrier at will. That objective has been achieved. Now the question is, what is going to be done with the ability?' One answer was the plays of Arnold Wesker's trilogy, which showed the limitations of the working class as well as its potential. Only Wesker, Bernard Kops and Michael Hastings could themselves be considered as having working-class origins; the theatre provided many of its own writers, former actors like John Osborne and Harold Pinter, and the producer Ann Jellicoe. There were complaints that the fashion for lower-class settings was excluding other writers like John Whiting and Dennis Cannan – though in Whiting's case the position was rectified by Peter Hall's commissioning of *The Devils* for the Royal Shakespeare Company's first season at the Aldwych in London. Nor were the middle classes without their spokesmen, a point made by a Sunday night debate at the Royal Court in November 1960 entitled 'Political Theatre – Yes or No'. On one side sat Robert Bolt and John Mortimer, in suits, on the other the casually dressed Arnold Wesker and Lindsay Anderson. Bolt and Mortimer defended their craft, while Anderson berated them for their lack of commitment – and condemned the audience as a pack of culture vultures for turning up at all.

Look Back in Anger was important for beginning a revolution in style rather than for its limited political content. The change in style showed itself in all sorts of ways – a vogue for the low-life musical, for instance, after the whimsies of Julian Slade's *Salad Days* (1954). Lionel Bart's first big hit with *Oliver* in 1960 owes a great deal to his training with Theatre Workshop. Kenneth Macmillan (who did the choreography for Osborne's *The World of Paul Slickey*) has said that *Look Back in Anger* led him to re-think his approach to ballet and try for a greater realism, rather than produce fantasy ballets like the French. The poor reception given to Benjamin Britten's *The Prince of the Pagodas* (1957), choreographed by John Cranko, may reflect the change in public taste. Macmillan's *The Burrow* (1958) was loosely based on *The Diary of Anne Frank*. In television drama the conditions of the medium and co-existence with actual documentary encouraged the realistic presentation of everyday life, though trimmed of the political overtones of Free Cinema. In fiction, working-class life began to be treated with a similar directness, with Alan Sillitoe's *Saturday Night and Sunday Morning* (1958) and *The Loneliness of the Long Distance Runner* (1959); Keith Waterhouse's *Billy Liar* (1959); David Storey's *This Sporting Life* (1960) and Stan Barstow's *A Kind of Loving* (1960). All these titles became notable British films.

The progress of Alun Owen's play *Progress to the Park* is typical of the possibilities that had opened up by 1960. It began life as a radio play, had a Sunday night performance at the Royal Court in 1959, directed by Lindsay Anderson, was then directed by Harry H. Corbett at Stratford East in November 1960, and appeared in the West End in May 1961. Alun Owen had himself been an actor, and the play is set in his native Liverpool against the background of tension between the Roman Catholic and Protestant communities. The cast was drawn from the new school of demotic actors created by Theatre Workshop: Billie Whitelaw, Roy Kinnear, Tom Bell, Brian Murphy, Barbara Ferris, John Junkin. The typical British actor, in fact, no longer tried to eradicate all traces of accent and speak with a voice studied from Oxford and the BBC; no more did he aspire to matinée-idol good looks: instead, Royal Court actors like Kenneth Haigh (the original Jimmy Porter), Alan Bates (the original Cliff in the same play) and Albert Finney projected a virile toughness. The Royal Court not only helped to breed a new style of actor, George Devine's assistants, Tony Richardson, John Dexter, Lindsay Anderson, Ian Johnstone and William Gaskill, represented a new breed of director as well.

In January 1960 Alan Brien reported:

it is the commercial managements who are now in a state of mild panic. Since July I have counted sixteen plays which threw in the towel after a few weeks' run. Some of them were abysmal rubbish. Most were mediocre stuff moderately well acted. . . . All of them were box-office failures. Yet the record of the unorthodox, long-haired, shoe-string fringe theatres on the whole is more impressive, both critically and financially, than that of the big-time, conventional, well-heeled, old-fashioned impresarios.

At the beginning of the 1960s the fashion for realism faded, as its imaginative limits were discovered. In 1961 Joan Little-wood left Theatre Workshop for a while, the stock of acting talent she had created having been dispersed by the success of Theatre Workshop's productions. Writing in 1962, John Russell Taylor summed up the immediate prospect:

If any general trend can be discerned, it is a gradual move away from naturalism, represented by the increasing employment of Brech-tian techniques derived from the heroic theatre (Osborne, Arden), increasing recourse to personal myth, possibly in a quasi-historical framework (Wesker, Delaney) or simply the use of more and more non-naturalistic language within a basically realistic framework (Owen, Exton, Shaffer). Only Pinter, the incorrigible individualist, stands aloof from all this: perversely, his plays are getting more and more realistic.

Peter Brook's experiments with 'The Theatre of Cruelty' in 1964 began a second phase of theatrical revolution.

The success of the first phase can be exaggerated. In 1960 Britain still had no National Theatre, neither a company nor a building; indeed, the reputation of the Old Vic, the National Theatre designate, was wavering. On the other hand the new director of the Stratford Shakespeare Memorial Theatre, Peter Hall, was preparing to challenge the Old Vic's position by opening a permanent London base at the Aldwych as the Royal Shakespeare Company. British theatre was the main benefici-ary of the energy released in 1956, but, as the next chapter shows, the whole cultural balance was shifting as the decade tilted away from that pivotal year.

CHAPTER SIX

CULTURE AND SOCIETY

*'These "cultural" questions
are questions about life.'*

E. P. Thompson
The New Reasoner No. 9

In October 1959 the Conservative Party won its third general
election in a row, increasing its overall majority to 100 seats.
Under Harold Macmillan the party had regained its confidence
after the Suez crisis, and although colonial troubles continued
to be an irritation – Cyprus, the murder of prisoners at Hola
Camp in Kenya – progress was being made towards an orderly
withdrawal from Imperial power. At the same time Macmillan
had taken a special place on the international stage by visiting
Moscow and Washington in preparation for a summit meeting
in 1960. Domestically, the small economic boom of 1955 had
lead to fears of inflation and so to a financial squeeze that held
up the expansion of industrial production, but the budget of
1959 was reflationary, and nicely timed to assist the Conservative victory in October. At the beginning of 1960 the Conservative government looked as though it would hold power for
ever, while the Labour Party was once more in disarray, torn
by internal disputes over the Campaign for Nuclear Disarmament, and Hugh Gaitskell's attempt to rid the party of its
historical commitment to the public ownership of the means of

production, distribution and exchange, enshrined in Clause Four of the Constitution. The apparently permanent power of the Conservatives, and the political wrangling of Labour, are encapsulated by two catch-words that preoccupied the latter half of the 1950s: the Establishment and Commitment.

That a summit meeting between East and West, though abortive, was at least held in Paris in May 1960 shows that the climate of the Cold War was changing, indeed, beginning to unfreeze. After the death of Stalin in 1953 there was a struggle for power that distracted the Russians from conducting a more dynamic as opposed to defensive foreign policy. Khrushchev gradually emerged as the victor, and in 1958 became both Prime Minister and Leader of the Party. Moving onto the offensive, Khrushchev decided to try to resolve the problem of Berlin, which was providing too easy an escape-route to the West, and the decade ended, as it had begun, with a crisis over the city. But Khrushchev did not get his way, and the new era of summitry and the election of President Kennedy in 1960 prepared the way for a new phase of the Cold War – just as dangerous as the old, as the Cuban missile crisis of 1962 was to show. The atmosphere had been changed by science. Russia exploded a hydrogen bomb in 1953; by 1955 American cities were in range of Russian bombers; and then, on 4 October 1957, Russia successfully launched the first satellite, Sputnik, and sent it coursing over the United States. This development was a severe shock to the West. For the first time Russia appeared to have the scientific advantage, and as the weight of nuclear terror increased on either side the need to talk rather than fight became more and more urgent.

The effect of the Western alliance, and especially the economic superiority of the United States, increased American cultural as well as political dominance. As in the case of *Encounter*, covert funds were used to promote pro-American views along the Western intelligentsia. Through the Museum of Modern Art in New York, CIA funds went into the promotion of the New York School of painting, which from 1956 onwards began to dominate the styles of native British art. It is also true, however, that in contrast to the meagre British Fifties, the expansive state of American culture, particularly its popular culture, was genuinely attractive to younger British artists, and to poets not schooled in the disciplines of the Movement.

In spite of the efforts of John Berger (who turned to fiction with *A Painter in Our Time* in 1958), Britain had not had a politically committed school of painters since the founders of the Euston Road School received their call-up papers at the beginning of the Second World War. The extent to which politics were regarded as a purely individual matter was summed up by the Artists' International Association's 25th anniversary exhibition in 1958. The AIA had been founded as a specifically anti-fascist organization, committed to the ideological battles of the 1930s. By 1958 it had become little more than an exhibiting organization. The painter Adrian Heath explained why in his catalogue introduction: 'The whole cultural climate of our country has greatly changed. An artist no longer feels called upon to justify his existence save by the work he produces. The AIA reflects these changes. As an organization it has completely lost its political characteristics. Its present members no longer feel that their status and rights as artists are threatened.' This political quietism was seen as a challenge by the recently founded *New Left Review*, which organized a show of realist painters at a radical coffee-bar, *The Partisan*, but it is true that the circumstances of the artist had changed, as Basil Taylor wrote in his review of the AIA show, 'the opportunities now given to an artist to bring his work before the public, especially if he is under forty (and even more so, in this youth-crazy time when the next crop of millionaires would seem likely to be fifteen-year-old rock-'n-rollers, if he is under thirty), have been greatly extended. There have also been far more commissions for public works in the past ten years than in the Thirties.' Public patronage had certainly increased, as Richard Wollheim commented in the *Spectator* in 1960: 'Since the war the Arts Council and British Council have conducted a campaign under the heading "Wanted – A British

Art". The rewards they offer are large enough for it not to be surprising that the number of suspects brought in yearly is steadily growing.' Increased public expenditure on art was matched by increased commercial activity. The number of private galleries dealing in contemporary art doubled between 1950 and 1960; the greater interest in painters both as personalities and business propositions led to attempted poaching between galleries that left the artist, as the commodity, with a higher price. At the same time the latter half of the 1950s saw a considerable change in the teaching practices of the art schools, which moved away from centrally administered examinations to individual school diplomas. The professional artist was thus able to supplement his income with part-time teaching that did not demand any compromise between his own work and what he taught.

As was said in Chapter 4, British art has always been susceptible to outside influences; in the 1950s that influence flowed more and more powerfully from America. This is not the place to give an account of the evolution of Abstract Expressionism in America in the 1940s. Suffice it to say that it was a radical alternative to the European tradition of geometric or constructivist abstraction, which in England continued in the work of Ben Nicholson and Victor Pasmore. Sam Hunter described the new work in *Art Since 1945* (1958) as 'the repudiation of purist abstraction, and the identification of an abstract means with emotion, fantasy, and the inner drama of the self'. Since the artist was freed of all objective reference to anything but the very canvas, the painting became an expression of the emotions of the painter recorded – to borrow Sam Hunter's word – by the drama of the act of painting. This is a generalization, but one justified by the splashed and dribbled tracery of Jackson Pollock. Freed of the object, painting became a question of emotion alone, and this is true of 'action painters' like Pollock, or the colour field painters like Mark Rothko. As if to magnify the emotional impact, the paintings got bigger and bigger. enveloping the spectator in visual and unspecific sensation.

British abstract painting rarely achieved the *élan* or daring of the Americans, but there was a growing sense of liberation derived from the American example. The key date is again 1956, when a large show from the Museum of Modern Art in New York visited the Tate Gallery. But the history of British painting from 1950 onwards is dotted with the conversions of individual artists to 'painterly' abstraction. As early as 1948 Alan Davie (Plate 5) saw paintings by Jackson Pollock, Mark Rothko and Robert Motherwell in Venice when Peggy Guggenheim (the patroness of early abstract expressionism) sent her collection on a European tour. The School of Paris also made a contribution in the early stages, with the exhibition *Art d'Aujourd'hui* in 1949, and British painters like William Turnbull, Eduardo Paolozzi and Anthony Hill were regular visitors to Paris. In 1953 the two influences came together at the *Opposing Forces* exhibition at the Institute of Contemporary Arts, which offered the alternative examples of Jackson Pollock and Jean-Paul Riopelle, geographically synthesized by the work of Sam Francis, an American living in Paris. Patrick Heron's selection for the 1953 Hanover Gallery show, *Space in Colour*, of Ivon Hitchens to hang beside work by Victor Pasmore, Terry Frost, Keith Vaughan, Roger Hilton, Peter Lanyon, William Scott, Alan Davie and himself, shows that there were also English sources for the abstraction that was evolving, and the 'St Ives' abstract painters like Frost and Heron never quite lost the 'landscape feeling' of their location.

The trend towards informal as opposed to geometric abstraction continued until 1956, which was the year, to quote Laurence Alloway in his introduction to *Dimensions* (1957), 'in which everybody got into the act of painting'. The final section of the Tate Gallery's show *Modern Art in the United States* contained works by sixteen of the New York abstract expressionist school, including Arshile Gorky, Franz Kline, Willem de Kooning, Jackson Pollock, Mark Rothko and Robert Motherwell – all painted between 1942 and 1954 – and the full wealth, range (and size) of contemporary American painting was revealed. The most startling conversion to total abstraction was that of the former Euston Road painter Rodrigo Moynihan

(Plates 1 and 2) but other noted converts were Patrick Heron and Bryan Winter. Two important British shows later in 1957 were *Metavisual, Tachiste, Abstract Painting in Britain Today* at the Redfern Gallery, and *Statements: a review of British abstract art in 1956* arranged at the ICA by its deputy director, Laurence Alloway. A single work by each of twenty-one artists was shown, and the catalogue contained a brief comment by each artist on his approach to abstraction. It is noticeable that only the constructivists Ben Nicholson and Peter Kinley actually mention action painting, probably because neither had a use for it, but comments from others show the extent to which the American lesson had been absorbed. Bryan Winter: 'I think of my paintings as a *source* of imagery, something that *generates* imagery rather than contains it.' Alan Davie: 'A synthesis must occur in your own mind.' Roger Hilton: 'The painter's works record his thought processes, his outlook. The greatest artist will be the one who most completely lets the medium shoulder the idea.' Adrian Heath: 'From the very beginning, from the first lines or spread of colour (which carry to the author unforeseen demands) the work itself must be consulted.' Caution about too freely acknowledging the influence of America is also apparent in Laurence Alloway's second major show in 1957, at the O'Hana Gallery in December, *Dimensions: British Abstract Art 1948–57*, whose catalogue has a careful chronology prepared by Toni del Renzio suggesting a non-American pedigree for the thirty-five artists represented.

The spread of abstract painting naturally disturbed John Berger – he said of the Americans at the Tate in 1956: 'These works, in their creation and appeal, are a full expression of the suicidal despair of those who are completely trapped within their own dead subjectivity' – but he was forced to admit by the time of the 10th *Young Contemporaries* exhibition in 1959 that abstract expressionism had won the day. 'One has an impression of talent, energy and toughness. The "sensitivity" of romanticism of the Forties has altogether been shoved out. These people are proud of having no illusions – they came in on the ground floor.' Action painting had found a way forward, around the stalled vehicles of academic modernism, where realism had not.

Having moved forward, abstract expressionism was itself susceptible to development and change, and again in response to American painting, particularly that of Ellsworth Kelly and Barnet Newman, it moved towards its 'hard-edge' phase, a phrase coined by Laurence Alloway to describe another show of American paintings at the Institute of Contemporary Arts in March 1960, where action painting had been superseded by formal arrangements of flat areas of colour with clean edges. The response to this development was clear in a British show at the RBA Galleries in September 1960, *Situation*, organized by a committee of artists chaired by Alloway, with an introduction by Roger Coleman of the Royal College of Art. The emphasis of the show was on large paintings in the American manner, and two of the contributors, Harold Cohen and Richard Smith, were actually working in America at the time. Roger Coleman *did* acknowledge the importance of American painting to British art:

The change in the definition of what a picture could be, that was brought about by American painting in the 1940s, is only the second, counting Cubism as the first, fundamental reorientation in the history of modern art. The British artists, if they have any concern with this moment at all, are unavoidably its heirs whether they have the capacity or desire to inherit or not. And, while some of the artists here are still in the process of assimilating what they have discovered through the Americans, the character of all the work is becoming recognizably individual. (Not recognizably 'British', however, the desire to be British by attempting to isolate British characteristics usually results, when its arises, in a full stop.)

If there are 'British' characteristics to be detected, say, in the work of Robyn Denny (Plate 10), then it is a preference for a sense of style and rigour over the emotional outbursts of the Americans; but it is essentially a continuation of the drive begun in New York to make, as Roger Coleman put it, 'the work of art a real object; something existing in its own right

192

and not merely because it happened to represent some aspect of what could only be, by definition, reality'.

It is fair to say that *Situation*, partly because it was an artists' rather than a dealers' show, and partly because it represented the most advanced position British artists had taken by 1960, did not attract a great deal of critical or public attention at the time. Pop art, that quintessentially 1960s movement, had its origins in an exhibition as far back as 1956, and indeed in meetings of the Independent Group of the Institute of Contemporary Arts from 1952 onwards, although it did not achieve public recognition until the following decade. The movement arose out of an avidity for – and in the case of Peter Blake, who graduated from the Royal College of Art in 1956, a nostalgia for – the artefacts of popular culture. Although this began as a specifically British movement, the artefacts themselves were mainly American since these represented the most industrialized forms of mass culture. 'Pop' material – and the phrase was familiar to adepts before 1956 – represented, like jazz and science fiction, another alternative to the Mandarin values of fine art. Richard Hamilton, a key member of the Independent Group, wrote in 1956: 'What is needed is not a definition of meaningful imagery but the development of our perceptive potentialities to accept and utilize the continual enrichment of visual material'; in other words art must be an inclusive, not exclusive process, and should accept all the resources of popular culture as well as what had been previously narrowly defined as fine art.

In 1956 Richard Hamilton participated in an exhibition at the Whitechapel Art Gallery, *This is Tomorrow*, an exploration of the possibilities of integrating the arts of painter, sculptor and architect, by a series of jointly designed 'environments'. Hamilton contributed to the first of these, with a collection of pop and pulp magazine imagery summed up in his collage *Just What is it that Makes Today's Homes so Different, so Appealing?* (Plate 12), which offers virtually the entire iconography of the Pop Art movement. Hamilton's work was generally misunderstood at the time, however. In reply to an enquiry about his definition of Pop Art he wrote in a letter in January 1957 that it was

> Popular (designed for a mass audience)
> Transient (short-term solution)
> Expendable (easily forgotten)
> Low Cost
> Mass Produced
> Young (aimed at Youth)
> Witty
> Sexy
> Gimmicky
> Glamorous
> Big Business

This was a prescient programme for the vices and virtues of the 1960s, as the next volume of this series, *Too Much*, shows.

The privileged alienation of the American abstract artist, and his apparent independence from the ideological squabbles of Left or Right – which made his work so useful for purposes of cultural propaganda – had a romantic appeal to British would-be Bohemians, who had no sympathy with Mandarin tastes, but also rejected the somewhat puritanical attitudes of the Left. As the austerities of the 1950s eased, romanticism began to revive among the young: it was derived from images of Parisian Left-Bank bohemianism, Colin Wilson's Outsider, and increasingly from the style of the American Beats – the epithet 'Beatnik' dates it to after 4 October 1957. Jack Kerouac's novel *On the Road* was published in Britain in 1958, and in the same year there appeared the British edition of Gene Feldman and Max Gartenberg's selection *Protest: The Beat Generation and the Angry Young Men* – although Wain, Amis, Wilson, Braine, Donleavy, Hinde, Scott and Osborne rather paled beside Kerouac and Carl Solomon, and especially Allen Ginsberg's poem *Howl*, first published in 1956. The Beat style fell in easily with jazz bands and CND; the first British poet to pick up the new manner was Christopher Logue, who experimented with poetry and jazz at the Royal Court, and contributed 'protest' poems to *The New Reasoner* and *Universities and Left Review*.

Much of the early British beat movement was a matter of style rather than content, although it was an important prelude to the conformist non-conformity of the 1960s. A more serious shift however was taking place in poetry, or, at least, was being called for in the critical writings of A. Alvarez. Alvarez, himself a Fantasy Press Poet (No. 15), was among the first to express dissatisfaction with the impasse in which the Movement had left poetry. (His personal dissatisfaction with the structure of English cultural life caused him to give up a regular academic career in 1956 in preference for critical writing and journalism.) Alvarez summed up the history of twentieth-century English poetry as 'a series of negative feed-backs' – the 1930s against the Georgians, the Apocalyptics against Auden, the Movement against the Apocalyptics:

All three negative feed-backs work, in their different ways, to preserve the idea that life in England goes on much as it always has, give or take a few minor changes in the class system. The upper middle-class, or Tory, ideal – presented in its pure crystalline form by John Betjeman – may have given way to the predominantly lower middle-class, or Labour, ideal of the Movement and the Angries, but the concept of gentility still reigns supreme. And gentility is a belief that life is always more or less orderly, people always more or less polite, their emotions and habits more or less decent and more or less controllable; that God, in short, is more or less good.

In his view, the gentility principle had led to the 'academic nullity' of the Movement.

Alvarez, however, was caught in his own critical system, for the poetry he was trying to promote had itself to be a negative feed-back from the Movement, expressed by his chosen label 'the New Romanticism'. His study *The Shaping Spirit* (1958) is another attempt to come to terms with Modernism in British and American poetry, and argues that only the Americans had been able to make use of the discoveries of their exiled compatriots, Eliot and Pound. But Alvarez did find a potential way forward for British verse from the example of D. H. Lawrence. Lawrence, as we saw earlier, was already being rehabilitated by the cultural critics; now Alvarez was arguing that his poetry was 'as important as any poetry of our time'. His reasons show that the debate on Commitment was being taken a stage further. Lawrence's 'excellence comes from something that is rare at best, and now in the 1950s, well nigh lost: a complete truth to feeling. Lawrence is the foremost emotional realist of the century.'

There is a significant distinction to be made between realism as concerned with rendering the externals of contemporary life in a new and challenging way – important and refreshing though that was, as we have seen – and the 'emotional realism' that Alvarez is driving at. In the end realism is not enough, which is why, having made the break with Mandarin conventions, the Movement poets lost their impetus, the realist painters returned to experiment, and the dramatists turned to Brecht and the Theatre of the Absurd. Alvarez, in a 1959 essay titled 'The New Romanticism', argued that the tide was flowing strongly towards this renewed emotionalism:

the public fancy has been caught again and again by one brand of Romanticism or another: by Beckett's and Ionesco's investigations of, respectively, the agonies and fantasies of isolation by Anouilh's and Tennessee Williams's continual harping on youth, corruption and the ravages of sex; by Jimmy Porter who is like nothing so much as another young Werther, though with more aggression and a taste for party politics; there was even a minute classic *v.* romantics battle when the Movement fought the Mavericks; and then there was that extraordinary compendium of Romantic attitudes, *The Outsider*.

In the case of Alvarez, this new romanticism found its expression in his selection – but more accurately in his introduction to – the Penguin anthology *The New Poetry*, first published in 1962. The introduction, quoted earlier, argued that poetry must go 'Beyond the Gentility Principle'.

What, I suggest, has happened in the last half-century is that we are gradually being made to realize that all our lives, even those of the most genteel and enislanded, are influenced profoundly by forces which have nothing to do with gentility, decency or politeness. Theologians would call these forces evil, psychologists, perhaps, libido. Either way, they are the forces of disintegration which destroy the old standards of civilization. Their public faces are those of two world wars, of the concentration camps, of genocide, and the threat of nuclear war.

In truth, Alvarez's essay was considerably ahead of the poems he introduced, as he was forced to admit when a heavily revised version of the anthology was published in 1966. Deference to the historical facts of the new poetry of the 1950s led him to include six of the *New Lines* poets, excluding only Robert Conquest, John Holloway and Elizabeth Jennings, but he balanced the former Movement poets by calling to his aid two Americans, John Berryman and Robert Lowell, who more nearly represented the poetry he admired: 'poetry of immense skill and intelligence which coped openly with the quick of their experience, experience sometimes on the edge of disintegration and breakdown.' Of the British poets one *New Lines* contributor, Thom Gunn, had, with his appreciation of violence, given a lead to Ted Hughes and Peter Redgrove who were working towards Alvarez's prescription. Before 1960, however, it was mainly prescription, and his case was considerably strengthened in the second edition, when he revised the choice of individual poems, and was able to add work by two more Americans, Anne Sexton and Sylvia Plath, as well as a number of British poets, including Jon Silkin. Alvarez was unrepentant. His original introduction, he said, 'was, at least in part, an attempt to read the entrails and prophesy the direction poetry might soon take.' His claim to have been proved right is tested in *Too Much*.

While 'Suez' had an irritatory effect generally on the British intelligentsia, 'Hungary' was of crucial importance to the small group of intellectuals who were still members of the Communist Party of Great Britain at the beginning of 1956. In *The Craft of Letters in England* (1956) Laurence Lerner could claim that

'Marxism is so out of favour in Britain nowadays that to write about it at all may seem quaint', but the activities of Marxist intellectuals in the following years were to be an important stimulus in cultural life. That they became free to do so after years of isolation and fruitless efforts in various 'Peace' organizations set up by the Cominform was largely the result of Khrushchev's speech to the Twentieth Party Congress in February 1956. Khrushchev denounced Stalin and Stalinism and called for greater individual liberty, and for greater scope for debate in intellectual and artistic circles. In April 1956 the Cominform was dissolved on the grounds that it had exhausted its function. Khrushchev's speech was made in secret, but in June 1956 the American State Department published a full text. Behind the Iron Curtain – which the West rightly continued to regard as Iron whatever Khrushchev's proposals for greater autonomy for satellite countries – the liberalizing effects were too stimulating, first in Poland, where a Russian invasion was narrowly avoided, and then in Hungary where a full-scale revolt was brutally suppressed.

In Britain the effect of 1956 was to end the almost automatic connection between being a Marxist, and being a member of the Communist Party. Questioning of the official party line began in the Historians' Group of the Communist Party, a meeting-point for intellectuals whose concern with the past history of the party led them to confront present reality: what *had* happened under Stalin, and why should it have been covered up? What *had* the British party been doing between 1939 and 1941, when the official line was to oppose the war with Germany? In July 1956, frustrated by their inability to open up a debate in party publications – the *Daily Worker*, *World News*, *Modern Quarterly* and *Labour Monthly* – two members of the Historians' Group, John Saville and E. P. Thompson, published a small cyclostyled magazine, *The Reasoner*. Contributors included Doris Lessing, Ronald Meek, Hyman Levy, Rodney Hilton and G. D. H. Cole. The Party bureaucracy ordered the editors to cease publication but they carried on, and in their third issue in November called for a

Culture and Society

Russian withdrawal from Hungary, just as the British Communist Party was officially endorsing the intervention. Saville and Thompson were disciplined by the Party, and resigned, as did nearly 7,000 others – one fifth of its membership. As a sop to the intellectuals, an enquiry was held into Inner Party Democracy, but at a special Congress held in April 1957 the official hard line against the intellectuals was reinforced, and the resignations, among them that of Christopher Hill, continued.

As a focus for this now extra-Party opposition, Saville and Thompson launched *The New Reasoner: A Quarterly Journal of Socialist Humanism* in the summer of 1957. Although rising from what Thompson later called 'the shambles of intellectual disgrace and moral collapse' of the British Communist Party, *The New Reasoner* did not follow the previous path of Communist apostates and switch to violent opposition. Its first editorial proclaimed:

We have no desire to break impetuously with the Marxist and Communist tradition in Britain. On the contrary, we believe that this tradition, which stems from such men as William Morris and Tom Mann, and which later found expressions in the cultural field, in such journals as *Left Review* and *Modern Quarterly*, is in need of rediscovery and re-affirmation.

This concern with culture was to be an important theme in the following years although, with the exception of some short stories by Doris Lessing, the literary contributions to *The New Reasoner* were generally mediocre.

At the same time as *The New Reasoner* was launched, another magazine with parallel concerns also appeared, the *Universities and Left Review*, first published from Oxford in Spring 1957, and edited by four Oxford graduates, Stuart Hall, Gabriel Pearson, Ralph Samuel and Charles Taylor. Here disaffection with the Labour Party was as important as distrust of the Communist. David Marquand commented in the first number:

Occasionally, as in the recent Suez Crisis, [Labour's] leaders can appear to speak with the old voice of righteousness, sending delicious draughts of adrenalin through the bloodstream, spurring their listeners to yell 'Fascist' at mounted policemen. But already that feeling is over. The Party has returned to its normal self.

Distrust of party politics was a well-established tradition among the cynical students of the early 1950s. The *Universities and Left Review* accepted that, and tried to find in the cultural field a substitute for the aridities of party political debate:

> it was inevitable that the post-war generation should identify social-ism at worst with the barbarities of Stalinist Russia, at best with the low-pressure society of Welfare Britain: a society in which creative, popular and intellectual initiative was at low ebb, bureaucracy – particularly in administration, trade unions, and the nationalized industries – at full flood.
>
> . . . Given the feeble level of political controversy, and its interne-cine character, who could argue with the young intellectuals, when they said – they are still saying it, with something of relief and something of regret – that politics was not 'about them'.

Universities and Left Review and *The New Reasoner* ran in parallel, with many cross-contributions, until 1959, when it became obvious that their efforts would be more effective if combined; and in December 1959 the *New Left Review* was launched, edited by Stuart Hall, with an editorial board merged from the founding magazines. The *New Left Review* was intended to be 'more than a journal, but not quite a movement' and, just as its title echoes that of the *Left Review* of the 1930s, its organization took a leaf out of that of the Left Book Club, by organizing local discussion groups, of which there were forty-two by the end of 1960. In 1958 a coffee-bar, *The Partisan*, was opened at 7 Carlisle Street, in Soho. The editorial offices were above, and in May 1959 appear to have suffered the attentions of the Secret Service when a mysterious burglar stole the magazine's records and subscription list. In 1960 New Left Books were launched, the first suitably titled *Out of Apathy*.

The New Left began as a movement of intellectuals, and it is not surprising that most of its leaders were academics, univers-ities being their only source of employment outside journalism or the BBC. Several, however, like Thompson and Raymond Williams who joined the editorial board of the *New Left Review* on its creation, worked in university extension schemes and adult education courses, and the social origins of the activists were generally working or lower middle class. They were therefore a special kind of *clericus*, having managed to rise meritocratically before the Butler Education Act of 1944 widened educational opportunities. Many of the beneficiaries of the 1944 Act felt the same social displacement as their predecessors, and so provided a constituency for the now politically-disenchanted older generation. Many of the new recruits in turn became academics, and the movement remained one of intellectuals, with a theoretical rather than practical influence in politics until the surge of radical feeling in 1968.

Disenchantment with party politics was by no means confined to ex-Communists, and the New Left found itself with some unusual allies in the one political cause that genuinely stirred people in the 1950s, the Campaign for Nuclear Disarmament. The campaign, in so far as it succeeded at all, was a success precisely because it was a single issue, non-party movement. It had its origins in the nuclear scare at the time of Suez, and was given a powerful stimulus by the launching of Sputnik. J. B. Priestley's article in the *New Statesman* of 2 November 1957, 'Britain and the Nuclear Bombs', crystallized the thoughts of several public men, chiefly non-party politicians, and the campaign was launched at a public meeting at Conway Hall in London on 17 February 1958, addressed by Priestley, the philosopher Bertrand Russell, the socialist historian A. J. P. Taylor, the Labour MP Michael Foot, and the right-wing military thinker Sir Stephen King-Hall. The pacifist Canon Collins was another prominent member of CND's committee. The meeting was attended by 5,000 people, who applauded disparaging references to the Labour Party as happily as they applauded rude remarks about the Tory government. The *New Statesman* was an ardent supporter of the campaign, and reported in May 1958 that

201

official circles are confused and alarmed about the Campaign for Nuclear Disarmament because it is a movement of a new pattern. It is unprecedented because it has no political group behind it; no showman's drum beats it up; it has no leaders serving personal ambitions; it is not inspired or indeed supported by the Communist Party, which is embarrassed by the obvious retort that the Soviet Union should also abandon nuclear weapons.

The case of CND – that Britain should recognize her position as a second-class power and renounce the use of nuclear weapons – was sufficiently broad to encompass both pacifists and non-pacifists, Communists and anti-Communists; rallies and meetings were a welcome change from the apathetic state of conventional politics. The cheerful amateurism of the organization attracted young people and gave them a chance to do something without abandoning their cynicism about professional politicians. Here at last was a focus for the energies frustrated by the Cold War abroad and the bureaucratic Welfare State at home. At Easter 1958 there was the first of the annual pilgrimages between London and the nuclear weapons research station at Aldermaston, a four-day march that gave physical expression to protest – and was a good way to spend the Easter holidays. The march justified blue jeans and black sweaters, and provided a welcoming audience for jazz bands, skiffle groups and folk singers. It occasioned poetry readings, the Free Cinema film *March to Aldermaston* (1958) and play performances – David Campton's three playlets *A View from the Brink* were performed on the 1960 march in church halls along the route while the marchers rested in their sleeping-bags. Alan Brien described the delights of the march in the *Spectator*: 'a tremendous stimulation of ideas and arguments and witticisms and friendships and love affairs. Perhaps it would be more tactful to keep this revelation a secret – but the Aldermaston March is the rare phenomenon of a physical and social pleasure which yet has an intellectual and moral justification.'

The problem of CND's virtues was that they failed to move either the professional politicians or, for that matter, those not committed to CND. At the end of 1958 the novelist Mervyn Jones commented in *The New Reasoner*: 'the Campaign owed its initial *élan* to its having roused the politically unattached. But some of them are already tiring, and anyway most of them are middle-class. I have nothing against the middle class, but the working class happens to be more numerous, and the failure to rouse it on a sufficient scale remains the Campaign's chief weakness.' In the end the campaign had to tackle party politics, and though the small Liberal Party accepted disarmament, the primary target had to be the Labour Party. After the Labour defeat in October 1959 the party was divided on disarmament and nationalization, for, while the New Left were advanced as far as disarmament was concerned, they sternly resisted Gaitskell's attempts to alter the constitution. Gaitskell in turn resisted disarmament, but at the Labour Party conference in October 1960 Frank Cousins, leader of the Transport and General Workers' Union, succeeded in getting a motion passed in favour of unilateral nuclear disarmament, against the opposition of the majority of MPs and the Labour Party's national executive. This however proved to be a political high point for the movement, for the vote was reversed the following year. CND itself split in October 1960 when Bertrand Russell resigned because of disagreements with Canon Collins over 'direct action', and went off to form the more militant Committee of 100.

Such, then, was the political background to the debates that began to go on around those key-words: Establishment and Commitment. The discussion of the Establishment was the broader of the two, as indeed was the term itself. The idea of social government through an unofficial institution called the Establishment had been in existence for a long time; the word goes back in its cultural context to the starting-point for discussion of contemporary British culture – the writings of Matthew Arnold – and it is in effect an extension both of the normally competitive relationships of generations, and the conspiracy theory of literary politics. The Conservative political commentator, Henry Fairlie, brought the word into common currency with an article in the *Spectator* of 23 September 1955 on the defections of the spies Burgess and Maclean, in which he claimed (rightly, it would now appear) that the men had been protected by 'the Establishment'.

As with literary conspiracies, the operation of the Establishment is more obvious to those outside than those within it. F. R. Leavis had a very clear idea of how it worked, as he told the *Listener* in November 1956:

the establishment in my (the obvious) sense of the word, is to be seen, I should say, in those who have the institutional positions and the power in the institutional system, and, by all the signs, stand solidly together – those, for instance, who, when the *Listener* prints a Third Programme talk of theirs, get (as Mr [John] Holloway did for his first talk) an editorial comment at the beginning of the number saying what an important service they are performing, and an appreciative note from the official critic at the end.

Belief in the existence of an exclusive and manipulative Establishment was encouraged in its critics by the class consciousness that remained such a powerful element in English life – class consciousness, or more accurately, snobbery. The snobbery that 'runs riot like the bay tree and throttles every kind of personality with its ivy tendrils', according to the anonymous author of a *New Statesman* profile of Cyril Connolly, accusing Connolly of the same. Quick to exploit a trend, the advertising industry launched a new campaign to promote the Establishment's house journal in February 1957 with the slogan 'Top People take *The Times*'.

'Is there a Power Elite?' asked the *Twentieth Century* magazine in October 1957, and the answer from A. J. P. Taylor, Anthony Hartley and Philip Toynbee among others was yes, and an élite very much the same as that intellectual aristocracy that had used the unifying influences of the public schools and Oxbridge to administer society for the past 150 years. Philip Toynbee pointed out that the Labour government of 1945–51 was not really an exception, for while 'the *political* power of the English upper class was genuinely suspended during the Labour years . . . the *social* power of that class was almost untouched, and will remain so until a genuine social revolution has been accomplished here.'

By 1958 the topic was sufficiently popular to merit a brief investigation on Independent Television, with Lord Boothby and Lady Violet Bonham Carter as the experts, and Paul Johnson and John Collet as the critics. J. B. Priestley weighed in with *Topside, or the Future of England*, which recorded the self-adaptation of the ruling class to 1945 through becoming a meritocracy with no values other than a belief in the value of staying on top. Finally, in 1959, the Establishment received a full-length discussion in a collection of essays under that title, edited by Hugh Thomas, with John Vaizey on public schools, Simon Raven on the army, Thomas Balogh on the Civil Service, Victor Sandelson on City business, Christopher Hollis on Parliament, and Henry Fairlie on the BBC.

The number of constituent elements in *The Establishment*, and the spread of political convictions of the contributors from Left to Right shows that Henry Fairlie could justifiably protest that by 1959 the term had been debased by over-use to meaning for most people no more than 'those in positions of power they happen to dislike most'. (By extension, however, the very popularity of the phrase showed the need for such a cliché.) Fairlie produced a more subtle description of the influence of the Establishment:

The idea of the Establishment is concerned less with the actual exercise of power than with the established bodies of prevailing opinion which powerfully, and not always openly, influence its exercise. The Establishment is not a power élite. If its members have any connections with power blocks in society, it is not these connections which give them their particular influence. If in their other activities they represent actual interests, it is not their representation of these interests which make them members of the Establishment. Indeed, the one significant fact about the Establishment is that it represents nothing in the national life. It has its roots in no class and no interest; it responds to no deep-seated national instinct. It is this rootlessness which is seen by its defenders as its main virtue, and by its opponents as its most depressing fault. Its defenders have, of course, found a euphemism for this rootlessness: they call it disinterestedness. It must be disinterested, they argue, precisely because it represents nothing.

Fairlie is protesting at the nullity of political life produced by the post-war consensus, a consensus reflected in the declining power of politicians *vis à vis* the bureaucrats and administrators – C. P. Snow's New Men, who administer rather than lead, and whose power extends from the Civil Service into the universities and the increasingly bureaucratized institutions of the arts.

Bureaucrats must be trained to administer their paper empires, and the Establishment had to hand a perfect instrument for that purpose: the public schools. The public schools were unaffected by the Education Act of 1944, except in so far as middle-class parents were partially relieved of the cost of supporting their children at university which made a public school education an even better investment. John Vaizey (later Lord Vaizey) calculated that there were no more than twenty public schools of true significance, with 100 more imitating them, to which the Establishment sent its children. High fees and a boarding education reinforced the separateness of this élite. The emphasis was on 'leadership' and 'tradition', virtues which once had maintained a territorial Empire. But the training for leadership was actually training for service in a strict hierarchy. Public schools might produce a few hot-house intellectuals, but in the main the public school product was conformist, socially conscious and repressed.

The chief advantage of a public school education has always been that it smooths the path to Oxford or Cambridge, and once there the Establishment child would encounter a broader social spectrum than at his school, though at least half the undergraduate population came from similar institutions. He might even meet a non-conforming teacher. The American sociologist, Norman Birnbaum, who found a job at the London School of Economics after McCarthyite pressure caused him to leave the United States, admitted in the *Universities and Left*

Review in 1958 that British universities did employ the occasional Communist or Marxist, but 'we enjoy a freedom mainly formal. Informal, but terribly effective, ideological pressures in fact limit our freedom. We are, formally, quite free to choose problems to investigate and equally free to formulate our conclusions. Informally, but practically, neither choice nor conclusion are free.' Such an ideologically frank protest was rare; the assumptions behind university education were not questioned, since the universities were doing what appeared to be their job. As Birnbaum put it: 'We think we are *educating* students to *understand* society; in most cases, we are *training* them to *manipulate* it.'

Experience in the manipulation of institutions was provided by the leisure activities of Oxford and Cambridge even more vigorously than by their tutorials. Both universities had excellent facilities for theatre and journalism, and it was a natural assumption that success (or even experience) in these fields was as valuable as a degree when the time came to make the short journey to London, to the BBC, Fleet Street, or even occasionally to practising the arts themselves. Undergraduate politics were a similar convenient means of making connections (and to be fair, enemies) that would last for life. Oxbridge was also the place in which non-public school recruits to the Establishment (like grammar-schoolboy National Service officers) could assimilate the appropriate manners and dress. The majority were glad to take advantage of their privilege, though there was the occasional renegade. Raymond Williams, a pre-war undergraduate who completed his Cambridge degree in 1946 after serving (as an officer) in the army, was the son of a railway worker. He commented that it was a swift passage from a weekly wage-earning family to an old university. 'It is then less the injustice of the British class system than its stupidity that really strikes one.'

Williams's pre-war experience may disqualify him as an example; in 1960 Dennis Potter's *The Glittering Coffin* tried to distil the resentment that Oxford could produce among many more recent scholarship boys:

the flowing dark gowns, coloured chapel glass, cavalry twill and cut-glass accents seem to have no links with the crowded Cowley-bound buses. The bells crash across those gentle, damp Sunday evenings, and the world seems of a sudden a mellow and dedicated place. 'Oxford is not a place', said a quiveringly fragile, aristocratic don at one college, in an alcoholic address to the gathered freshmen, 'but a way of life.' Looking at this decidedly odd creature swaying nervously with the college port, frightened grammar schoolboys could only agree. The magic soon wears off, however.

Potter was the son of a coal-miner, and he published *The Glittering Coffin* while still an undergraduate at New College. His own feelings were heightened by his embarrassment over his participation in a television investigation by Christopher Mayhew for the BBC, 'Does Class Matter?' He was invited to repeat what he had already written in the *New Statesman* about the difficulties of working-class entrants to middle-class ways who 'cannot stomach the two languages that sharply divide up the year, the torn loyalties and perpetual adjustments, the huge chasm between the classes'. His remarks were picked up by *Reynolds News* which headlined 'Miner's Son at Oxford Ashamed of Home. The Boy who Kept His Father Secret'. (The incident was dramatized in Potter's 1965 television play *Stand Up, Nigel Barton*.)

However much Dennis Potter might protest at the social influences of Oxford, though, his articles were written for the *New Statesman*, and it is likely that *The Glittering Coffin* was read chiefly by members of the middle class. 'Culture' remained a middle-class province, even after there had been a significant intake of new recruits, as Raymond Williams pointed out in *The Long Revolution* (1961). Instead of bridging the chasm, the middle class itself became divided between a majority and minority culture.

The appearance of contributors from new social groups within the culture, which has attracted attention in recent years, has been normally through the institutions of this minority. Most of the new writers from families of clerical and industrial workers are in fact not being read by the social groups from which they come, but the dissident middle class. The expanding audience, for novels and plays, certainly includes members of new social groups, but in general they are simply being absorbed into the existing majority public. The danger of this situation is that the minority public may soon be the only identifiable group with an evident and particular social affiliation – defined largely through university education.

A 'university education', meanwhile, had to be at Oxford or Cambridge to obtain maximum advantage for the potential recruit to the Establishment. This was obvious where formal institutions were concerned, but the links between Oxbridge and London operated on an almost unconscious level: in 1960 Faber and Faber launched a new series of anthologies to promote the work of new writers; of the six contributors to the first volume of *Introduction* half came from Oxford, half from Cambridge. In 1963 a group of rising writers, broadcasters and journalists published a joint account of what had been their formative years, 1945 to 1951. The contributors to *The Age of Austerity* all came from Oxford or Cambridge – and many of them have continued to rise within our contemporary Establishment.

The most directly influential cultural institution for an Oxbridge graduate to enter was the BBC. The BBC had the greatest potential for producing a homogeneous, middlebrow society, and in the middle 1950s seemed to have turned the social solidarity of wartime into a respectful deference for authority and tradition. 'The Royal Family' – a popular phrase with the BBC – suggests just the domesticated virtues it tended to recommend. The BBC tolerated dissent and modest controversy because its discussion programmes were designed to produce synthetic debates that muffled issues between balancing statements; just as only 'acceptable' speakers were allowed to take part in current affairs programmes, only artists and critics who had already succeeded contributed on the arts. Henry Fairlie wrote in *The Establishment*: 'It is a significant comment on the confused state of British opinion that in recent years the BBC has no more enthusiastic defenders than the

Labour Party, although it has done more than any other body to buttress the most conservative institutions in the country, to create and perpetuate reverence for the orders, the privileges and the mysteries of a conservative society.' The BBC, however, appeared less homogeneous to insiders than to outsiders. Richard Hoggart reported in the *Universities and Left Review*:

One commonly hears BBC workers on the floor (producers, writers, editors) speak about the higher officials in a way which recalls the Other Ranks of the Armed Forces discussing the upper ranks. And there is often a wide difference in background. The upper echelons, we hear, are the Corporation's 'career administrators' – what can they know of the imaginative side of script-writing and production, or of the high-pressure competition in sports or variety programmes? . . . Or one is told that the 'Oxford/Cambridge' axis is too powerful. With all this one hears that, to avoid Establishment repercussions, the BBC will not take enough chances; that 'when in doubt, cut it out' is the axiom.

The BBC, as a healthy and vigorous Establishment, knew that it had to adapt to changing circumstances if it was to survive. Having lost the battle to prevent the introduction of commercial television, it was able to use its rival's greater liveliness to justify an unbending on its own part – though in the early days, as Richard Hoggart pointed out, 'great numbers of people simply assume that the BBC is "Them". By contrast, commercial television is – or seems to be more nearly – "Us".' Independent Television's early current affairs programmes, *Free Speech*, *Under Fire*, *This Week*, *What the Papers Say* had a refreshing effect on the BBC's own output. The Suez crisis was important to both organizations in establishing their credentials as formally independent commentators. They gradually freed themselves of the 'fourteen-day rule' which limited the broadcasting of all but official pronouncements on matters of public controversy, the BBC most notably by insisting that Gaitskell should have his say following Eden's statement on Egypt on 3 November 1956.

Competition seems to have done the BBC good. In 1957 the lively current affairs programme *Tonight* was launched, originally as a means of filling the period between six and seven in the evening when ITV had tried to steal a march on the BBC by beginning broadcasting early. The expansion of television, however, led to a curtailment of radio, particularly in the Third Programme, which had its hours cut in October 1957. This caused such alarm among the Third's tiny audience that a campaign was started to prevent the Third being closed down altogether. There was some cultural compensation when in February 1958 BBC-TV launched the arts fortnightly *Monitor* presented by Huw Weldon and offering early opportunities for experience to film directors like Ken Russell and John Schlesinger. In 1959 a whole new era began for the BBC when Hugh Carlton Greene was appointed Director-General.

That the BBC *was* able to change its identity from the stuffy institution it was in the early 1950s to the more adventurous organization that it became in the 1960s suggests both that Establishments are adaptable, and that their influences may not always be a bad thing. But the BBC changed very slowly and, though it was responsible for transmitting them to a much wider audience, it was responding to new ideas rather than originating them. The protestors against the Establishment were mainly young writers, artists and journalists who were, many of them, on the way to becoming part of the Establishment themselves. Anti-Establishment feeling was part of the 'anger' of the times and might be dismissed as no more than frustrated ambition if there were not concrete evidence that an Establishment, indeed a series of Establishments, existed. In his study *Elites and Society* (1964), T. B. Bottomore saw the problem as affecting more than Britain:

If we now look at the Western democracies of the present day we shall see that, while they conform well with the competition model of democracy, they are deficient in respect of these other conditions: there is not a rapid circulation of the personnel of the élites, which are

211

still recruited predominantly from the upper class of society; the outlook of the élites has changed only slowly and the old aristocratic view of the functions is kept alive by their recruitment from the upper class, by the élite theories themselves, and by the prevailing social doctrines of 'getting on' and reaching 'the top'; and lastly, the 'levelling' of conditions in Western societies has gone on so slowly that the rulers are still very sharply distinguished from the ruled.

In Britain the sociologist W. L. Guttsman – almost certainly inspired by the general discussion that had been going on about the existence of an Establishment since 1955 – published an elaborate survey in *The British Political Elite* (1963). He concluded that there had been a gradual concentration of greater power in fewer hands in government and industry, in spite of the expansion of the activities of both:

In the cultural and social field also, large organizations and great enterprises are controlled by a constantly decreasing total of directors and governors. Such tendencies can be clearly observed in most spheres of the 'cultural' life. In publishing, concentration is most marked in the magazine field where two vast enterprises share today almost the whole market. In the theatre world, the ownership of a declining number of houses rests in few hands, and with ownership goes, ultimately, effective artistic control. Film production and distribution is likewise heavily concentrated. Outside the commercial sphere, grant-giving bodies, especially the Arts Council, have great strategic power. The BBC is still the greatest of the mass-media enjoying a partial monopoly. ITV, with one foot in the commercial world and with the other in the world of culture and entertainment, occupies a similar position.

Guttsman concluded that, although the traditional aristocracy had declined in power, the upper middle class had not; indeed the involvement of academics and civil servants in decision-making was on the increase. It was these who occupied most of the positions of power, and who through private education were able to pass it on to their sons. Noel Annan's intellectual aristocracy was certainly showing no sign of dying out.

As a footnote to this discussion, it is worth pointing out that the Establishment had an infallible means of self-perpetuation, and self-defence. It simply absorbed its critics, or else set them up as a rival Establishment. John Wain explained that misleading label Angry Young Man:

In England there is a time-honoured method of dealing with opposition. First of all, you try to squash it; then, if it refuses to be squashed, you institutionalize it. Give it a name, turn it into an institution, and you find yourself absolved for ever from the responsibility to answer its criticisms.

The Angry Young Man, though partially neutralized by the system, was an important progenitor of the debate that occupied a somewhat narrower band of people in the late 1950s: the question of Commitment. The idea of being *engagé* figured strongly in the post-war writings of Jean-Paul Sartre, but the issue in France was virtually exhausted before Commitment became a point of discussion in England. A key document is Lindsay Anderson's essay 'Stand Up! Stand Up!' published in the Autumn 1956 issue of *Sight and Sound* – it is significant that this essay should appear in a film magazine and not a literary journal. Anderson tries to focus the undifferentiated anger of John Osborne:

The young people who respond so unmistakably to *Look Back In Anger* are responding to its outspoken attacks on certain venerable sacred cows, and also to its bitter impatience with the moral vacuum in which they feel public life, and cultural life, is today being conducted. The class resentment is only part of it. If there 'aren't any good, brave causes left' (or if that is the feeling in the air) the fault is not so much that of the Right, the Tory element in politics and art, as of the Left, the progressives, the Liberals in the best sense of that long-suffering word. The manner in which the British political Left has muffed its chance to capture the imagination and allegiance of the nation is too obvious to need dwelling on: from the peaceful revolution of '45 to 'You Can Trust Mr Attlee', and Mr Gaitskell in pin-stripe trousers helping with the family washing-up, the descent has been sure, steady, and well publicized. Less easily – or at least less often – remarked has been the steady draining away of vitality from what we may call the cultural Left, its increasing modishness, and its more and more marked aversion from emotional simplicity or moral commitment.

Anderson's article was reprinted in the first number of *Universities and Left Review* as 'Commitment in Cinema Criticism', alongside Peter De Francia on 'Commitment in Art Criticism', and Commitment rapidly became the watchword of the New Left.

Inevitably, opposition to the Old Left was the concomitant of Commitment, for the Labour Party was as much a target for criticism as Whitehall or the BBC. E. P. Thompson made the connection in *The New Reasoner*: 'It is the bankruptcy of the orthodoxies of the Old Left, and particularly their imprisonment within the framework of Cold War ideology and strategy, which has contributed to the characteristic political consciousness of the post-war generation – the sense of impotence in the face of the Establishment.' The paradox in the relations between the Old and New Left was that, in terms of pure politics, the New were more conservative than the Old; it was they who resisted the social-democratic arguments of Anthony Crosland in *The Future of Socialism* (1958) and Gaitskell's attempts to revise the Labour Party's constitution.

The reintroduction of a political dimension to literary values had no appeal to Cold War purists of the Movement like Robert Conquest, who dismissed the new fashion as a hangover from Stalinism:

The few writers who 'grapple with great public issues' – i.e. who present intolerable over-generalizations instead of realities – are mainly either near-Communists or people who regard everything of which they disapprove as the results of a vast social conspiracy – not to put too fine a point on it, crackpots. The train of thought in political commitment is as follows: (1) I am against injustice, (2) therefore I am a 'socialist', (3) because 'socialism' is the way to prevent oppression any action to preserve it is justified, (4) including injustice.

In reality, the New Left was very wary of involvement in practical politics, and for reasons that Robert Conquest's own

experience in poetry might have led him to appreciate: just as
the Movement poets reacted against the poetic principles
derived from the 1930s, so the New Left found that the
Establishment, both literary and political, was dominated by
men of the 1930s. As John Mander has pointed out in *The
Writer and Commitment* (1961): 'In the political field, especially
on the Left, the truth of this is striking. Mr Hugh Gaitskell, Mr
Richard Crossman, Mr Tom Driberg were all near contemporaries of Auden at Oxford.' For those in the New Left who were
ex-Communists, the disillusion that had struck so many in 1939
had not been felt until 1956 – but the result was the same. E. P.
Thompson wrote in the first number of *Universities and Left
Review* that there was a gap between the intellectuals' ideals
and what could be achieved. 'How, then, are we to leap the
gap? I no longer believe that this is accomplished by joining
anything.' Intellectuals who join the Labour Party 'seem to get
swallowed up in seas of expediency. They concern themselves
not with what is potential but with what is in the short-term,
politically practicable.'

Disillusion with past practical politics, combined with frustration at the present bureaucratic organization of the trades
unions and the Labour Party – the Labour Establishment –
meant that the political energy of the New Left had to find a
fresh channel. It also meant that while in practical terms
Socialism lost ground, as the General Election of 1959 demonstrated, the political thinkers of the New Left had no way of
transmitting their ideas into political practice. *Conviction*,
MacGibbon & Kee's follow-up in 1958 to *Declaration*, edited
by Norman MacKenzie, was a far more coherent collection
than its predecessor; the unresolved anger of *Declaration* was
replaced by closely argued essays calling for a rethought and
recommitted Socialism, but as the Campaign for Nuclear Disarmament showed, the late 1950s were a period of anti-politics.
Instead of joining things, the New Left put its energies into
sociology and cultural criticism.

Sociology was a relatively underdeveloped subject in Britain
during the 1950s, especially at Oxford and Cambridge. Its

principal stronghold was at the London School of Economics, and the subject had expanded with the post-war expansion of the LSE where, significantly, it proved an attractive subject to working-class and lower middle-class students. From the London School of Economics the subject spread to the provincial universities, where lectureships were established, with professorships (and correspondingly larger departments) at Leeds, Nottingham, Birmingham and Liverpool. In the context of the cultural patterns in Britain in the 1950s, Oxford and Cambridge's resistance to sociology was almost predictable.

It is symptomatic of the underdeveloped state of sociology that the two most important works of the period were cultural studies produced by literary critics, not sociologists: Richard Hoggart's *The Uses of Literacy* (1957) and Raymond Williams's *Culture and Society* (1958). These were independent studies and, though both writers were contributors to *Conviction*, they did not meet until 1960. Jointly, however, these studies became the most influential cultural investigations of the 1950s – and not only for the New Left. Apart from the intrinsic interest of the subject, it is easy to see why Hoggart's book should have such appeal. It opens with a warm and personal account of working-class life in the urban North of England in the 1920s and 1930s. It is in the tradition of Orwell, and shares some of Orwell's nostalgia for the apparent solidarity of working-class existence, whose core is 'a sense of the personal, the concrete, the local: it is embodied in the idea of first, the family, and second, the neighbourhood.'

Insofar as Hoggart's account is based on his own childhood, *The Uses of Literacy* can even be linked to the childhood reminiscences popular with contemporary novelists, but the lost innocence of Hoggart's scholarship boy could be more readily identified with than L. P. Hartley's go-between, since many of his readers now found themselves where Hoggart had been, 'at the friction point of two cultures'. Hoggart's concern for the problems and responsibilities of those, like Dennis Potter, for instance, who had been educated away from their class, is the second theme of the book, and he sees their

216

responsibilities as changing. With the political achievement of the Welfare State behind them, the greatest need for the 'saving remnant' of the working class is

> to reassess the position, to realise that the ideas for which their predecessors worked are in danger of being lost, that material improvements can be used so as to incline the body of working-people to accept a mean form of materialism as a social philosophy. If the active minority continue to allow themselves exclusively to think of immediate political and economic objectives, the pass will be sold, culturally, behind their backs.

This concern for cultural, rather than political values, brings Hoggart to his final theme, one familiar to the 1950s – the New Barbarism (Hoggart's phrase is 'shining barbarism') of admass culture spreading through television, imported teenage tastes from America, pop songs, entertainment and pulp literature aimed at the lowest common denominator, 'the ceaseless exploitation of a hollow brightness', and 'sex in shiny packets'. A proper concern for culture, the right use of literacy, was the only defence.

Raymond Williams's *Culture and Society* is a quasi-historical rather than quasi-sociological study, tracing the use of certain concepts, '*industry, democracy, class, art* and *culture*' from 1780 to 1950. The concern for words, and the concern for culture, betray the Leavisite origins of his approach, and Williams acknowledges his own short-lived magazine *Politics and Letters* as a starting-point. But the end date of 1950 shows that he has a contemporary purpose, and his choice of material reveals contemporary interest. Like Hoggart, he writes respectfully of D. H. Lawrence, an early exile from the working class who, in the 1950s, begins to re-emerge from his wartime unpopularity as a new hero of the Left. Lawrence opens Williams's modern section, and Orwell closes it. In a final section Williams becomes openly polemical.

Williams, like Hoggart, is involved with the idea of community, and like Hoggart he identifies communal virtues with his

217

own experience of working-class life. He acknowledges the tendency of cultural critics, from Goldsmith in *The Deserted Village* (1770) onwards, to place their golden age at a point just beyond accurate reminiscence, but nonetheless finds many of the now lost virtues present in his own boyhood in the 1930s. His ideal is a *common* culture, but

> this is not possible until it is realized that a transmission [of ideas] is always an offering, and that this fact must determine its mood: it is not an attempt to dominate, but to communicate, to achieve reception and response. Active reception, and living response, depend in turn on an effective community of experience, and their quality, as certainly, depends on a recognition of practical equality. The inequalities of many kinds which still divide our community make effective communication difficult or impossible.

The principal division, in cultural terms, which Williams identifies, is between the working-class ethic of solidarity, and the middle-class ethic of service. He admires the service that has done so much to limit the depredations and injustices of capitalism, but service is uncreative – and in explaining why, Williams reveals his social alienation:

> I was not trained to this ethic, and when I encountered it, in late adolescence, I had to spend a lot of time trying to understand it, through men whom I respected and who had been formed by it. The criticism I now make of it is in this kind of good faith. It seems to me inadequate because in practice it serves, at every level, to maintain and confirm the *status quo*. This was wrong for me, because the *status quo*, in practice, was a denial of equity to the men and women among whom I had grown up, the lower servants, whose lives were governed by the existing distributions of property, remuneration, education, and respect.

And, Raymond Williams concludes, with an apparently unconscious use of another key-word, 'one cannot in conscience then become, when invited, an upper servant in an establishment that one thus radically disapproves'. The invitation to climb the educational ladder to Oxford or Cambridge is open to individuals only, and the working-class scholarship boy (like Williams) should accept it. 'But he cannot then be expected to agree that such an opportunity constitutes a sufficient educational reform.'

Williams's argument shows a more subtle understanding of the relations between classes, and the cultural problems they create, than any mechanical Marxism; in 1960 he attempted a fictional, though partly autobiographical, treatment in his novel *Border Country*. *Culture and Society* prompted a great deal of discussion – in 1961 Williams said that he had read 50,000 words of comment on the book. *The Long Revolution* (1961) was planned as a continuation of *Culture and Society*: 'questions in the theory of culture, historical analysis of certain cultural institutions and forms, and problems of meaning and action in our contemporary situation' – a summary that is virtually a complete plan of research for the New Left – and culture remains central to his arguments:

The condition of cultural growth must be that varying elements are at least equally available, and that new and unfamiliar things must be offered steadily over a long period, if they are to have a reasonable chance of acceptance. Policies of this degree of responsibility seem impossible in our present cultural organization. The encouragement of valuable elements is restricted to what is little more than a defensive holding operation, which is better than nothing, but hardly likely to make any general change. The rest of the field is left to the market, and not even to the free play of the market, for the amounts of capital involved in financing our major cultural institutions restrict entry to a few powerful groups, so that both production and distribution are effectively in very few hands.

The New Left is often criticized for its lack of political achievements, but the great expansion of the operations of the Arts Council after the Labour Party regained power in 1964 was at least in part a result of arguments such as that of Williams. In 1960 Arnold Wesker made a more direct attempt to make the labour movement aware of its cultural responsibilities by starting a drive for trades union support for the arts. Resolution 42 at the 1960 TUC conference recognizes that responsibility, although, as the following volume *Too Much* describes, 'Centre 42', which arose from it, was finally to prove unsuccessful.

Both *The Use of Literacy* and *Culture and Society* celebrate an idea of wholeness, of an undivided community that might produce unalienated artists and an unalienated art. The ideal is derived from aspects of working-class life as Hoggart and Williams had experienced it, but the problem remains of how such an ideal might be translated into actuality. Culture was the medium, but as Hoggart's protests against the New Barbarism show, culture could corrupt. Nor was writing about the working class necessarily a way to recover their virtues, as John Mander pointed out:

Many working-class novels and plays in the past reflected precisely that closed, static, fatalistic view of the world which was the reaction of the working class to its capitalist environment. Strictly speaking, nothing could be more anti-Socialist than Miss Littlewood's sentimentalizing of this way of thinking. It is the guarantee of the Establishment, the very foundation of Conservative political success; for it amounts to an abdication of social responsibility on the part of the working class.

On these grounds, neither *A Taste of Honey*, *Room at the Top*, nor *Look Back in Anger* were responsible contributions either. Reviewing Clancy Sigal's semi-documentary in the manner of Orwell, *Weekend in Dinlock* (1960), Angus Wilson put his finger on why the New Left were in danger of over-sentimentalizing the working class:

Most of them are working-class in origin, but that only gives them a new guilt. How are they to compound for the gulf in communication that has sprung up between them and the class they came from? By not wholly forsaking the old primitive high tea and kipper gods of their forefathers. Many of them – Mr Sigal is one – see the sentimentality of this, but they are still tied to the polarity of the narrow working-class way of life versus coffee-bar intellectualism, as we [of the Old Left] were between the same working-class mores and our own country-house cocktail-party horizon. Anything else is a deadening bourgeois world; and the New Left have the added horror that a large percentage of the working-class has already entered it. It is easy to laugh at this as *naïve*, but it is the strength of the New Left as of the Old that, for all its *naïveté*, its concern remains the central problem – how to extend a variety and richness of life to more people.

This variety and richness could not be communicated through a debased political language, it had to be communicated by a committed art. Stuart Hall argued: 'The political intellectual is concerned with the institutional life of the society: the creative artist with the attitudes, the manners, the moral and emotional life which the individual consummates within that social framework. It seems to me that the beginning of a common socialist humanism is the realization that there are not two distinct areas of interest, but the complementary parts of a complex, common experience.'

It is for these reasons that the elusive problem of what constitutes Commitment is more readily answered in terms of artistic endeavour than political action, and just as the large question of society was considered in cultural rather than political terms, the question of personal Commitment became a matter of subjective judgment. The danger in the large term was that sociological analysis became confused with literary criticism, and literary criticism with political thinking; the danger in the small term was that Commitment placed the critical emphasis more on the artist's sensibility than his individual works.

Some artists, at least, were aware of the distinction between art and sociology. Karel Reisz saw this as the essential difference between Free Cinema and the Grierson school of Documentary. Old-style documentary realism 'implies that there is a sociological truth which it is the artist's function to interpret, to make the spectator *feel* a scientific fact. This makes the artist a sort of public relations officer for the more serious sociologist. But this is simply not how art works. There is a difference in kind between a sociological fact and poetic truth, and the artist had better remember it if he wants to keep his audience.' On the problem of artistic sensibility John Osborne's statement in *Declaration* – and Osborne is a prime example of the importance of personality – makes the position clear. 'I am a writer and my own contribution to a socialist society is to demonstrate those values in my own medium, not to discover the best ways of complementing them.' These arguments are consistent with what must be called the *ideal* of Commitment; in practice it was a quality rather than an entity that could be extrapolated from an individual work, and the New Left were not so naïve as to believe that individual works could do anything more than influence the climate of opinion. Stuart Hall wrote in the theatre magazine *Encore* in 1959: 'it would be reassuring to think that a couple of showings of *O Dreamland* would bring the Rank Organization to a dead stop, that *We Are the Lambeth Boys* would prevent race riots in Notting Hill, and that by now every new housing-estate would have had its open-air performance of *Chicken Soup With Barley*. It simply isn't as easy as that.'

On the other hand, the works that Hall mentions, indeed all the approaches to art and life that have been drawn together in this book under the label 'Realism', indicate a respect for their subject matter that neither idealizes it nor fails to criticize the conventional view of life that pretends such truths are extraordinary. A directly propagandist attack on the Establishment, such as Osborne's musical *The World of Paul Slickey*, failed, not simply because it was a bad musical, but because its direct propaganda made it bad. By contrast, John Arden's pacifist message in *Serjeant Musgrave's Dance* (set in nineteenth-century England, but raising issues to do with Cyprus and CND) makes its point by presenting the pacifist as the man who feels he has to kill. Similarly Wesker's trilogy begins by exploring the disintegration of Communist belief from the 1930s, centres on the alienation of the working-class intellectual, and ends with the defeat of a William Morris ideal, but does not therefore regard the future as impossible. Even those who diffidently or dismissively replied to the *London Magazine*'s questions on Commitment in May 1957 (questions set in typically negative and 1930ish terms), Maurice Cranston, D. J. Enright, Roy Fuller, William Golding, Philip Larkin, John Osborne, Stephen Spender, John Wain, and Colin Wilson, could not avoid confirming the writers' *moral* commitment to his material, however divided they were about drawing that material from contemporary events.

The weakness of Commitment was its lack of definition, though on occasion the issue could be made ridiculously clear cut, at least by its critics. In 1958 the Oxford University Labour Club decided to put on a production of Brecht's *The Caucasian Chalk Circle*. Brecht represented the ideal of the committed artist, and Dennis Potter, who acted in the play, has written that the idea of mounting the production was 'the result of an urgent desire to formulate the language of "commitment"'. Whatever the undergraduates learned from the production is not recorded, but the University authorities seem to have perceived a serious threat from the play, for they tried to forbid the performance.

By admitting the aesthetic autonomy of the artist, the New Left avoided the trap of trying to impose an ideological conformity. Such a Stalinist attitude, after all, was what many of them had only just escaped from. Instead, the subjective nature of Commitment led them towards a new kind of romanticism. The design historian, Reyner Banham, detected this in the very layout of *The Partisan* coffee-bar: 'Quite apart from the overt historicism of the proposition to recreate "the character of older coffee-houses" and the mousy monasticism implicit in the proposition that one needs a special environment to be Left in, the functional programme presented to the architects was congested, with a profit-making coffee-bar doubling as a meeting-hall and art gallery, and aesthetically confused by the decision to replace Right romanticism ("We didn't want it to look like an espresso bar") by the romanticism of the Left ("Something of a French tabac").'

While the debate about Commitment went on in *The Partisan*, on the march to Aldermaston and in the queues outside the National Film Theatre, the Establishment carried on in its estate. The point about conspiracy theories is that they are hard to prove, but there are times when the unconscious assumptions of authority are revealed: in cultural matters Establishment values frequently come to the surface over questions of censorship. Again, the assumptions are hard to test, because formal censorship, the forbidding of something already created, is much rarer than the self-censorship which realizes that there is no point in adopting a certain course of action, or proposing a certain idea, because there is no chance of its being accepted. Cases of direct censorship by the BBC, for instance, are rare – forbidding the Goon Show comics to do imitations of Winston Churchill, for instance, or disciplining the producer who allowed the poet George Barker's 'True Confessions' to be read on the Third Programme – but it is evident that the BBC throughout the 1950s was careful to follow public opinion (or what the BBC took to be public opinion) rather than lead it. In these circumstances there was no need for formal censorship, as Malcolm Muggeridge pointed out in 1959:

By appearing to be free of government control, its subservience is the more effective. And, in any case, the sort of individuals chosen to occupy the higher control posts ensures that, without any special directives, the Corporation may be relied on always to operate on the side of conformism. The party line does not have to formulated; it beats naturally in their hearts, and speaks in their mouths, and wanly illumines their eyes.

In the cinema, there was a more elaborate relationship between voluntary and formal censorship. There was always of course the formal sanction of a police prosecution for obscenity, but for practical day-to-day matters responsibility lay with the British Board of Film Censors. This was a purely voluntary system established by the film industry itself, for the real power to license films rested with the individual local authorities. Since 1912, however, with occasional exceptions, local authorities had accepted the certificates of suitability issued by the Board of Film Censors, and film-makers had submitted to its judgment, although they could, if they wished, apply directly to a local authority for a certificate, as happened from time to time with the London County Council. The system worked well, in that the film distributors thought it the least of all possible evils, the local authorities were not bothered with film censorship, and the government stayed out of the matter, though it was able to exercise pressure discreetly by appointing retired politicians as censors.

Progressive film-makers, however, were less pleased with the system, even after the introduction of the 'X' certificate in 1951 which allowed for greater sexual frankness (and of course greater sexual exploitation). Sex was only one of the subjects from which the film censors were concerned to protect the public; the Royal Family, politicians, religion, and indeed anyone in authority such as policemen or teachers were not allowed to be satirized or shown in a bad light. Violence was permissible, depending on its meaninglessness. Political censorship was difficult to detect, though a number of East German films were refused a certificate, and Sergei Eisenstein's *Battleship Potemkin* did not receive a certificate until 1954, twenty-nine years after it was made. In 1960 the Board of Film Censors demanded cuts in 300 of the 550 feature films submitted to it, and eight were refused a certificate altogether. These figures apply only to films that were actually made; film producers usually took the precaution of submitting scripts of proposed films to the Board of Censors for advice, and it is likely that this pre-censorship was more effective than any post-production work with the censor's scissors. The Free Cinema film-maker Lorenza Mazzetti submitted a script for a film about Teddy Boys and was told by the Board of Censors that it would not receive a certificate unless the film ended by roundly condemning them. The film was never made. Such a clear example of the effect of censorship is rare; Tony Richardson described its more subtle effects in *Encounter* in 1960.

What is so frightening about the Board's activities is not the petty tyrannies, the sudden and often bizarre suspicions, but its confirmation of the timidities of Wardour Street. Distributors as a whole are conventional enough. They shy away from certain political, social and religious subjects, they shirk definite attitudes. The result is the anaemic feebleness we see so often on the screen. The cinema is reduced to purveying commercial fantasies devoid of any real connection with human beings and the society they live in.

In literature the innocent public was protected by the common law, but the opinions of local police officers, custom officials and magistrates could be capricious, as in the case of the destruction of Boccaccio's *The Decameron* at Swindon in 1955. In 1954 a flood of horror comics from America led to proposals for a Harmful Publications Bill that would tighten the censorship of literature considerably, while at the same time a series of prosecutions under the existing law caused more liberal writers and publishers to agitate for reform. The unsatisfactory state of the present law was demonstrated by the trial early in 1954 of a publisher of erotic paperbacks called Reiter, who in defence of his own merchandise submitted a list of five novels recently published by reputable firms, which, he said, were just as adventurous as his own. Reiter was found guilty, and accordingly the five reputable publishing firms found themselves in the dock; two of them were found guilty, two were acquitted, and one formally acquitted after the juries at two trials could not agree.

Alarmed by these developments, the Society of Authors set up a committee, chaired by their President, A. P. Herbert, to promote a bill that would replace the 1857 Obscene Publications Act. The measure was resisted by Home Office Ministers past and present, but the proposals for a bill, drafted by Norman St John Stevas (Conservative), author of the only legal textbook on the subject, *Obscenity and the Law* (1956), and steered by Roy Jenkins (Labour), were slowly pushed through the House of Commons. In 1958, after a Select Committee had reported on obscene publications (it revealed among other things that the Customs had a blacklist of some sixty books, including all Genet's works), the government introduced its own Bill and there was a long battle to replace the government's draconian measures with more liberal clauses. The battle reached a climax in 1958 when A. P. Herbert threatened to stand in a crucial by-election (and so ensure a government defeat) unless the Obscenity Bill was given a second reading. The new Obscene Publications Act was finally passed in 1959.

The new law had certain advantages over the old for serious publishers. Booksellers were better protected, and it was no longer possible for a magistrate to order books to be destroyed without informing the publisher. It also reduced the penalties if publisher, author or bookseller were found guilty. A book now had to be considered as a whole, and although a book might be judged to be likely to 'deprave and corrupt' its readers, this was not necessarily an offence if it could be shown that the book was justified 'as being for the public good on the ground that it is in the interest of science, literature, art or learning, or of other objects of general concern'. Most importantly, this justification could be established (or refuted) by the introduction of expert witnesses for the defence or prosecution. In October 1960 these advantages were put to the test for the first time.

The prosecution brought against Penguin Books for publishing an unexpurgated edition of D. H. Lawrence's *Lady Chatterley's Lover* was in fact the ninth brought under the new act, but all previous cases had clearly involved pornography, and only one of them, *The Ladies' Directory*, went before a jury before *Lady Chatterley*. It was, and the prosecution referred to it as, a test case. From the point of view of testing the operation of the law the case had its disadvantages, for the novel was plainly serious literature and the explicit nature of the sexual passages might be condemned on grounds of language alone, whereas truly pornographic literature could be erotic while being far less obvious. (That the novel chosen for prosecution should be by D. H. Lawrence is appropriate in the light of the fresh interest in his work.) Penguin Books decided to publish the novel in unexpurgated form in order to complete their publication of all Lawrence's major works on the thirtieth anniversary of his death. When it became apparent that a prosecution was likely, Penguin avoided involving a bookseller by simply handing twelve copies to the police. The other 200,000-odd waited in store until the outcome of the trial.

The six-day trial at the Old Bailey caused a great sensation, but it was not quite the struggle between the forces of progress and reaction that its terms made it appear. This was partly because the prosecution could find no expert witnesses (or did not try to find any) who would say that a novel by a distinguished British author published by a distinguished British firm should be condemned. The defence on the other hand had an army of witnesses, including the Bishop of Woolwich, the Master of the Temple, the President of the Publishers' Association, educational psychologists, teachers, theologians and a whole range of literary critics and academics (including Hoggart and Williams) prepared to speak in favour of publication. Thirty-five expert witnesses were called, and another thirty-five stood ready. In all 300 had been approached about giving evidence; only one, F. R. Leavis, declined. The Establishment, therefore, had to be represented by the prosecuting counsel, Mr Griffith-Jones, Senior Treasury Counsel at the Old Bailey, although it was strongly felt that the judge, Mr Justice Byrne, did all he could to assist the prosecution case.

It was evident from the prosecution's opening speech that Penguin's offence had not been so much to print a book with rude words in it (all of which were in print elsewhere at the time), but to make these words available in 200,000 copies at 3s. 6d. each. A small 'private' edition for the élite might have gone unnoticed (and most of the witnesses appear to have read the unexpurgated version before Penguin set it in type), but the public must be protected for its own good. According to the prosecution *Lady Chatterley's Lover* 'sets out to commend sensuality almost as a virtue. It encourages, and indeed even advocates, coarseness and vulgarity of thought and language.' Mr Griffith-Jones then went on to make to the jury a famous, and probably fatal, remark: 'Is it a book that you would have lying around in your own house? Is it a book you would even wish your wife or your servants to read?' As the trial went on, and witness after witness defended Lawrence's language and ethical purpose, the prosecution concentrated more and more on the fact that the sensual pair were unmarried, so that it became as much a trial for adultery as obscenity. In spite of the new obligation to consider the work as a whole, the sexual description bore the brunt of the prosecution's attack. One witness however, journalist and television personality Francis Williams, gave an interpretation of the book that suggests the authorities might have had unconscious reasons for objecting to Lawrence's book:

He cast in the role of the husband this intellectual person of long-standing tradition, a property-owning person in a newly industrialized area, but the crippling to him was in his conception a crippling of modern society which had begun before the First World War, but which had, in his view, been greatly increased after. I think it is significant that the first meeting with Mellors is when Lady Chatterley is going to visit one of the oldest pieces of wood in England, a piece of the old Sherwood Forest, and Sir Clifford Chatterley sees it as his duty to preserve this. I believe Lawrence is trying to convey his belief that in fact the intellectual upper classes were no longer able to preserve that which was absolutely great in the old tradition of England, and that it was Mellors who was likely to further that preservation.

It is unlikely that the jury understood this as a reference to the impotence of the Mandarin pastoral tradition, but it only took them three hours to decide that Penguin Books were not guilty.

No one will ever know, however, as C. H. Rolph writes in his book on the trial, 'whether that meant "not obscene", or "obscene but justified"'. Censorship and self-censorship continued; in the theatre the duties of the Lord Chamberlain's office were not abolished until 1968. In August 1960, his officers paid a solemn visit to a performance of Les Ballets Africains in order to decide whether it was a ballet, in which case the bare breasts of the female dancers did not come under his jurisdiction, or a play in mime, in which case they were illegal. The Lord Chamberlain pronounced that the performance was a ballet, and the popular press published quantities of photo-graphs to prove it. In such ways is the cause of artistic freedom advanced in Britain.

In his editorial for the sixth issue of the *New Left Review*, written shortly after the Campaign for Nuclear Disarmament had briefly captured a majority at the Labour Party conference at Scarborough, Stuart Hall wrote: '1956–60 has been "The Thirties" of the present generation.' The 1930s, rather than the 1940s, were the important decade for the later 1950s, and it is appropriate that in the closing month of 1960 Julian Symons should publish the first of many studies of that decade, *The Thirties: A Dream Revolved*. Symons was an important and active member of the generation of committed intellectuals formed by the 1930s, and though he set out to write a tolerant and objective account of the period, his own admitted involve-ment kept breaking through. It is not a conscious attempt to rewrite the history of the period, but the book's own confusion of purpose conveys the self-accusations which many intellec-tuals felt at the start of the 1940s and had continued to feel. (John Lehmann's second volume of autobiography, *I am my Brother*, also published in 1960, is a much more concerted effort to 'correct' the received myth of the political involve-ments of the period.)

Symons illustrates the disillusions of the 1930s by referring back to an even earlier literary decade:

'Its creators are tragically dead, or have made more tragic recanta-tions, for we are patient of every affectation save theirs, and tolerate any artistic heresy save the one they practised thirty years ago.' The words used by A. J. A. Symons on the Nineties art-for-art's-sakers now ring uncomfortably true of the young Left-wing writers whose art was partly a form of mental therapy and partly produced with the services of an imaginary classless future. The future, as the artists of the time conceived it, seems now to be a dream.

It is possible also to refer forward, to point the parallels between the 1930s and the 1950s, for the 'Auden' generation was a myth just as much as the Angry Young Men who followed. Symons parallels Auden's *Poems* (1930) and *The Orators* (1932) with Amis's *Lucky Jim* as works 'which have an absolute importance and value at the time of their publication because they express cohesively a set of attitudes which have been waiting for an expositor'. 1936 and 1956 are both pivotal years for their respective decades, and we may see the parallel between the Peace Pledge Union and CND, the Group Theatre and Joan Littlewood's Theatre Workshop. It is also true that, however much working-class life became a subject for literature and theatre in the 1950s, the *audience* remained middle-class, and the New Left in the 1950s found, as their predecessors had done, 'the ideal working-class audience of their imaginations turning in disconcerting fact to groups of middle-class aesthetes, sociologists and do-gooders'.

Symons is caught between admiration for the idealism of the 1930s, and its failures. The editors of the original *Left Review*

abdicated from their responsibilities as editors in the sense that their chief concern was not to raise the level of writing among their working-class contributors but to extirpate the heresies found among the bourgeois writers of talent who were sympathetic to Communism. We have learned now that writers cannot artificially transform themselves in this way, that social criticism must proceed from the knowledge and limitations of an individual personality, and not from the attempt of that individual to adapt himself to the stand point of an ideal state. In the Thirties writers, or some writers, learned this lesson painfully, and with unhappy results.

The contemporary reference shows that Symons, like all cultural historians, is writing about the present as much as the past.

I may protest that today I am impartial, but of course that is not true. . . . The old political Adam shows himself, I am sure, in all sorts of assumptions. Looking out from whatever comparatively comfortable hidey-hole he has found in the lickspittle Fifties, any denizen of the Thirties must be astonished by the targets in the sights of young

231

Left-wing artists nowadays. To draw a bead on the Establishment, the Royal Family, on the antics of gossip-column writers – are they really worth powder and shot? Should Kingsley Amis be quite so blandly happy in his adoption of an extremely anti-intellectual attitude, isn't the word *triviality* hanging ominously about?

Symon's contrast between the 'generous impulses' of the 1930s and 'the barren knowingness of the Fifties' demands some answer. If the idealism of the 1930s ended in disillusion, then the knowingness of the 1950s must be preferable, since disillusion is so psychologically damaging, as the various cultural responses of the 1940s indicate. That is not a justification for cynicism, but the realists of the 1950s took a hard look at the forms of society they had inherited, and in destroying the conventional acceptance of an ordered homogeneous Mandarin culture at least opened up the possibility of future change. Anger, however confused, is a more positive response than nostalgia or despair.

Nor were, finally, the younger generation of the 1950s as negative as some of their criticisms of the Establishment and the Welfare State suggest: the search for an articulate form of Commitment represents an idealism that tried to build on the knowingness learned of the disillusions of the Cold War. Julian Symons received a reply, as it were on behalf of the New Left, in John Mander's review of his book for the *New Statesman*. Mander pointed out that though Symons was critical of the 1950s, he made no mention of the 'revolution' of 1945:

Was 1945 a revolution, though? It is a leading question. It is at this point precisely that the gulf yawns between the Old Left and the New. If it was, then the battle is behind us, and we are living in paradise unwitting. If it was not, then somebody must have betrayed it, and who else can that be but the Old Left, the men of the Thirties? . . . Where the Old Left still speaks of tactical successes, the New Left sees only strategic defeat. . . . If I were asked to name one respect in which the New Left has it over the Old . . . I would say this. Much of what Orwell criticized in the Thirties – the practical and private joking, the cult of homosexuality – had its origin in the English public school. This has now vanished, with astonishing completeness. In the Thirties

232

the working-class intellectual was a bit of a joke; Orwell was unsparing about him. It is difficult nowadays to think of younger left-wing intellectuals who do *not* come from working-class or lower middle-class homes. They are less ambivalent in their social attitudes. The New Left may have evolved no very coherent ideology as yet, but it lacks this particular confusion.

The Bloomsbury intellectuals who gathered at Hamish Hamilton's party for Edmund Wilson in 1945 had had their day; the confusion that existed in the New Left conception of Commitment was the difficulty of balancing revulsion from formal ideology (that common theme of the 1950s) against the solipsism of viewing politics and culture entirely as a personal gesture, a problem played out at length in the 1960s.

If, to quote E. M. Forster, '1939 was not a year in which to start a literary career', 1961 held much more promise. The conditions of a literary career had of course changed a great deal, and it is more likely that the young artist of 1961 was considering work in the theatre, the cinema or television rather than in literature *per se*. He or she was also far more likely to be interested in painting or sculpture, rather than in writing novels. Some, indeed, would be entering the new profession of 'arts administrator', and those who were literary artists were driven more and more into the academy. The word was giving way to the image, and the old-style man of letters was losing ground (though he has still not entirely lost it). The British intellectual of the old school received his just memorial in Nigel Dennis's *Cards of Identity*:

Here is one of the family at work. . . . In the passing of these old houses, nothing is to be more regretted than the loss of the library – and, with it, the sort of occupant you now see. Before we discuss the room, I would like you to look very closely at this individual. His bent shoulders, his pinched and nervous face, his tremulous grasp of his quill pen indicate that he will not be in contemporary society very much longer. I am not *too* well up in these matters, but I am assured that without him and his predecessors we should not have any culture at all.

NOTES ON SOURCES

I refer here only to material that has been quoted in the text, except where a general reference to a secondary source is appropriate. Where the context is clear in the text I have not repeated the reference here. (NY) means New York.

CHAPTER ONE

The epigraph is from Winston Churchill's speech on the end of the war in Europe, 8 May 1945. Edmund Wilson's response to London in 1945 can be found in his *Europe Without Baedeker*, Secker & Warburg and Doubleday (NY) 1948, and his *Letters on Literature and Politics*, Farrar Straus & Giroux (NY) 1977. He is quoted from *Europe Without Baedeker*. John Lehmann's autobiography *I am my Brother* was published by Longmans in 1960 and Reynal & Co (NY).

J. B. Priestley's protest was published in the *New Statesman*, 2 July 1949, Donald MacRae's in the *Political Quarterly*, January 1949. T. S. Eliot's *Notes Towards the Definition of Culture* was published by Faber & Faber in 1948 and Harcourt, Brace Jovanovich (NY). The last number of *Horizon* was dated January 1950, T. C. Worsley's comment was published in the *New Statesman*, 10 December 1949. Alan Ross's *The Forties* was published by Weidenfeld & Nicolson in 1950.

James Redfern's comment on the ballet is in the *Spectator*, 1 March 1946, Desmond Shawe-Taylor's complaint about opera singers in the *New Statesman*, 18 October 1947. Ernest Newman's comment in the *Sunday Times* appeared 8 May 1949. Peter Ustinov's protest about the theatre is in the *Listener*, 30 January 1947, James Agate is quoted from *Ego 9*, published by Harrap in 1949. J. B. Priestley was writing in the *New Statesman*, 1 September 1945, T. C. Worsley in the *New Statesman*, 8 January 1949.

Anna Kavan is quoted from *Horizon*, January 1946, the warning on bookstocks and the letter on artists' materials are taken from the *Spectator*, 1 November 1946. Malcolm Muggeridge's attack is in the *New English Review*, May 1946, J. B. Priestley's Fabian pamphlet *The Arts Under Socialism* was published by the Turnstile Press in 1947.

Cyril Connolly's description of the British scene is in his editorial for *Horizon*, April 1947. George Elvin's comment on the film industry is in the *Listener*, 1 April 1948, the *New Statesman*'s 19 March 1949. The post-war history of the Old Vic is based on Irving Wardle's *The Theatres of George Devine*, Cape 1978. The pseudonymous publisher's letter is in the *New Statesman*, 12 July 1947, Michael Joseph's comment on new writers' problems in the *New Statesman*, 3 April 1948. Denys Val Baker's *Little Reviews Anthology*, 1945, 1946, 1947/8, and 1949 were published by Eyre & Spottiswoode. V. S. Pritchett is quoted from the *New Statesman*, 10 November 1950. Arnold Wesker is quoted from *The Tulane Drama Review* Vol. II, No. 2. The *New Statesman*'s comparison with Munich is in the 6 October 1948 number.

The account of the first phase of the Cold War is based on Daniel Yergin's *Shattered Peace*, André Deutsch and Houghton Mifflin, Boston, 1978, and Louis Halle's *The Cold War as History*, Chatto & Windus 1967. V. S. Pritchett was writing on the future of fiction in *Penguin New Writing* No. 32, 1947. John Spink's article in *Horizon*, January 1943, is discussed in *Under Siege*, page 79. Alan Pryce-Jones is quoted from *The Craft of Letters in England*, edited by John Lehmann and published by the Cresset Press in 1956. Connolly was writing in *Horizon*, July 1947. *The God That Failed*, with an introduction by R. H. S. Crossman, was published by Hamish Hamilton Ltd in 1950.

Raymond Williams is quoted from the magazine *Politics and Letters* No. 4 1948.

Pamela Hansford Johnson's *A Summer to Decide* was published by Michael Joseph Ltd in 1948. Harold Laski's *The Secret Battalion* was published by the Labour Party in 1946. R. H. S. Crossman was writing in the *New Statesman*, 24 January 1948. Priestley was writing in the *New Statesman*, 2 October 1948. George Orwell's *Nineteen Eighty-Four* was published by Secker & Warburg and Harcourt, Brace Jovanovich (NY), who had both also published his *Animal Farm*. George Woodcock's *The Writer and Politics* was published by the Porcupine Press in 1948. Orwell's answer to Randall Swingler appeared in *Polemic* No. 5 1946, his *The English People* was published by Collins in 1947. Doris Lessing's *The Four Gated City* was published by MacGibbon & Kee in 1969.

J. B. Priestley is quoted again from his pamphlet *The Arts Under Socialism*, Turnstile Press 1947. Stephen Spender was writing in *Polemic* No. 2 1946. Elizabeth Bowen is quoted from *Why Do I Write?*, Percival Marshall 1948, Alan Ross from *The Forties*, Weidenfeld & Nicolson 1950. Geoffrey Faber is quoted from the *Spectator*, 5 November 1948.

CHAPTER TWO

The epigraph is from an editorial in the *Listener*, 22 July 1948. Tom Harrisson was writing in the *New Statesman*, 28 September 1946, Cyril Connolly is quoted from *Horizon*, April 1947, his scheme for redeeming hacks was floated in *Horizon*, January 1948. Harrison's letter to the *Listener* was published 30 January 1947. Geoffrey Barnes is quoted from the *Listener*, 26 September 1946.

Geoffrey Bridson's *Prospero and Ariel* was published by Gollancz and gives a first-hand account of the BBC Features Department. *From the Third Programme* was published by the Nonesuch Press in 1956. Rayner Heppenstall's *Portrait of the Artist as a Professional Man* was published by Peter Owen Ltd in 1949. V. S. Pritchett is quoted from the *New Statesman*, 22

March 1947. Harman Grisewood is quoted from his autobiography *One Thing at a Time*, Hutchinson 1968. W. E. Williams was writing in the *Listener*, 20 October 1947, Peggy McIver in *Pilot Papers* Vol. 2 No. 3, September 1947. Bruce Belfrage in the *Spectator*, 5 October 1951. George Orwell is quoted from *The English People*, Collins 1947, and *Polemic* No. 2; the article is reprinted in the fourth volume of *The Collected Essays, Journalism and Letters of George Orwell*, edited by Sonia Orwell and Ian Angus, 4 Vols. Secker & Warburg 1968, and Harcourt, Brace Jovanovich (NY). Derek Stanford is quoted from *Inside the Forties*, Sidgwick & Jackson 1977. B. Rajan was writing in *Politics and Letters* No. 2/3 1947, A. D. Peters in *The Battle of the Books*, edited by Gerard Hopkins, Allan Wingate Ltd 1947. Philip Hendy is quoted from the *Listener*, 25 July 1946.

The *Listener* is quoted from the editorial comment of 22 July 1948. Evelyn Waugh's *Brideshead Revisited* was published by Chapman Hall in 1945 and Little, Brown & Co. (NY). 'Bruce Truscott' (E. A. Peers) published *Redbrick University* first in 1943, and then in a revised version with Penguin in 1951. Richard Hoggart's *The Uses of Literacy* was published by Chatto & Windus in 1957 and Oxford University Press (NY). Roy Lewis and Angus Maude's *The English Middle Classes* was published by Phoenix House in 1949. David Glass is quoted from the *Listener*, 5 April 1951. Sir Walter Moberly's *Crisis in the University* was published by the Student Christian Movement Press in 1949, Michael Oakshott's review in the *Cambridge Journal*, June 1949. *No Cause for Alarm*, by Virginia Cowles, was published by Hamish Hamilton Ltd in 1949 and Harper (NY). A. J. Ayer's *Language, Truth and Logic* was reprinted by Gollancz in 1946 and Dover (NY). Graham Hough was writing in the *New Statesman*, 5 April 1947, Karl Popper's *The Open Society and Its Enemies*, 2 Vols., was published by Routledge & Kegan Paul in 1945. Iris Murdoch is quoted from her essay in *Conviction*, edited by Norman MacKenzie, and published by MacGibbon & Kee in 1958. 'Oxonian' was writing in the *New Statesman*, 26 June 1948.

Stephen Spender's comment on the English literary tradition appeared in *Horizon*, March 1949. T. S. Eliot's *Notes Towards the Definition of Culture* was published by Faber & Faber in 1948, and Harcourt, Brace Jovanovich (NY). F. R. Leavis's *Education and the University* was published by Chatto & Windus in 1943, and G. W. Stewart (NY). His comment on the Cambridge English Faculty is quoted from his Clark Lectures, *English Literature in our time and the University*, published by Chatto & Windus in 1969. John Gross is quoted from *The Rise and Fall of the English Man of Letters*, Weidenfeld & Nicolson 1969. Connolly was writing in *Horizon*, November 1946, Kathleen Raine in the *New Statesman*, 8 October 1949, John Wain in *Penguin New Writing* No. 40. J. B. Priestley is quoted from his Fabian pamphlet *The Arts Under Socialism*, Turnstile Press 1947.

Much of the material on the Festival of Britain is taken from the official guides and catalogues published by the Festival Office, and the Arts Council's annual reports, but Mary Banham and Bevis Hillier's symposium *A Tonic to the Nation*, published by Thames & Hudson in 1976 to coincide with the exhibition at the Victoria and Albert Museum, is very useful. The London School of Journalism's advertisement appeared in the *New Statesman*, 3 March 1951. Mary Banham is quoted from *A Tonic to the Nation*. John Summerson was writing in the *New Statesman*, 6 October 1951, Misha Black is quoted from *A Tonic to the Nation*, as is Reyner Banham. Le Roux Smith Le Roux was writing in the *Listener*, 5 July 1951. The Festival Exhibition of large paintings, '60 for '51' was reassembled as '25 from '51' at the Sheffield City Art Gallery in 1978, with a very useful catalogue by James Hamilton. Evelyn Waugh is quoted from the *Listener*, 31 May 1951. *Poems 1951*, edited by John Hayward, was published by Penguin in 1951. J. B. Priestley is quoted from the *Listener*, 10 May 1951, Desmond Shawe-Taylor from the *New Statesman*, 2 June 1951. Michael Frayn's essay on the Festival appears in *The Age of Austerity*, edited by Michael Sissons and Philip

Notes on Sources

French, published by Hodder & Stoughton in 1963, and republished by Oxford University Press in 1986.

CHAPTER THREE

The epigraph is from Roy Fuller's 'Dedicatory Poem' in *Epitaphs and Occasions*, published by John Lehmann Ltd in 1949. Rayner Heppenstall was writing in the *New Statesman*, 14 April 1956. A. J. P. Taylor reviewed *Encounter* in the *Listener*, 8 October 1953. Lehmann gives an account of his post-war career in *The Ample Proposition*, published by Eyre and Spottiswoode in 1966 and Reynal (NY). Edward Shils was writing in *Encounter*, April 1955. Noel Annan's essay apears in *Studies in Social History*, edited by J. H. Plumb and published by Longmans in 1955.

Enemies of Promise was published by Routledge in 1938 and is discussed in the prologue to *Under Siege*. Nigel Dennis's novel *Cards of Identity* was published by Weidenfeld & Nicolson in 1955 and Vanguard Press (NY). The revised *Brideshead Revisited* was published in 1960 by Chapman Hall and Little, Brown & Co (NY). Terence Rattigan's *Collected Plays*, 3 Vols., 1953 and 1964 were published by Hamish Hamilton Ltd and Random House (NY). Norman Marshall's *The Other Theatre*, John Lehmann Ltd, 1947, gives a useful account of London's avant-garde theatre. John Osborne's letter is in the *New Statesman*, 15 March 1952. The producer of *Personal Enemy* is quoted from *Banned!* by Richard Findlater, MacGibbon & Kee 1967, which gives a full account of the activities of the Lord Chamberlain's Office.

E. Martin Browne was writing in *Penguin New Writing* No. 31. T. C. Worsley is quoted from the *New Statesman* for 6 January 1951 and 29 November 1952. Kenneth Tynan is quoted from a review reprinted in *Curtains*, Longmans 1961. The influence of Ionesco and Beckett is discussed at greater length in chapter 3 of *Too Much*.

Evelyn Waugh's *The Ordeal of Gilbert Pinfold* was published by Chapman Hall in 1957 and Little, Brown & Co. (NY). L. P.

Hartley's *The Go-Between* was published in 1953 by Hamish Hamilton Ltd and Knopf (NY). Waugh's *Sword of Honour* trilogy was published by Chapman Hall and Little, Brown & Co (NY). Graham Greene's novels are published by Heinemann, as are Anthony Powell's. C. P. Snow's *Strangers and Brothers* series is published by Macmillans and Scribners (NY). Snow's first 'Two Cultures' article was in the *New Statesman*, 6 October 1956. William Cooper's *The Struggles of Albert Woods* was published by Cape and Doubleday (NY).

Anthony Quinton was writing in the *Listener*, 22 July 1954. Angus Wilson is quoted from *The Wild Garden*, University of California Press Berkeley 1963. *Hemlock and After* was published by Secker & Warburg and Viking (NY), who also both published *Anglo-Saxon Attitudes*. His discussion of the state of the English novel comes from an article in the *Listener*, 29 April 1954.

Encounter and the *London Magazine* are quoted from their editorials for June and May 1956 respectively. *The Craft of Letters in England* was published by the Cresset Press in 1956.

CHAPTER FOUR

My text was completed before the publication of Blake Morrison's *The Movement: English Poetry and Fiction of the 1950s*, Oxford University Press 1980, but I have found it a valuable corrective. The epigraph is from A. Alvarez's introduction to his anthology *The New Poetry* published by Penguin in 1962.

V. S. Pritchett was writing in the *New Statesman*, 3 October 1953, J. B. Priestley is quoted from the *New Statesman*, 31 October 1953. John Wain's *Sprightly Running: Part of an Autobiography* was published by Macmillan in 1962 and St Martin's Press (NY), Humphrey Carpenter's *The Inklings* was published by Allen and Unwin in 1978. John Wain's comment on the danger of literacy cliques is from his essay in *Declaration*, edited by Tom Maschler and published by MacGibbon & Kee in 1957.

Louis MacNeice is quoted from the *Listener*, 2 September

Notes on Sources

1958, and Canto V of *Autumn Sequel*, published by Faber & Faber in 1954. C. Day Lewis is quoted from 'New Year's Eve' in *Poems 1943–47*, published by Cape in 1948. George Barker was writing in the *New Statesman*, 8 July 1950. G. S. Fraser is quoted from his essay in *The White Horseman*, edited by Henry Treece and J. F. Hendry, published by Routledge in 1941, and then from his essay in *The Craft of Letters in England*, edited by John Lehmann, Cresset Press 1956. Fraser's comment of 1949 comes from *Penguin New Writing* No. 37. Dylan Thomas's *Collected Poems 1934–1952* were published by Dent in 1952 and New Directions Inc. (NY). Kathleen Raine was writing in the *New Statesman*, 14 November 1953. Howard Sergeant launched *Outposts* in 1944; *Images of Tomorrow*, edited by John Heath-Stubbs, was published by the Student Christian Movement Press in 1953. Dannie Abse was writing in *Poetry and Poverty* No. 4. Alan Ross is quoted from the British Council Pamphlet *Poetry 1945–50*, published by Longmans Green in 1951. Alan Pryce-Jones was writing in the *Listener*, 25 August 1949.

John Cotton's monograph *Oscar Mellor: The Fantasy Press*, published by the Didman Press, Hitchin, 1977, is a useful brief account, with bibliographical details, of the activities of the Fantasy Press. Eric Homberger's *The Art of the Real: Poetry in England and America since 1939*, published by Dent and Rowan and Littlefield, New Jersey, in 1977 is, as the sub-title suggests, a critical account with much useful information. Donald Hall is quoted from *Poetry from Oxford 1953*, edited by Martin Seymour-Smith, Fortune Press 1953. James Devaney's *Poetry in Our Time* was published by the Melbourne University Press, Carlton, and Marjorie Boulton's *The Anatomy of Poetry* by Routledge, both appearing in 1953. James Kirkup's *A Correct Compassion* was published by Oxford University Press in 1952, Francis King's *Rod of Incantation* by Longmans in 1952. Richard Church's review is in the *Listener*, 9 October 1952. *Springtime*, edited by G. S. Fraser and Iain Fletcher, was published by Peter Owen Ltd in 1953.

The third volume of John Lehmann's autobiography, *The*

Ample Proposition, published by Eyre and Spottiswoode in 1966, gives a full account of John Lehmann Ltd and *New Soundings*. John Wain is quoted from *Sprightly Running, op. cit.* The quotations from *New Soundings* are taken from microfilm of the original scripts held in the BBC's Radio Script Library. Hugh Massingham was writing in the *New Statesman*, 8 July 1953. Albert Hunt's letter appeared in the *New Statesman*, 15 August 1953; his theatrical activities in the 1960s are described in chapter 6 of *Too Much*. John Wain is quoted from *Twentieth Century*, December 1956. Anthony Hartley is quoted from his articles for the *Spectator*, 8 January 1954 and 27 August 1954; the editorial 'In the Movement' appeared in the *Spectator* for 1 October 1954.

D. J. Enright's *Poets of the 1950s* was published by Kenkyuska Ltd, Tokyo, in 1955. Robert Conquest's *New Lines* was published by Macmillan in 1956. *Mavericks*, edited by Howard Sergeant and Dannie Abse, was published by Editions Poetry & Poverty in 1957. David Wright was writing in *Encounter* for October 1956, Robert Conquest replied in the December 1956 issue.

Anthony Hartley was writing in the *Spectator*, 27 August 1954. John Holloway's *Language and Intelligence* was published by Macmillan in 1951, *The Victorian Stage* by Macmillan in 1953. Philip Larkin's *The North Ship* was published by the Fortune Press in 1945, *XX Poems* was privately published in Belfast in 1951, and *The Less Deceived* was published by the Marvell Press, Hessle, East Yorkshire, in 1956. *The Whitsun Weddings* was published by Faber & Faber in 1964. Kingsley Amis is quoted from 'Something Nasty in the Bookshop' in *New Lines*, included in his *Collected Poems*, published by Hutchinson in 1979. The history of the Group can be found in Edward Lucie-Smith's introduction of *A Group Anthology*, which he edited with Philip Hobsbaum for Oxford University Press in 1963.

General accounts of British post-war art are to be found in Herbert Read's contribution to *Art Since 1945*, Thames & Hudson 1958, Alan Bowness's to *Art of Our Time*, edited by

Notes on Sources

Will Grohman, Thames & Hudson 1966, and Edward Lucie-Smith's *Movements in Art Since 1945*, revised edition, Thames & Hudson 1975. Denys Val Baker's *Britain's Art Colony by the Sea*, George Ronald 1959, is a brief history of the St Ives school. *The Forgotten Fifties* opened at the Graves Art Gallery, Sheffield, in March 1984. M. H. Middleton was writing in the *Spectator*, 11 July 1952. John Berger was writing in the *New Statesman* of 4 April 1953 and 19 January 1952, he is then quoted from the *Spectator* of 10 October 1952. Berger's criticism of the Unknown Political Prisoner competition was made in the *New Statesman*, 21 March 1953, Herbert Read's reply in the *New Statesman*, 28 March 1953. David Sylvester was writing in the *New Statesman*, 16 November 1957.

John Berger's *Permanent Red* was published by Methuen in 1960. Kingsley Amis is quoted from his comment in *Poets of the 1950s, op. cit.*, Philip Larkin is quoted from his introduction to *All What Jazz*, Faber & Faber 1970. Angus Wilson was writing in the *Spectator*, 11 February 1955, Kingsley Amis in *Books and Art*, October 1957.

Hurry on Down was published by Secker & Warburg and Knopf (NY), *Lucky Jim* by Gollancz and Doubleday (NY), *Under the Net* by Chatto & Windus and Viking (NY), as was *The Bell* in 1958. Malcolm Lowry's *Under the Volcano* was published by Cape in 1947 and Reynal & Hitchcock (NY). William Golding's novels were published by Faber & Faber, who also published Laurence Durrell's *The Alexandria Quartet* with Duttons (NY).

Walter Allen was writing in the *New Statesman*, 30 January 1954, Kingsley Amis in the *Listener*, 29 July 1954, the hostile review of *The Less Deceived* is in the *Listener*, 15 November 1956. William Cooper's *Scenes from Provincial Life* was published by Cape in 1950. *Happy as Larry* was published by MacGibbon & Kee; *The Ginger Man* by the Olympia Press in Paris in 1955 and Neville Spearman, London, in 1956; *The Primrose Path* was published by Longmans Green in 1955, *The World's Game* by Eyre & Spottiswoode in 1957, *The Breaking of Bumbo* by Faber & Faber in 1959.

John Wain's comment on the 1930s is in *Outposts* No. 13 Spring 1949, Anthony Hartley was writing in the *Spectator*, 26 January 1953. John Wain's review of Philip Tonybee's *Friends Apart*, MacGibbon & Kee 1954, is in the *Spectator*, 19 March 1954. 'Remembering the Thirties' is included in Donald Davie's *Collected Poems 1950–1970*, Routledge & Kegan Paul and Oxford University Press Inc (NY). John Holloway is quoted from the *London Magazine*, November 1959. G. S. Fraser is quoted from his introduction to *Poetry Now*, which he edited for Faber & Faber in 1956. Anthony Cronin was writing in *Encounter*, April 1956, Philip Larkin is quoted from *Listen*, Vol. 2 No. 3. Donald Davie is quoted from his essay 'Remembering the Movement', reprinted in *The Poet in the Imaginary Museum*, edited by Barry Alpert, Carcanet Press, Manchester, 1977 and Persea Press (NY). Hugh MacDiarmid's *A Drunk Man Looks at the Thistle* was published by Blackwood, Edinburgh, in 1926. G. S. Fraser's *The Modern Writer and His World* was published by Derek Verschoyle in 1953, Donald Davie's review is in the *Spectator*, 11 September 1953. Bernard Bergonzi was writing in *Listen*, Vol. 2 No. 2.

Eric Homberger is quoted from *The Art of the Real, op. cit.* Donald Davie's 'Rejoinder to a Critic' is in *New Lines* and his *Collected Poems 1950–1970, op. cit. Lucky Jim's Politics* was published by the Conservative Political Centre in 1968, Richard Wollheim was writing in *Encounter*, October 1956. George Scott's *Time and Place* was published by the Staples Press in 1956. John Berger is quoted from his introduction to the catalogue *Looking Forward*, Whitechapel Art Gallery, 1952. *New Lines 2*, edited by Robert Conquest, was published by Macmillan in 1963. Donald Davie is quoted from *The Poet in the Imaginary Museum, op. cit.*

CHAPTER FIVE

The epigraph is from John Osborne's *Look Back in Anger*, published by Faber & Faber in 1959. An account of political developments in Britain during the 1950s is to be found in Alan

Sked and Chris Cook's *Post-War Britain*, Penguin 1979. Paul Johnson was writing in the *New Statesman*, 12 January 1957. Leslie Paul's *Angry Young Man* was published by Faber & Faber in 1951; John Osborne is quoted from his essay in *Declaration*, edited by Tom Maschler and published by Mac-Gibbon & Kee in 1957.

The Outsider was published by Gollancz 1956; a new edition with an introduction by Colin Wilson was published by Picador-Pan Books in 1978. An account of the publication is given in Sheila Hodges's *Gollancz: The Story of a Publishing House 1928–1978*, Gollancz 1978. 'Personalism' is discussed in *Under Siege*, pages 130–1. Connolly's *The Unquiet Grave* was published by Hamish Hamilton in 1944. Kingsley Amis was writing in the *Spectator*, 15 June 1956. Peter Crowcroft was writing in the *New Statesman; The Fallen Sky* was published by Peter Nevill Ltd in 1954. Kenneth Tynan's review is reprinted in *Curtains*, Longmans 1961.

Room at the Top was published by Eyre & Spottiswoode and Houghton Mifflin (NY) in 1957. Braine's article appeared in the *New Statesman*, 8 September 1951; he is then quoted from Kenneth Allsop's *The Angry Decade*, published by Peter Owen Ltd in 1958. All the quotations, until Allsop's book is referred to again, are from *Declaration*, edited by Tom Maschler, MacGibbon & Kee 1957.

That Uncertain Feeling was published by Gollancz in 1955 with Harcourt, Brace Jovanovich (NY), *Living in the Present* by Secker & Warburg in 1955. *The Entertainer* was published by Faber & Faber in 1961. *Religion and the Rebel* was published by Gollancz and Houghton Mifflin (NY) in 1957, *Ritual in the Dark* was published by Gollancz and Houghton Mifflin (NY) in 1960.

George Devine is quoted from Irving Wardle's *The Theatres of George Devine*, Cape 1978, which is a full account of the history of the English Stage Company. John Russell Taylor's *Anger and After*, Methuen 1962, and John Elsom's *Post-War British Theatre*, revised edition, Routledge & Kegan Paul 1979, give valuable accounts of the English theatre of the 1950s as a whole. Peter Zadek is quoted from the *New Statesman*, 4 May 1957, Derek Granger was writing in the *London Magazine*, December 1956. T. C. Worsley is quoted from the *New Statesman*, 12 April 1958.

Charles Barr's *Ealing Studios*, Cameron & Tayleur with David & Charles 1977, is a full account of the studios' activities. *The Decline of the Cinema* by John Spraos, Allen & Unwin 1962, has much statistical information. Penelope Houston was writing in *Sight and Sound*, Summer 1955. George Stonier was writing in the *New Statesman*, 5 April 1958. Elizabeth Sussex's *Lindsay Anderson*, Studio Vista 1968, has much information on the Free Cinema movement. George Stonier was writing in the *New Statesman*, 31 January 1959, Penelope Houston in *Sight and Sound*, Spring 1959. Isabel Quigley was writing in the *Spectator*, 26 June 1959, Walter Lassally in *Sight and Sound*, Summer 1960.

Alan Brien was writing in the *Spectator*, 18 September 1959, T. C. Worsley in the *New Statesman*, 21 February 1959. Alan Sillitoe's *Saturday Night and Sunday Morning* was published by W. H. Allen in 1958 and Knopf (NY), *The Loneliness of the Long Distance Runner* by W. H. Allen in 1959 and Knopf (NY), Keith Waterhouse's *Billy Liar* was published by Michael Joseph in 1959 and W. W. Norton (NY), David Storey's *This Sporting Life* was published by Longmans in 1960. Alun Owen's *Progress to the Park* was published in *New English Dramatists* 5, Penguin 1962. Alan Brien is quoted from the *Spectator*, 15 January 1960. John Russell Taylor is quoted from *Anger and After*, op. cit.

CHAPTER SIX

The epigraph is from an article by E. P. Thompson in *The New Reasoner* No. 9. The quotations in the section on painting come, unless otherwise stated, from the catalogue of the exhibitions referred to. Basil Taylor's review of the AIA show was in the *Spectator*, 18 April 1958; the AIA is discussed in

Notes on Sources

Under Siege, pages 167–9. Richard Wollheim was writing in the *Spectator*, 12 September 1960. *Art Since 1945* was published by Thames & Hudson in 1958. Richard Hamilton is quoted from the catalogue to his retrospective exhibition at the Tate Gallery in 1970.

Protest, edited by Gene Feldman and Max Gartenberg, was published in Britain by Souvenir Press in 1958. A. Alvarez is quoted from his introduction to *The New Poetry*, Penguin 1962; his *The Shaping Spirit* was published by Chatto & Windus in 1958, his essay on the New Romanticism appeared in the *New Statesman*, 29 August 1959, the revised edition of *The New Poetry* was published by Penguin in 1966. He is quoted finally from his introduction to *Beyond All This Fiddle*, Allen Lane 1968.

The Craft of Letters in England, edited by John Lehmann, was published by the Cresset Press in 1956. An account of the Historians' Group is given by Eric Hobsbaum in his essay for *Rebels and their Causes*, edited by Maurice Cornforth and published by Laurence & Wishart in 1978, a more sympathetic version of events than in Neal Wood's *Communism and the Intellectuals*, Gollancz 1959. E. P. Thompson is quoted from *The New Reasoner* No. 10. The *New Statesman* editorial in support of CND was published on 10 May 1958. Alan Brien is quoted from the *Spectator*, 12 April 1960, Mervyn Jones from *The New Reasoner* No. 6. The story of CND is told at greater length in *Too Much*.

F. R. Leavis is quoted from a letter to the *Listener*, 1 November 1956, the profile of Connolly was published in the *New Statesman*, 13 March 1954. *The Establishment*, edited by Hugh Thomas, was published by Anthony Blond Ltd in 1959 and C. N. Potter (NY). Norman Birnbaum was writing in the *Universities and Left Review* No. 5. Raymond Williams is quoted from *The Long Revolution*, Chatto & Windus 1961 and Columbia University Press (NY). Dennis Potter's *The Glittering Coffin* was published by Gollancz in 1960. *The Age of Austerity*, edited by Michael Sissons and Philip French, was published by Hodder & Stoughton in 1963. Richard Hoggart is quoted from the *Universities and Left Review* No. 5.

T. B. Bottomore's *Elites and Society* was published by C. A. Watts Ltd in 1964, W. L. Guttsman's *The British Political Elite* by MacGibbon & Kee in 1963. John Wain is quoted from *Sprightly Running*, Macmillan 1962 and St Martin's Press (NY).

E. P. Thompson is quoted from *The New Reasoner* No. 9, Robert Conquest from *International Literary Annual* No. 1, edited by John Wain and published by John Calder Ltd in 1958. Chatto & Windus published Richard Hoggart's *The Uses of Literacy* in 1957 with Oxford University Press (NY), and Raymond Williams's *Culture and Society* in 1958 with Columbia University Press (NY).

John Mander's *The Writer and Commitment* was published by Secker & Warburg in 1961. Angus Wilson was writing in the *Spectator*, 29 January 1960, Stuart Hall in the *Universities and Left Review* No. 3. Karel Keisz was also writing in the *Universities and Left Review* No. 3. *Declaration*, edited by Tom Maschler, was published by MacGibbon & Kee in 1957, Stuart Hall was writing in *Encore*, September/October 1959. Dennis Potter is quoted from *The Glittering Coffin, op. cit.*, Reyner Banham was writing in the *New Statesman*, 8 November 1958.

Malcolm Muggeridge was writing in the *New Statesman*, 14 February 1959, Tony Richardson was writing in *Encounter*, July 1960. The account of the Lady Chatterley case is taken from C. H. Rolph's *The Trial of Lady Chatterley*, Penguin 1961, and J. E. Morpurgo's *Allen Lane, King Penguin*, Hutchinson 1979.

Stuart Hall was writing in *New Left Review* No. 6. Julian Symons's *The Thirties, A Dream Revolved* was published by the Cresset Press in 1960 and Dufour Editions, Penn. John Mander's review appeared in the *New Statesman*, 10 December 1960. Nigel Dennis's *Cards of Identity* was published by Weidenfeld and Nicolson in 1955 and Vanguard Press (NY).

INDEX

249

Index

Belfrage, Bruce, 43
Belgrade Theatre, Coventry, 172
Bell, Tom, 184
Bellow, Saul, *A Dangling Man*, 71
Benjamin, Arthur, 60
Benn, Anthony Wedgwood, 145
Benthall, Michael, 84
Berger, John, xv, 128–9, 130, 131, 146, 188, 191; *A Painter in Our Time*, 188; *Permanent Red*, 132
Bergonzi, Bernard, 111, 142
Berlin, 13, 25, 187
Berlin, Isaiah, 51
Berliner Ensemble, 85, 169
Berryman, John, 197
Betjeman, John, 121, 195
Betrayal of the Left, The (Gollancz), 27–8
Bevin, Ernest, 24
Birnbaum, Norman, 206–7
Black, Misha, 58
Blake, Nicholas, 67
Blake, Peter, 193
Blin, Roger, 168
Bliss, Sir Arthur, 61
Blond, Neville, 165
Bloomfield, Paul, 95
Bloomsbury circle, 2, 3, 39, 43, 52, 67, 74, 95, 233; death of, 35, 233; influence on 1950s, 2; Leavis's image of, 64; socialism of, 114
Blue Lamp, The (film), 175
Blunt, Anthony, 94
Board of Trade, 19, 23, 56
Boccaccio, *The Decameron*, 226
Bohemianism, 103–4; and the BBC, 40–1, 42; and coffee bars, 68–9; death of, 35, 103–4; revival of, 194
Bolt, Robert, 174, 183; *The Critic and the Heart*, 173; *Flowering Cherry*, 173; *A Man for All Seasons*, 173
Boltons Theatre, 10
Bomberg, David, 130
Bonham Carter, Lady Violet, 205
Boothby, Robert John Graham, Lord, 205
Borkenau, Franz, 26
'Borough Bottega' style, 130
Bottomore, T. B., *Elites and Society*, 211–12

Boulton, Marjorie, *The Anatomy of Poetry*, 109
Bowen, Elizabeth, 21, 35, 71, 86
Boyars, Arthur, 102, 111
Boyle, Edward, 145
Braine, John, 157–8, 194; *Room at the Top*, 157–8, 220, (film) 180, 181
Brando, Marlon, 170
Braque, Georges, 124
Bratby, John, 129, 130, 131
Brecht, Bertolt, 85, 169, 196; *The Caucasian Chalk Circle*, 223; *The Good Woman of Setzuan*, 166
Bridge on the River Kwai, The (film), 177
Bridson, Geoffrey, *Prospero and Ariel*, 42
Brien, Alan, 182, 184–5, 202
Bristol Old Vic, 166
Britain Can Make It exhibition, 15
British Board of Film Censors, 224–6
British Council, xvii, 13, 29, 44, 73, 96, 188
British Film Institute, 177, 178
British Lion Film production company, 175
British Painting 1925–1950 exhibition, 62, 126
Britten, Benjamin, 8, 60; *Billy Budd*, 60; *Peter Grimes*, 1, 8; *The Prince of the Pagodas*, 184; *The Rape of Lucretia*, 8, 165
Brook, Peter, 13, 61, 168, 185
Brooke, Jocelyn, *The Military Orchid*, 12
Browne, Wynard, 82
Burgess, Guy, 94, 204
Burnham, James, *The Managerial Revolution*, 50–1
Burton, Richard, 181
Bush, Alan, 60
Bush, Thomas, 61
Butler, Reg, 131
Butler, Richard Austen *see* Education Act
Byrne, Mr Justice, 228

Calder, Alexander, 131
Cambridge Journal, 49
Cambridge Opera, 8
Cambridge University, xvii, 2, 90;

251

Index

Index

Index

Index

Index

267